Necklace of 59 human teeth brought back by Jack Renton. A detailed description appears on pages 289–90.

The

WHITE
HEADHUNTER

NIGEL
RANDELL

CARROLL & GRAF PUBLISHERS
New York

For Tessa Fowler

Carroll & Graf Publishers
An imprint of Avalon Publishing Group, Inc.
161 William Street
New York
NY 10038-2607
www.carrollandgraf.com

First Carroll & Graf edition 2003

First published in the UK by Constable
and imprint of Constable & Robinson Ltd 2003

ISBN 0–7867-1256-2

Printed and bound in the EU

Contents

Acknowledgements

This story was slowly excavated on a number of visits over eight years, to a group of Pacific islands that see few tourists. The Solomon Islands, in particular, has been without government or infrastructure for over seven years and were it not for the hospitality of a number of people, Melanesians, missionaries and expatriates, my task would have been impossible. In particular I would like to thank Robertson Batu, Stewart Diudi, Ashley Kakaluae, Nathan Kera, Falataou Levi, Charlie Panakera, Dorothy and Loata Parkinson and finally, my long-time guide and mentor, Tessa Fowler, for housing me, feeding me and often interpreting for me. I owe special thanks to my brother James who, over a number of years, looked after me in Sydney on my return from the islands and helped me with ordering the material – tapes, transcripts and photocopies that gradually leaked out of the guestroom to invade his house.

If this book can lay any claim to being unique then it is

entirely due to the contributions of oral historians in the Solomons and Vanuatu. In particular I would like to thank Nelson Jack Boe, Anathanasias Orudiana, Jacob Selo, Grace Sosoe, Malachi Tate, Stewart Diudi, Peter Afoa and John Tamanta. I am particularly grateful to Mike McCoy who undertook the initial interviews.

During the years of research and writing there are a number of people in England and Australia whose help, encouragement and advice I would like to put on record. So my thanks to Dr Ian Byford, Andrew and Wendy Evans, Richard Gibb, Sara Feilden, Clare Littleton, Niall McDevitt, Ron Parkinson, Ben Timberlake, Dr James Warner, Chris Wright and, in particular, Genna Gifford.

For their courtesy and patience I owe a particular debt of thanks to Lawrence Foauna'ota of the Solomon Islands National Museum, the staff of the Western Solomons Cultural Centre, Kirk Huffman of the Vanuatu Cultural Centre, Wendy Morrow of the National Library of Australia, and finally, the staff of the Mitchell Library in Sydney.

Like many first-time authors who know little about publishing, I was entirely dependent upon my agent for an introduction to this world. So to Andrew Lownie I owe a debt of thanks for his guidance, perseverance and enthusiasm and as all authors need an experienced editor, I believe that I was particularly fortunate. With candour, kindness and a sense of humour, Carol O'Brien shepherded me through all the hoops.

List of Illustrations

———○———

Jack Renton
Courtesy of The Mitchell Library, Sydney

Renton fishes for a shark
Courtesy of The Mitchell Library, Sydney

Recruiting, Panchumu Mallicolo
Courtesy of The National Library of Australia, Canberra

Sulufou*

The newly recruited on their way to Queensland
Courtesy of The National Library of Australia, Canberra

Recruiters and boat crew, New Hebrides
Courtesy of The National Library of Australia, Canberra

Kwaisulia of Ada Gege

Ancestral head
© *Royal Anthropological Institute*

Kanaka labourers arriving at Bunderburg
Courtesy of The National Library of Australia, Canberra

Levuka Harbour, Fiji, 1881
Courtesy of The Mary Evans Picture Library

Cutting sugar cane on a Queensland plantation, 1883
Courtesy of The Mitchell Library, Sydney

Santa Isabel tree house
'The Western Pacific', Walter Coote, 1883

Ingava of Roviana lagoon
'Man' Magazine Vol 14. 1907

Nuzu Nuzu
© Royal Geographical Society

War canoes in full cry
'The Savage South Seas', Elkington, 1897

A fully manned war canoe from Roviana
© The Royal Geographic Society

HMS Royalist bombarding Ingava's headquarters, 1891
Courtesy of The Mary Evans Picture Library

Jock Cromer's recruiting ship, *Fearless*
Courtesy of The National Library of Australia, Canberra

Skulls – A bush reliquary *

*All © Nigel Randell

The necklace is reproduced on page i by kind permission of the National Museums of Scotland.

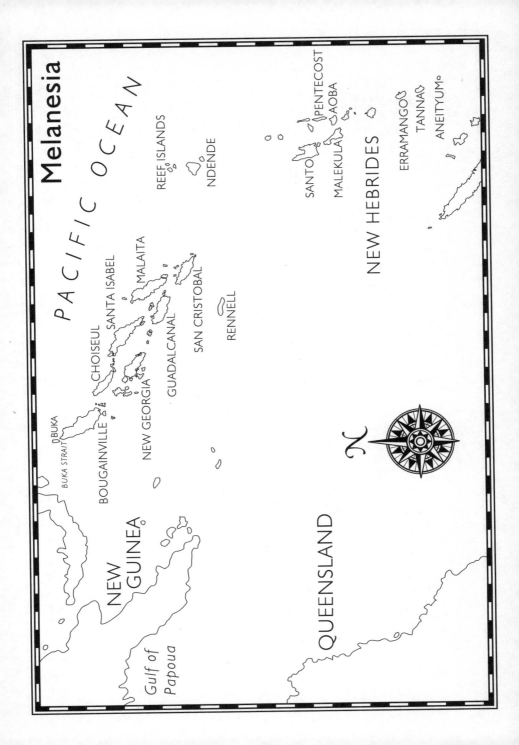

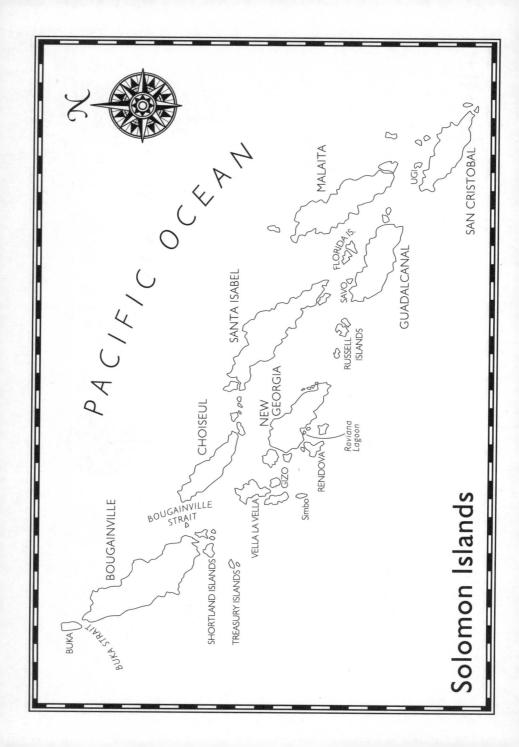

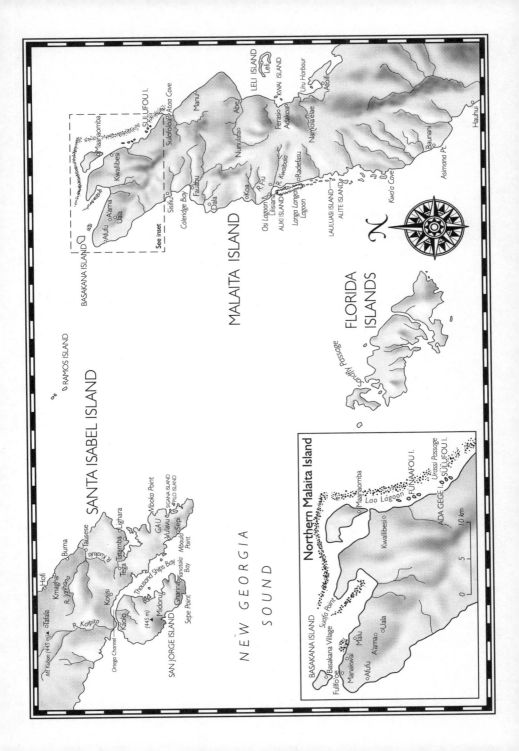

Introduction

THE South Pacific, as a real place, had almost disappeared. For two centuries this vast expanse of ocean and its thousands of little islands formed the backdrop upon which was projected all the baggage of European wish-fulfilment. It was not the writings of Banks, Bougainville, Cook or Rousseau, beguiling though they were, that touched an escapist chord in nineteenth-century Britain, but a literary genre that held enormous appeal for the newly literate masses contemplating their baleful futures in the Industrial Age. The 'Beachcomber Memoirs' were true stories of ordinary seamen who had reinvented themselves on an alien shore. Men (and it was always men) who, by accident or design, had chosen a different life.

Throughout the century a stream of books, articles and serializations flooded the market on both sides of the Atlantic – ten such books in English were published between 1831 and 1847 alone. Many are remarkable, not least because they capture, even in the rough ethnocentric prose in which most are written, a moment in time – the genuine, unrepeatable moment of fear and wonder when, both black and white, floundering across a chasm of disbelief, struggled to acknowledge their common humanity. For the 'visited', without the conceptual tools to deal with the unknown, this must have been an epiphany – nothing would ever be the same again. Unlike the discoveries of Galileo, Newton or Darwin and the gradual dawning upon Europe's intelligentsia of a different worldview, these visitations would have been earth shattering.

During my wanderings in the South West Pacific, I became haunted by the belief that, for every beachcomber's visit, a parallel narrative must have existed. *Their* story, as opposed to *ours*. I was sure that it would be a narrative that in an indirect way, would tell us something about ourselves and therein lay the attraction. These were cultures where there was a unique system of passing on what they knew. With no written language, their brightest children, male and female, became the store-houses of their beliefs, traditions, genealogies and history. Knowledge was passed from grandparent to brightest grandchild. To quote one anthropologist: 'This skipping of alternate generations in the transmission process has unquestionably aided in maintaining the original purity to a unique degree'.

One evening in the Solomon Islands I was speculating about the existence of such accounts to a group of acquaintances when one of them immediately remarked that he knew of just such a story. In the 1860s a young Scotsman had washed up on the shores of the island of Malaita. There, under the protection of a powerful chief, he had lived for eight years. I knew the story. Jack Renton had published an account of his adventures in a series of articles in the *Brisbane Courier* soon after he had been rescued. What I doubted was whether there existed any parallel narrative.

I was assured that there did. Highly doubtful I nonetheless advanced a small sum of money to fund a research trip and left the country.

Three months later, back in England, a small package arrived. The tapes, translated and transcribed, were fragmentary, episodic accounts of the life of a young white man in the village of Sulufou on the island of Malaita one hundred and forty years ago. This patchwork of narratives recounted in remarkable detail the young man's gradual assimilation into their culture to the extent that he became one of them and clearly, from the tone of the accounts, a figure of considerable affection and significance. Of particular interest were the accounts of his fighting abilities and it was clear that his considerable reputation appeared to be related to his capacity as a killer. The only disagreement was over the number of his victims. Some accounts said sixty, others considerably fewer. The description of the manner in which he had been coerced into a career as a headhunter appeared entirely plausible. Clearly these narratives were worth a return visit.

Perched on an artificial island in the middle of a lagoon, Sulufou is a large village dominated by an Anglican church built of weatherboard. I was taken to the communal men's hut and asked to wait. It was open on three sides and furnished with a few benches. On the back wall hung a framed photograph of a young white man. Dressed in his Sunday best he looked barely out of his teens. The portrait had clearly been taken in a photographic studio over a century ago. He wore a waistcoat, a double-breasted jacket with cloth buttons and his narrow silk tie appeared to be clipped to a starch collar. His hair was neatly cut with a parting to one side. He looked directly into the lens, relaxed, confident, a full mouth, even features, stocky and faintly agricultural – the complete antithesis of the hollow eyed Kurtz-like figure I had been expecting. Looking at me from his place of honour was the only white man who had embraced the heart of darkness and emerged to tell his tale.

And what a tale it was. Over the next few days I interviewed over a dozen inhabitants of the village of Sulufou – the leading oral historians. Each recounted some aspect of Jack Renton's time with them – his arrival, his education, his relationship with his protector, his abilities both as an innovator and a warrior, the manner of his leaving and the aftermath.

Unearthing the narrative required an understanding of how knowledge is communicated in this part of the Pacific. Village history does not reside in the public domain but is owned by various individuals and families – a copyright legitimised by an ancestral connection to a major participant in the narrative. I suspected that most of the older inhabitants of Sulufou were well acquainted with the Renton story, however only the copyright holders had the right to narrate the authorised version of a particular event. As a researcher in this marketplace of memories I had to navigate my way through a maze of owners. A story about Renton would stop abruptly and I would be passed on to another family who owned the rights to what followed. Inevitably there were dead ends; copyright owners had died without passing on their piece of this history to the next generation and others had left the village. Once there must have existed a seamless narrative, now it was a mosaic of tantalizing fragments.

Back in Sydney I was able to compare these accounts to Renton's own. At the time of his rescue in 1875, a number of descriptions of his experiences were published, most gleaned from members of the ship's crew who had interviewed him at length during the journey back to Australia. His own account was serialised in the *Brisbane Courier* a number of months later.

This forty-page document was his first and last word on the matter and, comparing it to the stories that I had gathered in Sulufou, it was not hard to understand why.

During the following four years of research in England, Scotland, Australia, the Solomon Islands and Vanuatu (formerly the New Hebrides) it became clear that Renton's actions and the friendships he forged were dictated by an awareness of events beyond the confines of his island exile, an awareness that inevitably mediated the content of his narrative and throws into sharp focus the disparity between the two.

This book is therefore not simply an account of the only European who ever went completely 'native', but also a narrative of Contact. Over a four-hundred-year period numerous groups had undergone the traumatic experience of the sudden appearance of the white man in their world. The inhabitants of Sulufou and the island of Malaita were one of the last people to be caught up in that drama. It is a drama chronicled by one of 'us' who, in manner, habits, language and identity had become one of 'them', and a man who did his very best to prepare the people he had come to love for the onslaught of white civilization.

1

The Island

———————— ◦ ————————

BY the 1860s it appeared on all the Pacific charts but, unlike the rest of the Solomon group whose coastal and inland features had been surveyed and named, this island existed only as an outline. The adjacent islands bore the names of Catholic saints, European territories or the sea captains who had first landed on their shores. Only one word was printed on the featureless outline of this island – a name that was testimony to the awe in which it was held by its neighbours and the ships that skirted its shores. The inhabitants may have known their island as Mala but to the rest of the world it was Mala'ita – 'Mala over there'.

Cigar-shaped, 120 miles long, lying north-east to south-west in the archipelago of the Solomon Islands, Malaita's mountains rise steeply from its storm-battered coastline to over three thousand feet. The interior is covered with a dense rainforest capped by a permanent canopy of grey cloud. It is a land of deep ravines eroded by fast flowing streams, limestone potholes and caves. These streams turn into short estuarine rivers, which empty into a coastline dominated by mangrove swamps infested with crocodiles. On the east and west coasts, two narrow reefs hug the coastline, their inviting lagoons protected by a sea wall marked out by a ribbon of churning surf.

By 1855 America and the Great Powers had completed their commercial and strategic flag-raising and the South Pacific had yielded up most of its mysteries. From their respective bases in Fiji and New Caledonia, Britain and France now turned their attention to the New Hebrides and the Solomons. The 600-mile necklace of islands was reputed to be rich in sandalwood but as the surveyors moved from island to island it was soon apparent from the rotting jetties and scarred landscapes that they had already been logged out. No economic case could be made for raising the flag on islands that had nothing to offer.

It was not a state of affairs that would last. In the 1860s large tracts of land in North Queensland were turned over to sugar production and, in the absence of any white settlers prepared to work for the wages on offer, the plantation-owners decided to exploit the one resource the islands possessed in abundance – manpower. Between 1865 and 1870, four thousand inhabitants of the Solomons and the New Hebrides were recruited on three-year contracts and shipped to Queensland. Labour trafficking, or 'blackbirding', now dominated maritime activity in the South Pacific and as the ships pushed farther and farther north, through the Solomons and up to the coast of New Guinea, only one island was spared their attentions.

Malaita's reputation appeared to be based upon captain Thomas Smith's widely read account of the voyage of the whaling ship *John Bull*. Published in 1840, Smith's narrative maintained that not only was he attacked when he attempted to approach the island but that, a few years prior to his confrontation, the twenty-man crew of another whaler had been captured and eaten by the islanders. Despite the fact that Smith gave no details of that particular encounter, revealing neither the ship's name nor when the incident was supposed to have taken place, his subsequent account of the capture of the captain and three seaman from the *John Bull*'s sister ship the *Alfred* placed his unsubstantiated claim in a completely different light. Malaita was clearly an island to be avoided at all costs and the lightly armed recruiting ships confined their activities to the adjoining islands of Santa Isabel, Guadalcanal and the Floridas.

In 1868, after three years of one-way traffic, the empty holds of the outward-bound ships filled up with the initial batches of recruits returning to the islands at the completion of their contracts. Escaping the stifling heat of their quarters below, the partially acculturated English-speaking natives clustered on the main deck and, as crew and passengers mingled, black and white started to view each other as fellow human beings. Exchanges between the two sides returned again and again to the journey's end and a world about which the crews knew absolutely nothing.

Not only were the stories they heard based upon a completely alien culture but the storytellers inhabited a different mindset. It was a culture that regarded objective knowledge as a slippery, subversive concept. The acquisition of knowledge through asking questions was seen as a heresy and liable to cause grief, alienation and conflict. In the shame-based societies of Melanesia, where a gerontocracy ruled, knowledge was a concrete thing; a commodity passed from generation to generation. In this profoundly hierarchical world one's own ideas lacked the authority of an ancestral witness. Knowledge was therefore acquired from those who 'knew' – be it a magic recipe, a spell, a dance step, a carver's motif, a ritual practice or a song. In this frozen, stone-age world, intellectual curiosity was an anathema. It was only beyond the boundaries of the known world that a man's creativity could take flight – after all, what was not known could not be contradicted and no authority would be challenged by the telling. Released from these constraints, Melanesian 'storying' could flower and, almost inevitably, as the listeners brought a concrete mindset to what they heard, the stories took on a life of their own. Fiction transmuted into incontrovertible fact and entered the canon of communal knowledge. For the experienced fabulist, schooled in the uses of enchantment and horror, the ever present but unknown world of Malaita provided wonderful opportunities.

There were tales of the Kakamoras, a pygmy race that lived in caves high up in the mountains. No more than three feet high with hair hanging down to their waists, they had the agility of a goat and the strength of three men. There were stories of the Luaulasi shark-callers, the headhunters of Lau, the Vinavina ghost society of child-stealers, of men and women blessed with precognition, of the spirits of the dead hovering, like fireflies, over a corpse before taking wing in pursuit of retribution. There were tales of the cannibal practices of the Kwaio and the Torbeda bush people who, armed with special potions, would stupefy and anaesthetize an enemy before carrying him off to witness his own death as they enlarged his anus and drew out his intestines.

Finally, with an eye for their European listeners, there was the story of a castaway who had been held prisoner for so long that he had forgotten his own language and appeared indistinguishable from his captors. Unsurprisingly, this story held a particular fascination for the crew members of passing ships, but it would be 1871 before that most valuable commodity, an empirical fact, emerged from the welter of fabulosity.

In 1871 the *Rose and Thistle*, recruiting on the nearby island of Santa Isabel, was given exact directions to the man's last known location. The ship made for the north-east coast of Malaita and lay-to opposite the village of Maanaomba. Accompanied by a dozen armed crew, Captain MacFarlane beached the ship's boat and, as the villagers retreated, made his way towards the village. A thorough search revealed a clue hidden in one of the huts – a small section of planking from a whaleboat.

Captain MacFarlane bided his time. On the village dancing ground he laid out the usual European inducements – multicoloured beads, rolls of calico and a few axes. After a short pause Rhomo, the chief of Maanaomba, emerged from the gloom of the surrounding vegetation. With the help of the Isabel interpreters an agreement was struck. In return for the gifts, MacFarlane gave Rhomo a letter to be forwarded to 'a white man' urging him to make his way to Sigana Island near Santa Isabel in eight weeks time.

However, much to MacFarlane's irritation, Rhomo neither confirmed nor denied the man's existence, merely agreeing to use his best endeavours to discover whether the rumour was true. As for the planking, the chief pointed out that the coast of Malaita was strewn with flotsam.

MacFarlane duly returned to Sigana Island at the appointed time and spent a fruitless week waiting for the mystery castaway. Any ideas that he might have entertained about returning to

Malaita to confront the temporizing Rhomo were extinguished following news of the massacre of the entire crew of a schooner that had been rash enough to attempt to barter for provisions in a bay only forty miles from Maanaomba. The island was definitely off limits.

Over the next three years the rumours persisted and grew more florid in the retelling. The castaway was no longer a slave suffering the daily humiliations of his status, but a man of rank who enjoyed special favours earned through his courage and his knowledge of the sea. He had been seen with his retinue in the Floridas and on Santa Isabel, negotiating with chiefs. He was well versed in the island's customs and indistinguishable in his manner, bearing and ornamentation from the other 'big men' who dominated inter-island trade. The castaway was no longer some ageing relic, fated to live out his life in the service of his captors, but a man in the prime of life who had been rescued as a child and raised by a chiefly family . . . but who was he?

In September 1875, four years after MacFarlane's fruitless rendezvous, a syndicated article appeared in a number of Australian newspapers. Written by Thomas Slade, one of the crew of the recruiting vessel the *Bobtail Nag*, it announced:

> An event of momentous interest to at least one individual occurred during the recent voyage to the island of Malayta [sic] one of the Solomon Group . . . On Saturday, August 7, the *Bobtail Nag* was cruising off this coast trading for yams, etc., with canoes which came off from the shore when it was elicited from a native that a white man was on shore at a village ten miles distant, living in the same style as the natives. It was concluded, of course, that he was detained, and Captain Murray determined to

obtain his release if possible. A present induced one of the canoes to carry a message ashore, promising to give them whatever they desired in the way of trade if they brought the white man down to speak with them.

The *Bobtail Nag* made its way down a coastline protected by a reef that lay a mile offshore. Bearing in mind the island's reputation, the crew had no intention of launching a ship's boat to breach any of the narrow passages that they passed on their way south. That night the ship hove-to approximately ten miles from its original anchorage.

At about 10 o'clock the following morning a canoe brought off a piece of rough slab bearing (in charcoal characters) a request from John Renton to be taken off the island. About 200 natives assembled in the vicinity and soon the white man was descried amongst them. As the ship's boat drew near the reef, two powerful natives were seen to lead him along without a vestige of clothing. After a long parley at a shouting distance, in which Renton acted as interpreter, they were induced to accept a number of axes and allowed him to come in the boat.

Although he has been upwards of eight years on the island, he is only a young man, being about 27 years of age. Renton is a native of the Orkney Islands and appears to have received a fair education for one of his position and possesses considerable natural intelligence, but the past ten years seclusion from the sound of the English language has temporarily interfered with the facility for expressing his ideas in his mother tongue, and frequently occasions the interpolation of a native word unconsciously.

To the crew, Renton's attitude towards his deliverance must have come as something of a surprise. Far from urging them to put as much distance as possible between himself and his captors, he urged them to stay. The previous day, as the ship had made its way down the coast, speculation had been rife and most imagined that they would be faced with some demented Crusoe-like figure. Now the crew sat watching a stark naked, deeply tanned, heavily muscled young Scotsman deep in conversation with their captain. Far from showing any interest in the details of his rescue he was pointing out the area's potential for recruiting and listing the trade goods his erstwhile 'captors' would expect in return. Given Malaita's reputation, Murray was extremely doubtful but agreed to stay for another day. Reassured, his guest was escorted below where, Slade observed, the young man found his introduction to clothing and footwear 'extremely distasteful'.

The following morning Renton proved as good as his word. Two of his captors were invited on board and, after an exchange of gifts, he made a short announcement in the native tongue. The effect was instantaneous. Both men became highly agitated, rushed to the ship's rail and started shouting to the crowded canoes milling around the *Bobtail Nag*. Murray, alarmed by the change of mood, was about to call the crew to arms when Renton stopped him, pointing out that it was being announced that he was leaving.

> At this juncture, [Slade recorded], it appeared that Renton had become a favourite with many of the islanders; the tidings were heard with great lamentation and with real tears. When the details of his departure became known to the villagers a large number of the

8

natives engaged themselves to come to Queensland for the sake of accompanying him.

Then, after supplying a few tantalizing details of island life, Slade's article ends. The bait had been set and offers for the full story soon arrived from newspaper and magazine publishers throughout Australia. Acting on behalf of the penniless young man staying in his house in Brisbane, Slade eventually sold the Australian and the worldwide ancillary rights to the *Brisbane Courier*. During the initial discussions with the editor it was evident that Renton was still having considerable difficulty expressing himself in English and he readily agreed to the proposal that his narrative be culled from a series of interviews with staff writers.

2

Escape from the *Reynard*

━━━━━━━ ○ ━━━━━━━

CHRISTMAS week 1875 saw the publication of the first part of *The Adventures of John Renton* and, true to its title, it dives straight into the narrative. Whether this was Renton's decision or the newspaper's, the effect is rather disorientating as the reader is invited to embark upon the extraordinary adventure with almost no knowledge of the protagonist – no details of his background, family, education, or his previous life at sea. In the 1920s, John Marwick, a local historian from Renton's home town of Stromness, unearthed a few fragmentary memories from the dwindling band of his contemporaries who remembered him flitting through their young lives over half a century previously.

Jack Renton was the eldest son of the local tailor. He seemed to have spent much of his time clambering about the fishing boats that crowded the little port. According to one of his contemporaries: 'he was second to none in his ability to shin up a mast and place his little cap on the masthead.' Others remembered an irrepressible extrovert, full of practical jokes, talkative, charming and athletic – in Marwick's words: 'with a personality that seemed to be particularly winning and it is quite clear that those brought into contact with him were attracted to him in a quite remarkable way'. But memories fade and Marwick was unable to add flesh and bone to the mysterious figure who, by then, was regarded as the port's most illustrious inhabitant. In reality there was probably little to distinguish him from the thousands of young men and women in the Scottish Highlands and Islands who, as teenagers in Victorian Britain, found that there was little to keep them at home. On his sixteenth birthday Jack Renton left for Liverpool and signed on a windjammer.

In January 1868, three years and six voyages later, he arrived in San Francisco from Hong Kong. Apparently tired of 'jamming', he decided to change to steam and, having done the rounds of the dockside agents, signed onto the steam packet *Pacific* sailing for Sydney the following day. He was living in a boarding house near the harbour and as he removed his sea chest into the hall to be ready for the morning the landlord invited him for a drink. The two large rooms on the ground floor were in fact a saloon full of sailors – some guests, others passers by. The landlord insisted on standing drinks all round and Renton's account begins in the boarding house.

> Everyone, particularly the landlord, was very friendly and I settled down to an evening of the usual seafaring talk. As the evening wore on I remember one of our crowd who was singing a song being interrupted by a stranger at the door. The landlord got up and left the room. A short time later he returned and shouted 'Time's up, gentlemen, please.' Everyone got up and ambled towards

12

the door. As I followed them the landlord motioned to me to stay. I didn't think anything of it as I was occupying a room on the premises. We sat down together he offered me 'one last one' before we turned in.

Drinking that glass of liquor was the last act I remember. When I came to I heard the familiar sound of the rattle of chains and felt the gentle motion of a ship under way. The smell of tarry rope and tobacco pervaded everything. I was lying in a ship's bunk. I had been shanghaied.

The ship was a leaky tub called the *Reynard* and she was bound for McKean's Island in the middle of the Pacific. I was not the only crew member who had been shanghaied but I was the only British sailor. The ship was Boston-registered as were most of the crew and it was engaged in the least interesting trade of all – guano traffic.

At this point Renton's narrative jumps straight to McKean's island. He has nothing to say about the 5,000-mile journey, his own feelings or the atmosphere on board the *Reynard*. In his defence, the reader is often left with the impression that his authorial voice has been stifled by the exigencies of popular journalism. Any linking narrative that he might have provided may well have fallen victim to the editor's red pen. This not only truncates the narrative but provides the editors with endless opportunities for digressions of their own. These musings follow the fashion of the time which was to make spurious analogies between the world of Renton's exile and other cultures. Mercifully the few weeks that follow are free of such interruptions.

From a distance McKean's Island looked like a palm-fringed paradise but as the crew walked inland the groves thinned out and within fifty yards of the beach they were faced with a wilderness of blazing rocks where nothing could grow to give cover from the sun's blistering glare. It was a landscape of dust and crumbling putty-coloured rocks – guano.

This solitary patch in the middle of the vast Pacific had become a sanctuary for numberless seabirds. There had been so many of them and they had stayed for so long that over the millennia their droppings had covered the land to a depth of over twenty feet. Those on the *Reynard* who had signed on voluntarily, in the mistaken belief that they would be enjoying the widely advertised delights of a South Pacific island, found themselves anchored beside a desolate wilderness populated only by themselves and the indentured labourers. Every morning these men left the ship to hack away at the soft rock. The dust flung up from their labours, the periodic thud of dynamite charges and the efforts to stow the slabs in the hold, covered everything and everybody in a grey pall. As the crew hung about the ship's rail staring at the thin veil of palm trees, morale started to sink and for those like Renton who had been shanghaied the talk turned to jumping ship.

The oldest of this group was Ned, the *Reynard*'s bosun, a man who had spent over twenty years at sea, most of them on whaling ships and sandalwood traders in the Pacific. As the chorus of complaints grew from those who had signed on, Ned drew Renton and two other men who had been shanghaied into his confidence. He told them that five years previously he had been on a whaler that had visited a nearby island. It was an inhabited Polynesian atoll where a couple of white men ran a trading post, a favoured stopover for sandalwood ships on the south-west Pacific-China route. Renton and the others were not convinced

14

and so the following day, once the captain was ashore, Ned took them to the chartroom. There, as he had assured them, barely fifty miles south of McKean's Island, lay Nikumaroro, a large kidney-shaped atoll.

Renton threw in his lot with the others although their decision had less to do with their present circumstances than with what they knew must lie in store. Ned's position as bosun had meant that he was well acquainted with the true condition of the ship. It was decrepit and very leaky. He had asked the captain repeatedly on the journey to McKean's Island for a stopover in Honolulu and later in the Christmas Islands so they could lay the boat up for week and recaulk the seams. His request had been refused and he had received no support from the other officers. The *Reynard* was now deeply loaded, making such an operation impossible in the future. As the cargo was bound for Georgia, the ship was due to attempt to sail eastwards round Cape Horn against the prevailing winds in winter time.

The atmosphere in the boat was poisonous and, knowing the danger of allowing any time for a secret shared by four people to leak out, Ned's preparations were already well advanced by the time he approached the others. He had selected one of the ship's lighters, a small whaleboat that was used to ferry the labourers to and fro. At night it was moored to the *Reynard* 's stern. He had concealed under the poop deck of the *Reynard* two small kegs, each containing eight gallons of water, together with a large tin of ship's biscuits. Finally, he had already earmarked some large hams in the galley.

Ned instructed each man to prepare his kit, as well as a stock of pipes, tobacco and matches. He explained that, although it would be safer to have more water and more food, everything would have to be smuggled off the ship in one trip – there could be no going back for more. The unrest on the ship meant that every night there was always an officer on watch, so their window of opportunity would be very brief.

They had transport, food and water but there was one item that was causing them all great anxiety; they had no compass. There were three on the ship – in the main cabin, the officers' stateroom and on the poop deck in front of the wheel. The first two would be impossible to remove without being detected and the third was always monitored by the officer on watch. His single circuit of the deck would leave them barely enough time to collect their supplies and slither overboard, let alone attempt to unscrew a compass. They would have to trust to the stars.

The next night they hid under the poop deck. Ned had calculated that they had four minutes to make their escape while the officer of the watch left the poop, toured the main-deck and returned. The stiff breeze bolstered their courage. Not only was it a westerly – the direction of their intended flight – but it rattled the rigging and the halyards and masked the sounds of their efforts to manoeuvre the kegs, oars and sails over the side and into the whaleboat. They accomplished their task in half the allotted time, unfastened the painter and drifted away from the *Reynard*'s stern. Besides their kit of clothing, blankets and tobacco they had two kegs of water, the biscuit tin, four hams and an old frying pan. The sails, mast, oars and an old harpoon they had stowed in the whaleboat under a tarpaulin when the labourers had returned.

They drifted a safe distance from the ship, hoisted the sail and, propelled by the westerly breeze, they sailed south-west, estimating their course by the stars. Dawn found them out of sight of the boat and as the sun rose they were all in high spirits. They reckoned their speed at five knots and calculated that it would take them less than two days to reach the atoll, if they were fortunate.

By 10 a.m. the wind had dropped and through the day they took turns at the oars and rowed as steady a south-west course as their dead-reckoning by the sun and Ned's timepiece would allow. That evening there was a breeze, but it was from a different direction so, anxious about drifting north, they continued to row through the night. Next morning it was dead calm – and so it remained for two days. All of them knew the problem and the risk they had taken.

McKean's Island lies only three degrees south of the Equator and the westerly Trades seldom reach as far north as the Line. Sailors know that a breeze is where you find it – for on either side of the Line is an airless patch known as the doldrums and, even with a compass, making it across these degrees of latitude is fraught with uncertainty. For three days not once did they have the opportunity to raise the sail. For three days they rowed across the slick, silent ocean. Even though they took it in turns to crouch beneath the canvas they started to suffer from the blazing heat and their limbs were cramped by the confinement.

Suddenly, one morning after a week at sea, there it was, dead ahead, welling up from the ocean. They could barely distinguish it in the morning haze but it was land – they knew it was land. With Ned at the helm they rowed towards it laughing and singing. After a couple of minutes Ned shouted to them to stop. The oarsmen turned. What they thought was land was drifting across the horizon, changing shape as it went and hiding itself in the thick morning air . . . they were to be hoaxed by a cloud on many more occasions.

They all agreed that it was now an imperative that they halve the rations – half a biscuit, a mouthful of ham and half a cup of water each. Two days later, on the horizon they saw a dark spot. It was more strongly defined than the clouds that had so often deceived them. But as they watched in the stillness and silence of a dead sea, the black patch rose out of the horizon and spread itself across the sky. It was a cloud of a different kind. Black, lurid, threatening – and in a moment it seemed to start to race towards them.

At first they were hopeful. Desperately short of water, they rigged the tarpaulin across the stern of the boat and, below the decline, held the kegs in readiness. It started to pour heavily and they had barely filled a quarter of a keg when a gale force wind set in, whipping the seas up around them and spilling the rain-water everywhere. Quickly they stowed the kegs and turned their little craft before the wind and under a close reefed sail, scudded for their lives, racing along with the heavy rollers that propelled them forward into the greyness. Ned alone, with his experience of whalers, was competent to steer the boat. He stood in the stern, lashed to the steering oar, whilst the others bailed incessantly in grim silence. That night was their worst so far. Ned could only guess by the phosphorescent gleamings of the wave crests, as they chased and overtook the boat, which wave to ride. All of them were aware that a false manoeuvre would leave them side-on to a sea wall that would overwhelm the gunwales and capsize them.

At dawn the storm passed, the sea was calm – calmer than it had ever seemed before and for a few hours they slept. That day was the start of a new chapter for when they awoke the full extent of their predicament immediately became apparent. Their tin had been upended and the few remaining biscuits were gone. All they had left were four ham bones and half a keg of water. Gone too were any illusions they had shared about their true position. The eighteen-hour storm had put paid to that. The sky was completely overcast, as it was to remain for the next two days as they drifted aimlessly waiting for the sun, crunching through the remaining ham bones and eking out the last drops of fresh water from their keg. They woke on the third day to see the sun creeping up over a cloudless horizon. Now, too weak to row, they rigged the sail across the gunwales to shield themselves from the sun's scorching rays.

For two days and nights, silent and listless, all four did nothing as their boat drifted aimlessly on the glassy, windless ocean. On the third day Renton and Ned watched as the other two filled a keg with seawater and slaked their thirst. For his part, Renton now developed the habit of clambering overboard from time to time and diving as deep as he could into the cooler depths. The water forced itself into his nostrils and ears and he rose from each plunge refreshed. He was sure that this was the reason his strength was outlasting the others, but he could not persuade them to do the same.

Another day passed and the two saltwater drinkers were becoming delirious. The sun seemed even hotter and now a steamy haze obscured the horizon. They had been drifting for seventeen days and for six of them nothing had passed their lips. As Renton looked at the others he could see that hunger and thirst were crucifying them. The bones of their wrists stood out like walnuts. Veins, normally hidden beneath tissue of muscle and fat, now stood out as livid grey rivulets, criss-crossing the tightening flesh on their legs and arms. Renton noticed that his saliva had become thick, creamy and foul-tasting. His tongue was swelling and he was finding it difficult to speak. Ned and the others seemed to be in worse shape, constantly swallowing and complaining in almost inaudible croaks that their throats were swelling up and that they were suffocating. The flesh on their chests and shoulders, though taut, seemed to be collapsing inwards and he could count all their ribs. Their calves, no longer muscled, were skin and bone, which made their knees look like large bony knots of gristle. This illusion was amplified by the fact that their feet and ankles had swollen to twice their normal size.

On one of his dives Renton noticed a moss-like growth on the whaler's hull, just below the waterline. He examined it closely. Its colour varied between light and dark green and it had the appearance of tufts of hair about an inch long. With Ned's knife he scraped it off and squeezed out the salty water. They shared out a few handfuls. It tasted like grass should taste, sprinkled with salt. Though it didn't ease their hunger it eased their minds and for a few hours Ned and Renton were spared the delirious mutterings of their two companions.

By the next morning one of them seemed much worse and lay motionless, wedged in the bows of the boat. In the stern lay Ned mumbling something into the ear of the other man. He then crawled across to Renton and, crouching beside him, murmured that 'something had to be done'. Then grabbing Renton's arm he gestured to the man in the stern who was feebly rummaging amongst the few articles of the ship's kit that they had managed to smuggle on board. The man produced a razor and strop and with a deliberation borne of exhaustion started to sharpen the blade. Renton turned back to discover Ned gnawing and sucking his own forearm, watching the preparations, gimlet-eyed. The intended victim still lay a few feet away, curled up and apparently unconscious. Renton knew what they all knew – they had even joked about it at the start of their ordeal. It was an unwritten law of the sea that sailors, faced with their predicament, had first to agree unanimously to the next step and only then, by the drawing of lots, would the selection be made.

He was about to bring the issue to a head before his companions completely lost their reason when his own survival instincts won over his scruples. He was, after all, a foreigner among a group of Americans and he was most certainly the plumpest. If he confronted them he might only make their choice that much simpler. He imagined the coming nights as the three others went slowly mad, of having to stay awake, wearing as many clothes as possible to protect himself from a sudden blow, of knotted handkerchiefs around his neck, of padding his sou'wester and wearing it over his cap. He scanned the horizon in the desperate hope that even at this eleventh hour the sight of land or the appearance of a sail might avert the inevitable.

Suddenly he became aware that something was disturbing the glassy surface of the ocean. Black, triangular and pointed, the dorsal fin of a tiger shark slowly glided towards the whaler. With a single convulsion it pushed itself forward to within a few feet of the watching Renton and eyed him with small pig's eyes. Then, as it veered away in a wide circle, the grotesque scenes of the previous half hour were forgotten as the other three, energized by the prospect of something to eat, quickly attached a line to the harpoon. For half an hour Ned stood poised ready to strike whilst the shark merely watched him from a safe distance.

It was clear that they would have to devise some means of enticing it closer. A piece of meat thrown onto the water at the end of a line would have fetched it, but they had no food. They would have to try live bait.

Seating himself on the gunwale, Renton fished for it with his own legs. The shark eyed the pink bait. Two of the pilot fish made a prospecting expedition and went back to report. Three times the shark approached, three times Ned readied himself and three times it slunk back again. Then suddenly it came up with a rush, turned quickly on its side and opened its jaws. Renton whipped his feet out of the water as Ned launched the harpoon into the shark's underbelly. It lurched in a spasm, thrashed and writhed, then attempted to dart away. The rope played out, tautened with a crack but held fast.

It flailed and plunged as the starving crew watched its battle against death. The harpoon had a killing hold and after a few minutes the shark weakened and slowly surfaced, wallowing gracelessly on its side. The crew hauled it in and waited for its death. It was impossible for them in their exhausted state to do anything more than secure the quivering carcass to the side of the boat. When the shark was still, each lunged with their knives, hacking off morsels of flesh and cramming them into their mouths – they hadn't eaten for a week.

Later they broke up the biscuit box and kindled a fire in the frying pan. Under it they placed a blanket saturated in seawater to prevent the boat from burning. They boiled strips of flesh, others they laid on the thwarts to dry in the sun. The water round the becalmed whaler was now awash with blood. Suddenly the shark seemed to come to life, the gunwale tilted and the whaler veered sideways. The astonished crew looked overboard, their shark had lost its tail! Two fins darted towards the boat. There was an audible snap of jaws as two tiger sharks tore into their prey, each thrusting back and tearing from side to side, pulling in opposite directions. Ned grabbed the harpoon and made frantic, ineffectual efforts to spear at the thrashing sea but the cannibal sharks were half hidden by the blood-filled water. Renton and the other two made desperate attempts to heave their prize on board as it was wrenched, pushed and torn. Eventually, minus its head, tail and much of its belly they heaved it in and, exhausted from their efforts they fell into a stupor around the bloody carcass, each tortured by a thirst that seemed worse for having eaten.

They slept for a while and when they woke the sky was over-cast and they watched the approach of clouds with mingled hope and apprehension – hope that they might be blessed with rain and apprehension because in their weakened state they knew that they did not have the strength to ride out another gale.

Their luck, however, had taken a turn. The evening brought a deeply overcast sky, the breeze got up and it rained in torrents. They spread the sail and the tarpaulin to catch as much water as possible and as it rained they turned their faces to the sky to catch what water they could in their parched mouths. Then they quickly filled the kegs and formed a pool in the tarpaulin. By morning the clouds had passed and as a breeze blew up they set the sail for the first time since the storm ten days previously. They felt in better shape than for days.

Now, however, as hope took over from despair, they realized their predicament. Two days of being blown about and ten days of drifting had left them completely lost, the best they could do was to sail westwards and hope. For two days, as they sailed blindly onwards, they broke every piece of wood they could safely dismantle from the boat without sinking it to cook the shark meat. Then they were forced to eat the sun-dried strips of flesh.

As for water they were particularly well off. The weather was unsettled without being stormy and it rained frequently. The moisture, however, damaged the shark's flesh, which started to putrefy and was soon so poisonous that even a small strip of meat proved indigestible. Their retching and vomiting left them sweaty and exhausted and took a heavy toll on the three elder men, leaving them even weaker. That night they heaved the putrefying remnants of the carcass overboard.

At the start of the fourth week, the sky was clear as they manoeuvred the bow of the whaler towards the western horizon, but the gesture seemed pointless because there was no wind. That afternoon as Renton swam round the boat scraping the last remnants of the moss-like growth from the whaler's waterline he heard a scratching noise from the other side of the hull. Fearing a shark he hauled himself onto the gunwale and collapsed into the boat. As he looked over the rail on the other side he saw a large turtle scratching at the hull with its flipper. Ned had heard it too and was making a few ineffectual jabs with the harpoon but his strength was gone and as he struck the point skidded across the turtle's leathery shell. The other two crew members were so weak they could only lie and watch.

Renton eased himself overboard. Holding his knife between his teeth, he grabbed at the turtle. But as he reached with one hand for his knife the turtle bolted and he found himself being dragged downwards, flipper in one hand, knife in the other. He lunged at the turtle's neck, as he did so the creature twisted and freed itself. Renton swam back exhausted. He no longer had the strength to clamber on board and Ned had to secure a looped line to one of the rowlocks to give him a toehold back into the boat.

The rest of the day passed dismally. Ned's two compatriots lay huddled under the tarpaulin in complete silence waiting for Renton's timepiece to herald the next sip of water. As for Ned, the smallest incident appeared to send him into a rage or a depression and as he staggered about his body appeared so beaten that it was having the greatest difficulty following his commands. That night they had their last sip of water and Renton knew that unless they sighted land soon the razor would reappear.

The following morning, as they crawled out from beneath the tarpaulin, they were confronted by a huge cumulo-nimbus cloud that billowed upwards to the heavens where, quite suddenly, it was planed flat by the icy jet stream that dragged the summit of the storm in its wake. It had the familiar appearance of a huge white anvil with a flat grey base from which, to the cheers of the four castaways, a torrent of rain poured down. They set a reefed sail, spread the tarpaulin and braced themselves for the storm to come. The wind increased to a strong breeze and Ned drove their little boat towards the storm but as the curtain of rain approached the wind swung round and, thankfully, slackened. The rain started to lash down, hissing loudly as it struck the sea and drummed on their tarpaulin with such force that they could barely hold it in position. Within five minutes the kegs were full and they lay on their backs, eyes shut and mouths open.

Despite their relief, the night passed dismally. It continued to pour with rain and for the first time in their thirty-three days adrift, darkness brought a drop in temperature of such severity that, despite their attempts to cover themselves with anything they could find, their emaciated bodies were racked with uncontrollable bouts of shivering. Exhausted, yet unable to sleep, they waited for dawn.

As morning broke the clouds began to lift and as the light flickered up from the east, the wind freshened from the same direction. Renton, aware of the futility of the gesture, nonetheless hoisted the sail and they ran before the wind towards the line where the sky and the ocean met on the western horizon that was gradually lit up by the slanting eastern sunrise. He scanned the line of cloud and sky and sea as he had for the last five weeks and for the umpteenth time imagined some line more sharply defined than the rest. It seemed that almost every day they had turned the boat's bow towards some dark speck. Even exhausted as they were, they had sometimes rowed for six hours at a time after what proved to be a cloud. But this morning as the sun rose, so did his hopes. This time the dark speck, instead of altering shape or fading away, continued unchanged in form and, for a moment, became more sharply defined. He called out to the others. They were so exhausted that they could barely stir themselves. Even when he urged them, only Ned had the strength to lift himself up to the gunwale. He assured Renton that it was the usual deception. It was low on the port side and they were effectively sailing parallel to it.

Renton brought the boat round but the wind barely filled the sail and progress was painfully slow. A distant shower passed like a curtain across the horizon, obscuring the dark speck, but when it had passed the speck was still there. Renton shouted to the others. As they watched, another cloud obscured the object and they waited in suspense for half an hour for the sky to clear.

When it did the speck was still there but their own progress was so slow that it appeared just as indistinct. Then the sky darkened and for over an hour as the breeze strengthened they were driven at a brisk pace through the ocean, but then it cleared and there, across three-quarters of the horizon spread a solid dark outline of land. Ned fell on his knees, Renton cheered, the other two wept. They had survived thirty-five days and here at last was salvation.

But now, just as they were in sight of land, the clouds passed, the wind dropped and they were becalmed. They sat and watched and waited. After an hour it slowly dawned on them that they were drifting on a current away from the distant shore. All of them except Renton were appallingly weak but if they wanted to live they would have to row.

All that day they strained feebly at the oars but when dusk came they seemed no nearer than before. Dusk in the tropics turns quickly into night and they collapsed where they sat, utterly exhausted. Now their main fear was that a gale might arise and carry them out of sight of their goal. They hoisted the sail and waited. A light breeze sprang up and all through the night, Ned, using the stars, kept the boat pointing towards land.

At the first light of day they all gathered in the bow, straining their eyes in the gloaming. They felt that this was the moment that would decide their fate. The morning was still, without a breath of wind and a dense fog surrounded them. But in the gathering heat of the morning sun it slowly evaporated revealing a high land that threaded its way both to port and starboard, off into the horizon. Whether it was an island or a continent they could not tell. They scarcely cared; it was land and that was enough.

The wind continued intermittently and they searched out the

light squalls that ruffled the sea, all the time fighting an offshore current. That day their progress was painfully slow but by late afternoon they were close enough to see a sight that electrified them. From various patches of the thickly wooded land rose small plumes of smoke. This land was inhabited; there would be food, shelter and possibly other white men. Ned said that it was just possible that they had reached the tropical northern coast of Australia.

As they came closer they saw a white ribbon of breakers, which appeared to stretch the length of the shoreline. An hour later they realized that this was yet another hurdle to overcome for the waves were breaking on a huge reef a mile from the shore. Soon they were close enough to hear the roar of the breakers. They stowed the sail and rowed slowly along the coastline looking for a channel.

Throughout that last night they stayed awake, maintaining their position, waiting for the dawn and the hope that they might at last reach land. But even before there was enough light to continue the search, their fortunes took one final turn. Through the morning mist a number of large dark objects loomed into sight . . . war canoes!

3

Landfall

We sailed to the north-east-by-east for 16 leagues and arrived at a good harbour that had a long reef at the entrance. They came out in 25 canoes with warriors who discharged their arrows. Some shots were fired at them, which killed some and wounded others.

Hernando Gallego, 1568

I T was to the misfortune of the castaways that they were about to wash up on one of only three islands, amongst the thousands in the Pacific, where attitudes towards the white man had been shaped by an encounter that had taken place two hundred years before Cook had set sail from Greenwich.

In the 1560s the Pacific ports of Guayaquil and Callao were rife with rumours of a land of gold that lay to the west and there was still no reason not to believe the story. After all, for forty years, since Atahualpa's vain attempt to ransom himself for a roomful of gold, the Inca Empire had surrendered up riches that had defied the imagination. Even in the 1540s, whilst the conquest of the interior was at its height, rumours of new lands of gold persisted. Somewhere on the vast continent lay a secret kingdom ruled over by El Dorado, the Golden Man. From the pen of a Spanish chronicler the beguiling legend was born.

> I interviewed Spaniards who had been in Quito . . . and asked them why they call that prince 'The Golden Lord or King'. They tell me that what they learned from the Indians is that the great lord or prince goes about continually covered in gold dust as fine as salt. He feels that it would be less beautiful to wear any other ornament; it would be crude or common to put on armour plated of hammered or stamped gold, for their rich lords wear these when they wish. But to powder oneself with gold is something exotic and unusually novel, and most costly, for he washes away at night what he puts on each morning, and that it is discarded and lost, and he does this every day of the year . . .

Here was a tale that combined both the mystical and the material. A tale that promised a land full, not just of riches, but of romance – a pure, inviolate world. Within a decade there was not a port in the Americas or Europe where there was not some new rumour of its provenance. It seemed that after Mexico, Peru and New Grenada there were countless men prepared to believe that anything was possible, be they Spanish, Portuguese, French or British. Stoking this credulity and multiplying the locations were numerous Indian tales of a rich and civilized people who lived just a few days' march away. El Dorado was 'beyond those peaks', 'beside a lake', 'in a hidden valley', or 'by a distant river's confluence' – anywhere but where these ironclad white men were currently encamped, questioning the local population. Gonzalo Pizzaro wrote, prior to setting out on one of the earliest expeditions: 'The Indians say that further on, if we advanced, we would come to a widespread and flat country teeming with people who possess great riches, for they all wear gold ornaments.'

The decades passed and, with the exception of the account of Orellana's attempt, which led to the crossing of the continent on a great river, few narratives remain of these journeys. For a conquistador, if there were no wonders to report or riches to discover, there was nothing. As Cortez explained to Montezuma's ambassadors when demanding another wagonload of tribute: 'We suffer from a strange disease of the heart for which the only known remedy is gold.' By the 1560s, in the face of these repeated failures, the new rumour started to circulate of a land that lay not to the east but westwards. It told of a journey made by the Inca king, Tupac Yapanqui, across the Pacific and the discovery of two islands from which he brought back shiploads of gold and silver, a copper throne and many black slaves.

De Castro, the governor of Peru, provided two ships with a total complement of 150 men, including seventy soldiers, four Franciscan friars, a number of slaves and two master navigators, Sarmiento and Gallego. The privilege of leading the expedition was granted to De Castro's twenty-five-year-old nephew Alvaro de Mendana whom he directed to sail to the unknown land, establish a colony and there, 'to convert all infidels to

Christianity'. Under the guise of evangelization, the small complement of professional miners and assayers betrayed the journey's primary purpose.

On Sarmiento's insistence that 'in fifteen degrees of latitude there were many rich islands' in November 1567 they duly set sail from Callao on a south-westerly course. Within a month the two prima donna navigators were locked in conflict. To Sarmiento's mortification, Mendana sided with Gallego and the expedition bore off west by north-west. Another month passed. Food and water ran low. The crew grew mutinous. On the sixty-second day they sighted a small barren island surrounded by reefs. Mendana sailed on and, as Gallego wrote in his log, this led 'to a murmuring among the soldiers, who said that, despite the risk, we should not have left the island. Being weary of the voyage, they showed great displeasure.' Two weeks later they found themselves in the grip of a cyclone and for six days they were swept south. On the seventh night the wind slackened and dawn found them facing a land that appeared so mountainous and limitless that they believed it to be a continent.

The delighted crew celebrated their deliverance by singing the *Te Deum* and Mendana named the land Santa Isabel, after the patron saint of their voyage. After eleven weeks at sea they landed in the Bay of Ghene. The descendants of the people who first saw the white man in the Pacific are now extinct, but in 1947 an anthropologist recorded an account from a few men who claimed to be related to the Ghene people. It is a testimony to the accuracy of oral history that this account mirrors the Spanish version of this historic encounter.

As soon as they saw the white men come ashore, they

thought that they must be ghosts. The white men shouted after them, but, in their terror, they ran into the bush. For days they stealthily came to find out what manner of beings these white men were, and also to find out whether they were real men or ghosts.

For days they could not make contact with the white men, but little by little they came nearer, as the white men showed signs of being friendly. Then a man gave himself up. He simply walked over to the white men and they received him with kindness. Not only were they friendly but they gave him some of their goods, they gave him mirrors and beads and pieces of cloth. Finally Belenbangara made his appearance, and he let it be known by signs that he was the chief of the people.

The official expedition account takes up the narrative:

He wore many white and coloured plumes on his head, very white armlets which looked like alabaster, and a small shield on his neck. He asked for a cap, offering one of his armlets in return. The General [Mendana] made him sit down, and asked him his name, and what he called the sun, the moon, the heavens and others things. And he gave them all a name in his language, which is quickly understood, as ours is by them, because they speak distinctly and not affectedly like the people of Peru. They were delighted in storing our words in their memory, and asked us to teach them.

Belenbangara, beguiled by the encounter, promised to provide food for the expedition, without being informed that he was expected to make provision for 150 famished men. Quickly realizing the full implications of his undertaking, he and his followers retreated into the bush. After several fruitless days at anchor and no food forthcoming, Sarmiento was delegated by Mendana to go ashore and find some. It was typical of this pious, insouciant and slightly feckless young man that he should entrust this task to a man known as the 'hammer of the Incas' with the instruction that 'He was to take nothing against their will, and to do them no harm, but to pursue his journey.'

Predictably, once Sarmiento had landed, he set out to capture Belenbangara. Anticipating this move, the chief set an ambush and the Spanish had to fight their way back to the beach. Another conquistador decided to flex his muscles. Gallego later wrote of this adventure: 'the General sent the Master of the Camp, Pedro de Ortega, to see if he could discover what land there was in the interior. He was absent about seven days on this service, and had many skirmishes with the Indians, wherein he burned many temples of the worshippers of snakes, toads, and other insects . . .' Clearly the Spanish were losing patience with their reluctant hosts.

Meanwhile 'the people watched how the white men built a great canoe. They were very much surprised at the speed of the great work.' The five-ton brigantine, made entirely from the local timber, was completed in eight weeks and sent out to explore the adjoining islands. Their attempts to land on a nearby island, which they named Guadalcanal, were met with spirited resistance but an anchorage was found and the main body of the expedition joined the brigantine. Their time on this island was to be no happier than on the one they had left. Again the Spanish took food by force, angering the islanders, who fought back. Prospecting expeditions into the interior had to be accompanied by large contingents of troops. Villages were burned, crops and livestock appropriated and islanders taken hostage in return for food or to act as guides.

Meanwhile the brigantine, under Gallego's command, sailed down to the south-eastern extremity of Guadalcanal where the mountainous outline of another island could be seen – Malaita. Against the advice of their two captive guides, who made it clear that they feared for everyone's lives, the Spanish made directly for the island. After some predictable skirmishes, Gallego's journal records the beginning of a legend: 'In this island we found apples of some size, oranges, a metal club that seemed to be a base kind of gold, and, besides, pearl-shell, with which they inlay the club they use in battle.'

A frisson of expectation now gripped the ship's company and the assayers urged Gallego to be more conciliatory. As they continued their journey up the coast the crew carried out a brisk trade bartering anything they could find for the warclubs. The handles were made of hardwood inlaid with mother-of-pearl, the head, held in place with fine grass plaiting, was a heavy golden nodule. The fever of excitement was momentarily cooled when the assayer Henriquez hammered two of the nodules together until they broke. However, the sharply delineated veins of gold exposed by cracking the pyrites left many of the Spaniards unconvinced. Even Mendana took comfort from the thought that ironstone 'is the mother of all metals'.[1]

After this brief attempt to be more conciliatory, Gallego's progress up the coast of Malaita was a continuing record of pillage, confrontation and death. Then, 'on account of the sickness of myself and some of the other soldiers we did not proceed further: and, keeping away to leeward, we arrived at the island of

Guadalcanal.' The journey down the coast of this island by the sick crew was to have profound implications: 'as we continued our cruise to return to the ships, we touched at some places where we had been before, the natives receiving us in a friendly manner, and giving us what they had, because they were so much afraid of the muskets we carried.'

Gallego returned to base to find the rest of the expedition, like his own crew, ill with malaria and other diseases. No gold had been found on Guadalcanal and their morale was disintegrating. Mendana called a meeting. There were three options, to continue exploring, to found a settlement or to return home. The party of Franciscans voted for the first, the soldiers for the second and the navigators for the third. The deadlock was only broken when the navigators pointed out that the ships were so worm-eaten that unless they left immediately they would never return. On 14 August 1568, a little over six months after they had first landed, the two ships set sail for Callao.

Initially the chroniclers were disparaging:

> Throughout the whole of these islands there is not to be found among the Indians a pot, jar or vase of any kind, either made of clay or anything else. In the course of these discoveries they found no specimens of spices, nor gold and silver, nor merchandise, nor any other source of profit, and all the people are naked savages . . . nor anything else, except little club-headed sticks of iron-stone. Nearly forty men died upon this voyage. God forgive them. Amen!

Yet, once home, in the port-side bars and bordellos, the *expedicionarios* had such tales to tell of an extraordinary adventure, of the discovery of lands thousands of miles away, of disease and death and strangeness. And with the retelling began the revisionism, as time and distance lent enchantment. Perhaps the golden warclubs had been the vital clue that they had all missed. Perhaps they had not looked hard enough. Hadn't the natives said that theirs was a small land compared to the great one that lay nearby? Spain's New World conquest had always yielded riches. The governor held an enquiry. Gallego maintained that there was evidence of the existence of gold and Mendana claimed that, when shown specimens, the natives recognized it and called it *aburu* or *tereque.*

And so the story took on a life of its own – of a great island, as yet unvisited, where riches could be mined in great quantities. It was the land of Solomon, adorned with the gold from Ophir. Theirs had been a romantic enterprise that deserved a romantic name. Within a decade the King of Spain was addressing Mendana as 'Our Governor of the Islands of Solomon'.[2]

If the whole enterprise had now fallen victim to Cortez's 'strange disease of the heart', their hosts had fallen victim to diseases of a far more prosaic kind. Along the eastern coasts of Santa Isabel and Guadalcanal the coconuts lay unclaimed on the tidelines, germinating on the once busy beaches. Within a generation all traces of human habitation had disappeared and all that remained were the bleached bones of the dead – there had been no one to bury them. But these were not just places full of purgatorial spirits but a coastline cursed with a sickness that had taken hold when the white man had left. No one doubted that he had been the cause but none dared return to their lands for fear that what the white man had left behind might still linger in the air.

In most pre-literate cultures each generation selects individuals in late adolescence who are taught by rote the genealogy and history of the community and on Santa Isabel, Mendana's visit was still part of the Ghene people's history barely fifty years ago:

> The white man stayed on the island for at least ten moons. The people called their ship 'nguanguao', and they said it was manned by ghosts and it carried diseases. Later, whenever the people saw a ship approaching they told their women and children to hide and the men prayed to the spirits, asking them to remove the nguanguao ship, this disease carrier.

To this day, on the east coast of Guadalcanal, whenever a man lights a fire, he takes the burning stick and blows hard on the cinders 'to blow the white man's diseases away'.

Through inter-island commerce, stories about Mendana's expedition spread throughout the archipelago – stories of his unpredictability, of his possessions, of his capacity to kill, not just with weapons from a great distance but by his very presence. Then for two hundred years he disappeared – thwarted by his inability to calculate longitude.

It was one thing to locate a group of remote islands in the Pacific, quite another to establish their exact position. On the early charts, the islands of Santa Isabel, Guadalcanal and Malaita exist with all the precision expected of a six-month survey. However, Mendana had gravely miscalculated their longitude, placing them five thousand miles east of Peru and two thousand miles short of their true position. From the seventeenth-century onwards the islands found a variety of resting places. In a map of 1646 they were identified 3,500 miles away in the Marquesas, later off the coast of New Guinea, once as far south as New Zealand and, for a time, the names covered almost every discovery made in the South Pacific until eventually they disappeared off the charts altogether.

It was to take a lifetime's work by John Harrison, a Yorkshire clockmaker, to solve one of the greatest scientific problems of the eighteenth century – the creation of the chronometer, a completely reliable instrument that would keep perfect time on board ship for months on end. By the 1790s every ocean-going vessel carried at least one set of Harrison-designed timepieces and the impact on Pacific exploration was immediate. However, for three islands with prior knowledge of the white man, this subsequent invasion was to usher in an era of increasingly desperate resistance.

In 1798 the British ship the *Anne and Hope* encountered seven canoes off the coast of Malaita. The ship's crew hung over the gunwales offering gifts and the canoes approached cautiously. As the seaman attempted to trade 'they stayed with us a little while,' the log-keeper reported, 'and then went away rather abruptly repeating the word "tabu".'

In 1802, three ships, the *Nile*, *Canada* and *Minorca* on their way from Australia to China, moored off the east coast of Guadalcanal. For the inhabitants they must have seemed like the harbingers of the dimly remembered holocaust for they immediately retreated to the bush. The next morning the ships were still riding at anchor just two hundred yards from the shore. Worse was to come as some of the ship's boats made for the beaches. The party made their way inland and, finding the villages deserted, helped themselves to fruit, vegetables and livestock. For two days the ships remained at anchor close to the shore and the population, fearing the decimation that might follow any further landings, assembled a war party of eight thirty-man war canoes.

On the third day the captain of the *Nile* signalled to the officers on the *Minorca* and *Canada* to join him for a meal and two ship's boats set out. On the shore this activity was interpreted as preparation for another incursion so the war-canoes were launched and formed into a line between the ships and the shore – a manoeuvre misunderstood by the crews of the three ships. Their logs recorded that the natives would not approach, 'although much enticed', and for over an hour the line held until, party over, one of the ship's boats left the *Nile* carrying the captain and officers of the *Minorca*. Once the launch was spotted, some canoes 'collected together and were in deep consultation', then a number advanced towards it. This was interpreted by watching seamen as an attempt to cut the returning boat off from its ship and, obeying the occupant's cries of 'Fire, fire!', the crews of the *Canada* and *Minorca* let loose with cannon and firearms. The official record was deliberately vague about the number of killed and injured, merely observing that 'many must be killed by the direction of the gun'.

Over the next thirty years it was the whaling ships that were to open up the world of the white man to the rest of the Solomon Islanders. When the Atlantic whaling grounds became less profitable the industry turned its attention to the Pacific. From May to November they pursued the migrating sperm whales through the South-West Pacific and the nearby islands became valued for their sheltered anchorages, their supplies of food and water, and their women. Contact was initially a simple matter, as few of the inhabitants could resist the offers of calico, beads, fish-hooks and, above all, hoop iron.

As one ship's captain reported, first contact followed a predictable pattern:

> Each canoe had a few coconuts, which they bartered for fish-hooks, beads and iron hoop. I prevailed upon two of the natives, who appeared to be chiefs, to come on board. They rubbed noses and hugged me . . . It was evident by their gestures that they took us for supernatural beings, and considered our dress to be part of our body. They threw themselves down on the deck, and kissed it repeatedly. On being taken to the cabin and seeing themselves reflected in the mirror, they screamed with terror, and implored me to allow them to go on deck. I offered them tobacco but they were ignorant of its use. On being shown how to smoke it, they were quite paralysed with fear – as far as I could judge from their appearance – they seemed to believe on seeing the smoke issue from a man's mouth, that he was on fire.

Only Guadalcanal, Isabel and Malaita continued to resist these blandishments. It may have been two hundred years since Mendana had sailed away but the deserted coastlines of Isabel and Guadalcanal were a constant reminder of the 'disease carriers'. These had been lands, in the words of one of Mendana's chroniclers, 'with so many villages on hilltops that it was marvellous . . . We saw much smoke in the plains, which is not surprising as the land is densely populated.'

On Malaita, the least accessible of the three islands, the cordon sanitaire was imposed with particular rigour. In 1829 there were rumours of twenty shipwrecked sailors being killed and eaten. In 1840 a ship reported from the area that they 'saw a great number of men on the beach striking the water with their clubs and showing other symptoms of hostility . . . They made signs for us to go away, pointing at the same time to three passages in the reef leading out to sea.' Another reported: 'The natives obstinately refuse all communication with strangers and if some disembark from ships they kill all those they are able to surprise.'

In 1858 a scientific expedition was briefly shadowed by a group of canoes as the ship made its way up the eastern coast of Malaita. Reviewing this encounter, the members of the expedition 'were unanimously of the opinion (which is not always the case in matters of personal impressions), that the inhabitants of Malayta [sic] were the wildest, most uncivilized race of men we had as yet encountered in our voyaging to and fro round the globe'. Now, ten years later, an encounter was about to take place that would eventually lift the curtain and reveal an island that was as strange as the imaginings of the many who had told stories about 'over there'.

*   *   *

As the four exhausted men drifted close to the reef, the canoes changed course, spread out line abreast and quickly closed on them. Then at a certain distance they stopped and waited. Ned immediately guessed that they knew about European firearms and were waiting to see what would happen. He pulled off his shirt and waved it at them. After a few moments the canoes slowly advanced, a few of the occupants paddling, the rest standing up, clubs, spears and bows and arrows poised. All were completely naked. Renton and his companions sat still, not daring to make any move that might be misinterpreted.

When they were encircled, the crews lowered their weapons as the helmsmen from each canoe shouted to each other. It soon became clear to the whaler's occupants that there was considerable disagreement amongst their captors about what to do next, though from the gestures of one of the helmsmen Renton gained the distinct impression that if this man had his way they would not be long for this world. He slowly bent down and picked up the cooking pot, which, together with his knife, he held out in front of him. The others followed suit, picking up anything they felt might be of value. At this point the debating stopped and the leader from each canoe jumped on board and, completely ignoring the passive occupants, set about ransacking the boat, passing every movable object to the encircling canoes. Everything was taken including their clothing and they were left with nothing except their trousers. They themselves were clearly the least important items in the boat, a fact that was reinforced when, having left four men to paddle the boat, the rest of the islanders continued on their journey.

The whaler was beached in front of a large crowd who had noticed its slow progress across the lagoon from the reef a mile distant. It was a type of vessel none had seen before. Renton climbed out unaided. For over a month he had been pitched and tossed in an open boat and suddenly he felt very giddy. As he stumbled on the firm sand beneath his feet there was a hush. He paused in the silence not knowing what to do next. Over a hundred pairs of eyes were watching him. Half a dozen, mostly elderly men, approached him. He stood very still. They touched his chest, examined his long hair, held out his arms and compared them to their own. Someone in the crowd shouted something. Two of the men looked at him and then looked at each other. Suddenly both men made a grab for his genitals. As

he doubled up to protect himself one of them shouted something and the crowd burst into laughter. He was then escorted to
a hut fifty yards from the shore where he turned to watch Ned
tottering towards him and the other two following on all fours.
The crowd visibly shrank from their presence. With their blistered, emaciated bodies, swollen joints and stick-like limbs they
appeared to Renton 'to be without human semblance'.

Fresh coconuts were stripped, sliced and placed some
distance from them. They crawled forward and tasted their first
vegetables for thirty-five days. As they ate the crowd grew.
Renton calculated that there were soon over two hundred. After
much discussion, the half dozen who had originally approached
Renton now came forward. It was clear from their gestures that
they wanted their trousers and whatever they wore underneath.
Ned made it quite clear that none of them had any intention of
surrendering this last vestige of their modesty. At this point the
crowd seemed to lose interest and wandered off towards the
beached whaler. The four men crawled into the shade of the
hut. They sat for a while and watched as about fifty men set
about destroying their only chance of escape. They appeared to
be after the nails. Exhausted, the four survivors slept for the rest
of the day and all through the following night.

Shortly after daylight canoe-loads of new visitors started to
arrive; news of their capture had obviously passed down the
coast. For Renton, that morning was remembered above all for
the feeling of being an animal in a zoo. They were still desperately hungry so what better way to entice the animals out of their
cage than by offering food. Small gifts of yams, fish and meat
were placed outside the hut. The four occupants emerged into
the daylight and gobbled up the morsels to the approving

44

murmur of the crowd. The next offering was placed at a slightly greater distance from the hut. Again the famished crew crawled out into the open, all except Renton. He stood up and walked down to the beach. To his surprise no one followed him. The crowd appeared fascinated by the antics of his companions scrabbling in the sand for the small offerings.

As he stood watching them, a young native walked up to him. He was tall, well built and Renton guessed him to be his own age. Unlike the rest of the visitors he was carrying an armful of yams and fish. He smiled at him and proffered the armful. Renton was confused. All he had experienced so far was clinical curiosity. What little food that had been offered was offered just to see what these strange creatures would do. Now he felt that he, the youngest and most active of the catch, had been singled out for special treatment. He thanked the young man, summoned up a rather wan smile and returned to the others with the food, who followed him back into the hut.

Half an hour later Renton peered outside. The crowd had disappeared but standing beside the demolished whaler was the young man, who motioned to Renton to join him. Together they walked a short distance along the beach. Then, looking back over his shoulder to make sure they were not being followed, the young man put his hand on Renton's shoulder and stood facing him. With a series of unmistakable gestures he made it clear that if Renton stayed he would have his throat cut. He then pointed down the beach to a large canoe a few yards offshore. It was full of waiting natives. With a series of reassuring gestures he motioned to Renton to follow him.

Renton did not hesitate very long. Not because of the behaviour of the young man but because he quickly realized that a canoe full of armed natives who had clearly come here for the express purpose of kidnapping him were not going to paddle away empty-handed. He could walk away or even try to run, but to where? He decided to go willingly – or at least give that appearance. He followed the young man.

It was a large canoe, over twenty-five feet long, its sides inlaid with pearl-shell from end to end. The elongated curving prow and stern rose to over six feet. He was placed in the stern, sitting with his back to the bows opposite a middle-aged man wearing a necklace. It seemed to be made of small shells – red, white, yellow and black – crocheted with connecting fibres into elaborate patterns. It fitted round his neck and the richly coloured strands hung over his shoulders and reached down to his waist. Renton's escort sat beside him and as the canoe moved off the two conferred for a moment. Then the older man leaned forward and yet again Renton was subjected to a physical examination, although rather more thoughtful and expert than the previous one. His hands met with approval, particularly the palms; his feet less so, though his examiner seemed fascinated by their softness and pinkness. And finally his teeth; these aroused much discussion. Renton noticed that theirs were black.

Twenty paddles moved to the rhythm of a grunting kind of chant and, except for the muffled click of each blade as it was drawn back against the canoe at the end of the stroke, no paddle made a sound. The barrier reef seemed to extend into the horizon about a mile from the shoreline. The lagoon was shallow; Renton estimated that it was no more then five or ten feet deep. Dark bands of coral could be seen through the emerald green water. In the gullies and hollows over which the canoe passed he could see through the clear water, the shoals of coral fish parading in startling combinations of translucent colours – angelfish, parrotfish, butterflyfish, pink coral trout, red cod and tiger-striped snapper. On the sandbanks and shallows, villages of various sizes sat just above the waterline, resting on neatly stacked foundations of rock coral.

What Renton was yet to discover was that these were artificial islands, unique creations, peopled by the dispossessed. From all over Malaita they had arrived, the victims of land disputes, individuals and families fleeing blood vengeance, escaped slaves, the exiled of family feuds and the survivors of inter-tribal wars – all seeking the opportunity to rebuild their lives under the protection of an island's founding family. Satellite islands could be built nearby with the permission of the family who owned the fishing rights to the water surrounding the village but only after a suitable period of vetting. Thus there grew up a society not unlike early medieval Europe with chiefly families enjoying baronial status and where, in place of tithes, the commoners were expected to undertake communal projects and, when necessary, take up arms.

Unlike the rest of the Solomon Islands where language and tribal groupings had occupied the land for thousands of years, these islands were recent creations. Gallego's account of his voyage in the brigantine along the east coast of Malaita made no mention of the artificial islands. Even today they are a remarkable sight and it is highly unlikely that the fastidious navigator would not have logged their existence if they had been there.

The early inhabitants hung onto this sliver of territory between the ocean and the mountainous coastline but they needed access to land and, above all, fresh water, so they fought and made peace and fought again until eventually the coastal tribes, exhausted by their constant belligerence, agreed to the unthinkable – they sold tracts of coastal land to the people of the lagoon. In a world where land was ancestrally bequeathed and therefore impossible to sell this was indeed succumbing to a new dispensation and was to create an enmity between the 'bush' and the 'saltwater' people that was exacerbated by mutual dependence.

Bush life was shaped around the wresting of subsistence from the land. Families depended upon a continuing harvest of starchy food with the staple diet consisting of taro, with yams providing a seasonal change. Gardening was exhausting labour as the land had to be cleared. The bases of the huge hardwood trees were burned and stone adzes used to chip away at the charred wood. This process of burning and chipping was slow work; each tree would take four days to fell. The cleared land could only be used for one planting, then left to lie fallow to renew the feeble fertility of the soil. There was little in the forest to supplement their diet except tree grubs, snails, frogs and lizards. What bush people always craved was fish.

The saltwater people invented hooks and lines, nets and fish traps and developed a variety of canoes. By controlling the seacoast they became wealthy. Trade with the interior passed largely through their hands. But although the ceded land had given them access to fresh water, there was too little of it to support agriculture and their diet lacked one important ingredient – starch.

The enmity between the two societies was permanent and lasted into the twentieth century. Jack London, visiting the lagoon in 1910, commented:

Practically the only truces are on market-days, which occur at stated intervals, usually twice a week. The bush women and the saltwater women do the bartering. Back in the bush, a hundred yards away, fully armed, lurk the bushmen, while to seaward, in canoes, are the saltwater men. There are very rare instances of market-day truces being broken. The bushmen like the fish too well, while the saltwater men have an organic craving for the vegetables they cannot grow on their crowded islets.

From a distance Renton observed that the smaller artificial islands looked like schooners at anchor. Their rock walls and the cluster of indistinct houses merged into a dark mass, but clear into the blue sky sprang two or three coconut trees. When first built, an island had just enough room for three huts – the minimum requirement for a family. A hut for the man, a hut for his wife and children and an open shed without sides where his canoe is stored, nets dried and fish prepared. When a family built an island they first made a raft of logs to transport its foundations. These were pieces of coral rock either lying loose or broken off the bed of the lagoon. The foundation was built to just above the high-water mark. Usually circular, the island was then topped with soil in some areas and shingle in others. Small saplings of coconut, banyan and breadfruit trees were planted in the soil, their roots helping to bind the whole construction together.

Renton was taken to the largest of these islands. Its foundation of large rocks was surrounded by upright logs cut from coconut trees and bound tightly together to form a stockade that stood about twelve feet high. The island was circular and covered about two acres. Breadfruit trees and coconut palms grew in clusters, mostly near the perimeter. The canoe moored beside a stone ramp that appeared to be the only place where the stockade was breached. Renton was escorted through narrow streets lined with people. He guessed the island probably had about three hundred inhabitants. He was shown to a large hut and fed yet again, whilst the whole village watched.

*   *   *

White visitors, nervously skirting the island's shores, may have been of the opinion that the inhabitants were 'the wildest and most uncivilized people' but these were a people merely demonstrating a strong sense of history. Indeed it was an island obsessed with history. Each tribal grouping had their own unique, complex and detailed 'Generation', a narrative which recounted the achievements of particular individuals who had contributed to the development and progressive evolution of each group. The first person who discovered the cause of a sickness and how to cure it, the person who invented fishing nets, or found many uses for different types of stone, or how to make a canoe, or the first man to carve beautiful things, or to build a particular kind of house, or the first man who discovered how to count. There are detailed biographies of the first man or woman who brought some particular benefit to their society: in short – the people who invented their world. Learned verbatim by chosen individuals and passed on from generation to generation, when many of these histories were committed to paper in the 1940s – most ran to over forty pages.

For the people of the village of Sulufou where Renton was to spend the next eight years, his time there was to be an epoch-making event that was to become part of their 'Generation'. It is an account currently shared amongst a dozen oral historians and runs to thirty pages, with each historian, as in much of

Melanesia, appearing to have the 'rights' to certain parts of the story. It is anecdotal, episodic, parochial, rich in detail and it provides a very different picture of Jack Renton from the sanitized account that he presented to his Victorian readers. Details of his early life on Sulufou are narrated by the village's only female historian, Grace Sosoe:

It was a strange time. Here was this young man – a boy really – who *looked* so different. His white skin, all sore and red and blistered in those early days. His tattered trousers, which he never took off so everyone wondered: were white men made differently from other people? Every evening men and women would leave Sulufou for the shore and a freshwater spring where they would bathe together but he was very shy and would sit in the pool with his trousers on! The people talked even more, particularly the women! In the end the men felt sorry for him and they found him a pool where he could bathe on his own. It's still there, still known as Renton's Pool. Then some people peeked while he was washing and soon everyone knew he was made like other people. He was just a boy then, a long way from his home.

In those early days Chief Kabou sent him off with the children and every day they would take him to the shore and teach him all the words of our world. And, because he was young, our language came easily to him. When the tide was out the children would play on the beach. They would go to the water and jump about or play at being grown up, or play war games, the things children do everywhere in the world. He liked being with them. He said it reminded him of his own home. He was the eldest of his father's children and had many younger brothers and sisters.

51

When he could speak a little of the language he taught them this special game – one from his own world. He got the children to plait coconut leaves into a ball. Then they got longer leaves until the ball was large. Then they bound it tightly with netting and put posts in the sand, two at each end. Soon all the children were playing football – long before it came to the rest of the Pacific!

Adult life on the lagoon started before dawn and by sunrise there was a regular procession of canoes making for the shore. Some people were bound for the market, others to attend to their livestock, still more to gather wood and fresh water for their daily use, but the earliest risers were those bound for their gardens. In this stone-age world, where digging was done with sticks and cutting with flint adzes, the work was time-consuming. During the day the only movement on the lagoon were the fishermen, either working alone or in two large canoes which each held between four to six men and a butterfly net, secured at either end by each canoe.

> They fish in water two or three fathoms deep [wrote Renton], and their manner is to bring the ends of the net gradually together, working the upper part from the canoes, while the progress of the submerged portions is effected by men diving to the bottom, and moving the weights forward as required. The two ends are brought together, and the circle is gradually diminished till the fish are so crowded together that their capture is easy.
>
> Another method of fishing, which they practise, is more remarkable. The water being very clear, everything can be seen at great depths; and when moving along, should a man see a big fish at the bottom, he does not

hesitate to capture it with his hands. He begins by beating the surface of the water with a paddle or a pole, when the fish, alarmed by the percussion, generally takes refuge under a stone at the bottom.

The man then takes a small stick in his hands and dives to the bottom. Once there, he pokes under it with his stick. This done, he rises to the surface and smells the end of the stick. So keen is his sense of smell that he can, at once, tell whether the stick has touched the fish. If such proves to be the case, down he goes again, and, thrusting his arm under the rock, he gropes for the fish, which he seldom fails to seize and bring to the surface.

At low spring tides the shallower parts of the lagoon, near the coast, were full of women and children gathering shellfish or crabs. At night, particular fishing grounds were dotted with points of light moving slowly about. Each canoe was carrying clusters of dried coconut leaves tied in tight bunches which served as torches to attract the crayfish. And every night a group of men remained on the shore to sleep beside the pig-pens whilst owls, hand-reared from birth, stood watch from the branches of nearby trees, trained to hoot at the footfall of any pig-stealer from the bush tribes. In the village, fish-hawks, captured whilst still chicks, hung in cages outside the men's huts. These birds, hand-reared like the owls, had been trained to strike fish in the lagoon and bring them back to their owners.

The edge of the lagoon is fringed with mangrove swamp, populated by white cockatoos and hornbills perched on the branches overlooking the shallows and waiting to strike. On the little beaches sandpipers run briskly back and forth, jerking their tails and uttering their little cries. Golden-backed plovers, migrants from China, stand on the rocks of the foreshore eyeing each retreating rivulet. Others settle in village clearings on the watch for insects. White gulls swoop down on shoals of fish and, as the sun retreats behind the mountainous coast, hawks and frigate birds take off from their eyries to wheel and hover in the evening thermals.

From Sulufou the reef is a mile distant, a thin, barely discernible white line. Only at night, when the wind is from the east, can the roar of surf be heard. More prominent is the gentle lapping of the tide waters against the rock wall of the artificial island which, together with the noisy flutterings and shrill cries of the big bat, or flying fox, are all one hears at night.

4

Savage Civilization

———————— o ————————

FAR from being pitched into a world of primitive chaos, Renton found himself living in a society bound by rules and rituals that governed the behaviour of every man, woman and child. Without writing, memory had to be perfect, tradition exact and each growing child was taught the form and function of countless rituals, dozens of songs and the ancestral histories that bound the community together. No people were more exact in their observance of etiquette: your attitude to your mother-in-law or paternal uncle, how you should balance a spear in the presence of a friend, what prayers you should invoke before you went fishing, what ritual you should perform if you saw a white man's ship out to sea, which bird or fish may be killed in which month.

This was a one-track, one-faith world that worked for people who saw no necessity for investigation. They were too busy living. They did not ask 'how?' or 'why?' For those questions start when man realizes that he might beat nature. It was a society where there was little discontent and no free thought. They did not criticize each other as characters, as abstract personalities related to some vague ideal as to what they 'should' be. They had no illusions about human decency or freedom. They simply existed in an accepted, totally unchanging world. Each living person was an 'is' and also a 'will be'. So when they died they were still an 'is' not a 'has been'.

Every human being had a soul which they described as *nunu*, whose literal translation was 'the shadow of a person as cast by the sun', but whose existence was recognized as being more amorphous. It was understood that, although the soul maintained a 'healthy' life, it did not activate it and that, particularly during the hours of sleep, the soul left the body. Thus no one was ever shaken out of their sleep in case their *nunu* was left behind and they sicken and die. A sleeping person was called and if they did not wake up they were left alone.

It was believed that the soul entered the body after birth during the period when the child could be seen to be developing an independent personality. This period, when they were believed to have a particularly tenuous hold on their *nunu*, was a time of particular anxiety for their parents who would avoid taking the child any distance from the family hut lest the *nunu* was left behind with disastrous results. Physical or mental handicap, delinquency or childhood rebellion against the strictures of the rigorously shame-based society were ascribed to the partial or total loss of a child's *nunu*.

Their religion was based upon the belief that God, the great outsider, having completed his creative work and laid down customs and traditional procedures, had retired from being an active god. His only ongoing connection with the living was his indirect control of their destinies through his servants – the legions of the dead. It was to them that the islanders turned when it came to those needs that required some power beyond their own abilities. To facilitate this each family hut contained a reliquary to house the decorated skulls of those family members who, in life, had been gifted – either as warriors, fishermen, magicians or child-bearers.

Consequently, the disposal of an esteemed dead relative was a ritual of great importance. The body was swathed in a thick shroud of leaves from the barringtonia tree. It was then eased into a canoe-shaped coffin, which was placed upright between forked posts a few feet above the floor in the men's or women's communal hut. In the bottom of the coffin was a hole into which a bamboo tube was applied and the junction chalked. The other end of the tube was sunk through the floor, terminating at the low water mark among the stones and shingle that formed the island's foundations. The body remained there for six months, decomposing but odourless. When the coffin was opened, the juices of the body would have drained away and the corpse would be perfectly desiccated. Before the body was buried on dry land, the head was broken off at the neck and stored away with the other heads in the family reliquary.

For these people, when life ran smoothly, there was no need to question the authority of one's judgements or choices and nothing happened by accident. So when calamity occurred they needed to know under whose auspices a particular act was carried out. Who was the origin of their misfortune? Or, as Bertrand Russell pointed out: 'One of the odd effects of the importance of the principle which each of us attaches to himself

57

is that we tend to imagine our own good or evil fortune to be the purpose of another person's actions.'

In Malaita the idea of causality was elevated into a religion and as a result death provided a constant source of tension and conflict, particularly as this was a society with no concept of disease, or death from natural causes. When death occurred, the survivors would consider the question: with whom was the dead person most unfriendly? If someone had quarrelled with them recently, this person would almost certainly be blamed. If not, suspicion would be directed towards anyone who was believed to have been envious of them.

At night, a priest and the dead person's closest relatives would hold an enquiry beside the corpse to establish the person responsible for his death. In the *Courier* articles, although dismissive of much ritual activity, Renton described what happened next in some detail:

A singular light issued from the head of the corpse, rising above it, floating and flickering in the air. After a while it made its way out of the hut and flitted away through the village and out over the water, increasing in magnitude until it assumed the brightness and semblance almost of a star. As it quitted the body and flitted through the village, the watchers silently followed it, embarking in their canoes, and grimly paddling after it into the darkness of the night. It might take them to some village miles away, or it might circle round and bring them back to the very hut where they started from, but in any case it would settle at last on the roof which sheltered the criminal. Arrived there its form would alter, and it would spread and swell till the whole hut roof would appear as if throwing off tongues of pale and livid fire.

The avengers would await the conclusion, coming noiselessly as near as possible; and before long the supernatural presence would affect the sleeper. He would be heard to moan and cry, oppressed with a nameless terror and bathed in sweat. Sometimes he would wake with a start, rush out and bury himself in the bush, or fling himself into the sea. Whatever at that moment might be his fate, the avengers would return to their homes as silently as they had quitted them. The man's fate was decided.

In another part of the family reliquary stood the heads that were the repository of *mana*. This common oceanic word denotes power or force and its meaning is more material than metaphysical. The heads of your enemies were the source of *mana*, and, unlike your ancestors, had the added advantage of being bound to serve you, not only in this life but the next. As one Solomon Islander put it: 'the heads of enemies had more soul value [*mana*] than anything else, and was believed that the more human heads one secured the better the time one would have when one passed into the spirit world.'

On headhunting expeditions each warrior would wear round his neck a small plaited bag containing the lower incisor from the head of his first victim. He could communicate with the ghost, who would warn him of danger or detect the enemy's hiding place. Another considerable inducement to stock the family reliquary was the belief that you were fated to pound excrement for the eternity of the afterlife if you had not taken a head before you died.

Heads were also the approved offering for numerous important occasions – the building of a canoe house, the launching of a war canoe, the opening of a ceremonial house or the start of a porpoise drive. The fortunes of communal undertakings depended upon the build up of *mana* through the presentation of heads. This often involved not simply their presentation but their preparation and decoration. The skulls were cleaned, dried and covered with a hard-drying black paste. After the over-modelling was completed, the skulls were decorated with shell-inlaid eyes and curving bands of nautilus shell pieces set on the brow, cheeks and jaw. Occasionally fibre hair was added. Each head captured by the community was decorated slightly differently and people could tell their provenance at a glance.

In this world where the relationship between the living and the dead was a life-long dialogue, where misfortune and death were ascribed to the supernatural activity of mortals and where the possession of certain body parts imbued power to the owner, it was inevitable that a person was viewed as more than the sum of his parts. Each individual, by virtue of their relationship with their ancestors, had the capacity to harm – with or without the assistance of a priest. Renton's description of mealtimes was an illustration of his initial bemusement at finding himself amongst a group of people who inhabited a completely different metaphysical universe: 'They would clear up every particle of the fragments of food. It was believed that should any false friend manage to obtain possession of even the particle of food of which they had partaken, or a hair of their head, or a paring of their nails, he held them in his power.'

This fear of those who might *siohi* (pick up) something that might serve their malign purpose, extended to a piece of earth on which someone had recently stepped, or a strip of coconut leaf that an individual had used to scrape themselves after bathing and, most importantly, the skins of the areca or betel nut which were chewed by both men and women. Inside every house at the foot of the centre post was a square formed with logs which served as a receptacle for all the scraps of betel nut and which were regularly incinerated. Defecation also caused particular anxiety as excreta was regarded as a particularly potent essence. Thus everyone went to considerable lengths to make sure they relieved themselves either in the rivers or the sea.

This reification of individuals was a particular source of fascination to Renton who recorded that: 'to my astonishment everyone believed that, armed with this article, all the individual needed to do was to secretly present himself at his ancestral shrine, and casting before his ancestors the purloined article, merely speak the name of the person he desired to injure to invoke an evil fate upon him.'

To his interviewers on the *Brisbane Courier* Renton expressed 'a distinct belief in the reality of the necromantic processes in question'. The effects could, indeed, be dramatic. Faced with his accuser, the victim would stand aghast, his hands up in front of his face, attempting to ward off the invisible, but lethal, implications. His cheeks would blanch and his eyes become glassy and trance-like. He would attempt to cry out but usually the sound would choke in his throat. His body would then begin to tremble and he would go into spasm and fall to the ground. After a short time, the victim would start to writhe, as if in mortal agony. Then, covering his face with his hands, he would begin to moan. At this point the accuser would leave and the victim would become quite composed as he was helped to his hut. Here he would lie, refusing to eat or drink. In Renton's words 'he might linger a few days in a rapid decline, but more frequently he would be smitten with unspeakable tortures and be a corpse within a few hours'.[1]

He gradually began to realize that this highly formalized society that appeared to be based on consideration, communality, respect for elders and a set of rules that reminded him of the world of windjammers was, in reality, driven by the fear of the lethal consequences of causing offence. It took him rather longer to understand that the reason why people often confided in him had nothing to do with his approachability or his easy-going nature. Quite simply, he had no ancestral presence, and in this paranoid society he represented absolutely no threat.

As many of the major ceremonies involved human sacrifice; most large headhunting raids also involved the attempted capture of women and adolescents. Servitude was not oppressive, although the captives were never in doubt about their status; they lived separately and were at the beck and call of their particular captor. Their lives were uncertain, knowing that at any time they might be selected for sacrifice. Nevertheless, they had some degree of security due to the economic role that was assigned to them and if they showed some abilities it was a reasonable guarantee against becoming a sacrificial victim. A slave's hope of survival depended on their personal capacity to become a useful and, if possible, an invaluable member of that society.

As men and women had their own compounds, so too the slaves, and on large artificial islands such as Sulufou, a satellite island would be built to house them. Here, women and children would be put to work carving fish-hooks made from turtle shell, stringing twine for fishing nets, weaving rattan cane and mixing dyes. Although warclubs, spears and bows were fashioned by their owners, the enslaved outworkers provided the supply of arrows. These were made in two parts – a top piece of palm wood set in a reed shaft. The ends were not feathered but notched and the arrowheads barbed with human or pig bone. The preparation of arrows used on headhunting raids, however, was an altogether different process.

The sight of an apparently empty canoe resting on wooden frames in the sand above the tideline opposite the slave island was one of the most graphic portents of a community preparing for hostilities. In the bottom of the canoe lay the body of a sacrificial victim with various parts of its anatomy already removed and particular bones fashioned into arrowheads. As the body putrefied in the blazing sunlight the moisture would drip from the uncaulked seams of the canoe into a shallow wooden tray situated beneath it. Along its notched rim, the arrowheads were positioned so that their points were soaking in the liquid. These were then dried and kept in protective leaf envelopes that would only be removed just before use. The arrowheads were deliberately carved in such a manner that the points would break off in the wound. To be hit by one of these tetanus-carrying arrows was lethal.

The slave island's occupants' most important function was to act as the tribe's mint. *Romo*, or shell money, was the standard form of currency used throughout Malaita. It was made from a small spondylus shell that possessed a red lip that was cut into discs, rubbed flat, pierced, polished and threaded on strings of different length according to different units of currency. It was used for the furnishing of bride price, for blood money, for the purchase of pigs and food and the payment of fees and fines – including redemptive offerings to ghosts.

Sulufou also possessed the monopoly of a unit of currency of much greater value than shell money; it controlled the rights to the culling of porpoises. Porpoise teeth were Malaita's Gold Standard and Sulufou's monopoly of the supply of these teeth formed the basis of its power on the north of the island. For all large purchases, be it land or war canoes, this was the currency of choice and its value was maintained by the people of Sulufou who, in true De Beers fashion, strictly limited the frequency of culls. On the slave island, the teeth were cleaned, strung, counted and stored.

Renton's adjustment to this highly complex society must have been far more difficult than he ever admitted publicly. In the *Courier* articles he gives the impression of a seamless transition from Scottish sailor to Malaitan native and, within a paragraph of his arrival in Sulufou, he appears totally acculturated: 'Being pretty handy at the principal native industries such as net and canoe making, and being active and willing, Renton began to find himself looked upon by the natives as almost one of themselves.'

The newspaper's readers must have felt slightly cheated at being denied any information about how this Scottish teenager engineered such a transformation. For Renton though, the motives were perfectly clear – to present himself and his hosts in the best possible light and to obscure the fact that his own status, during those early months, was no different from any island captive.

According to oral history there was no providential rescue on the beach at Maanaomba. The scene twenty-four hours after the capture of Renton and his companions was little different from that which had characterized relations between black and white for more than three centuries, the only difference being that the potential purchasers were black and the goods being paraded were white. The oral historians of Sulufou are quite clear:

> When Renton was captured at Maanaomba he was bought by a chief called Kamilla who took him to Maanakwai [fifteen miles to the west]. He stayed there for maybe a month. The story of Kamilla and his light-skinned boy spread along the coast of Malaita and Kabou set off to see him. When he arrived he told Kamilla that he wanted the boy and Kamilla sold him.

At this point oral history becomes a little coy. The Solomon Islanders are now as sensitive about their slave-owning past as most western countries, probably more so, bearing in mind that the population of Sulufou converted en masse to Christianity only fifty years ago. Thus 'slave' becomes 'boy' and 'slave-owner' becomes 'father'.

> His father kept a close eye on Renton and he had to follow his father all the time who told him everything. He was very strict and told Renton that Malaita was a dangerous place and that he shouldn't go off with anyone or he'd end up dead. [Clearly Kabou was anxious to protect his investment.] If people went out fishing, his father would make him go along too so that he could learn. Renton didn't listen to his father's advice because he didn't understand and so he used to wait around until

all the people came back from fishing for kakarai [herring-sized fish] and they would give him some to take to his master because they felt sorry for him.

During the first months he couldn't speak the language so he wasn't much use to the village. He was allowed to play with the children of the village. Sometimes when they were playing they would all go to a certain place and sit on a big stone. There, all the children would teach him our language and when he first learned to speak our language he used to draw things on a big flat wooden post made by the villagers. He'd draw all kinds of things, men, animals, crocodiles. Sometimes he would draw things from his own world and the people would look at these things without understanding them. Other times he told stories of the white man's world but the villagers never believed him.

One day Jack was standing with his basket when the fishermen came back and they said, 'Hey! You sit around doing nothing while we're out fishing and you come here with your basket. Why don't you learn to do something?' Jack went back to Kabou and told him what the people had said about him doing nothing and asking for fish. So Kabou sent him off to learn net-making, how to make floats and fish-hooks and how to fish. When the kakarai came back, Kabou told Jack, 'Go. Take your net and your canoe.' Jack went out to the spot where the fish were. When he came back to the village many men were waiting. Jack said: 'All you men here, bring your plates and we'll divide up these fish.' So they all brought their plates and Jack gave out a portion to all of them.

Jack Renton became good at fishing and after a while his father sent him out on his own and he would just sit around whilst Jack went out and did everything for him.

Sometimes Jack would have to cook food for five or six of the bigmen as they sat around the *kustom* house. All the men in the village said, 'My word, his father has him well trained.' Jack didn't like doing all these things for the bigmen. He had to do it, but he didn't like it.

This account's lack of explicitness about Renton's true status is unable to disguise the significance of the central incident and the reason why it is recounted. Clearly the male population of Sulufou initially tolerated Kabou's lenient treatment of his white-skinned slave but after a while drew the line at his freeloading, feeling that he should be sent to the slave island to learn some skills.

There is a revealing passage early in the *Courier* articles, which gives an indication of why Kabou was so keen to purchase Renton. When he first arrived, Renton was intrigued by the nickname conferred upon him by the oldest inhabitants. They would watch him closely, occasionally calling out, 'Doorey! Doorey!' As he learned the rudiments of the language he discovered that they had known a white man, a prisoner like himself, who had lived with them for many years. Further questioning revealed a more exact chronology. The white man had been captured in the lagoon with a group of seamen forty years previously. All had been killed – except Doorey.

As details of the incident emerged Renton realized that what he was being told was a version of the fate of the whaleboat *Albert*, one of a large collection of stories known by seamen the length of the Pacific seaboard, stories that told of lost expeditions and discovered treasure, of castaways, mutinies, survival in open boats, of death from drowning, disease, starvation and, top of the list, that most dreaded of all – a cannibal death.

Captain Cook's fate had been the precursor. A day after his death in Kealakekua Bay, two Hawaiians paddled out to the *Resolution* with a number of small packages containing Cook's scalp, a boneless thigh, his arms and his hands. The rest of his body, the choice cuts, had been divided up and eaten. When, thirteen years later, Captain Bligh, one of the witnesses, found himself captaining a twenty-three-foot open boat at the start of one of the epic journeys in maritime history, it was not the absence of land that dictated its length, but the captain's mortal fear of cannibals. Timor was the nearest outpost of civilization, so it was to Timor that they would sail. This same fear drove the survivors of the whaleboat *Essex*, sunk by an enraged bull whale, to ignore the prevailing winds and a 500-mile westerly journey to the Marquesas in favour of a 3,000-mile journey south and east. By the time they were discovered off the coast of Chile the skeletal survivors had been reduced to the status of those they had striven so hard to avoid. They were, according to the crew that rescued them, 'found sucking the bones of their dead mess mates, which they were loath to part with'. From Valparaiso to Vancouver, the dockside taverns hummed with the retelling, each version more lurid than the next.

For Renton, the fate of the crew of the whaleboat *Albert* ranked high amongst the cannibal death stories he'd heard during his travels. In 1829, short of fresh food and water, the ship hove-to beside a lagoon off the island of Malaita. Two small whaleboats were dispatched through a passage in the reef, but as they closed in on the shore, they were suddenly cut off by four war canoes that had been concealed in the lee of one of the artificial islands. Both boats were overwhelmed, their crews dragged onto the beach and dismembered. The remaining crew members of the *Albert* watched helplessly from the ship's rail as fires were lit and their messmates cooked and eaten by a multitude of howling savages.

Renton had learned enough by this stage to know that this final act was fiction. The inhabitants had a horror of cannibalism; it was an appellation they reserved for their traditional enemies, the despised bush people. But why, asked Renton, had there been a policy of killing all white people? He was told that many generations ago, white men had visited Malaita but had been driven away. When stories emerged from nearby islands of sickness and death amongst those who had had contact with the white men, the people of Malaita reasoned that they had been spared because they had not permitted them to land. White men were not killed for their things, but because their very presence brought death. So why, asked Renton, had Doorey survived?

More out of curiosity than compassion, the villagers of Sulufou had decided to test out the prevailing orthodoxy by sparing one member of the *Albert*'s crew. He was moved to the slave island and tethered to a post in a small wattle compound with two pigs for company. After a couple of days and with the two pigs still in good health, they threw him some food. After another week they built him a cage. As the days passed and the inhabitants of the slave island remained fit and well, Doorey, still in his cage, was set to work. He quickly mastered the basics of stone-age carpentry and proved to be a particularly quick and gifted carver.

Released from his cage, moved to Sulufou and let loose with the few iron tools in their possession, he revolutionized woodworking in the village. According to the elders, 'Doorey's handiness made him highly considered and he lived in great repute for many years.' Renton realized that the villagers had made a fortuitous choice. From the crew of the *Albert* they had singled out the one man who could really be of use to them – the ship's carpenter. However, after almost ten years, Doorey decided he was not considered highly enough and decamped to live on another island that promised him greater status. The villagers of Sulufou could not tolerate this loss of face so one day, while out on a tree-felling expedition, Doorey had been ambushed and killed.

Now, as Renton looked round Sulufou with new eyes, Doorey's legacy was everywhere to be seen. Unlike Maanaomba or Kamilla's village of Maanakwai where houses and furniture were constructed to the basic principles of crossbeams lashed together with rattan cane, here on Sulufou, beams were supported with dovetail joints; timber battens with halving joints; chairs and tables with mortise and tenon; and all were secured with wooden dowelling. Renton now understood that he owed his life to Doorey and that much would be expected of him.

Six months into his stay and reasonably proficient in the language, Renton was sent off into the bush on a large tree-felling expedition. When they set up camp in the selected grove of hardwood trees he was offered one of six steel axes. These were regarded as the community's most valuable possessions and had been obtained by trading with the natives of a nearby island.

The logs were dragged to the shore and floated across to the village where a communal undertaking started that seemed to involve almost all the adults in the village. Each fifty-foot log was split into planks, then an army of women, many brought in from the slave island, worked on each plank with stone and shell adzes and rough volcanic rock until each was smooth and true. Triangular crossbeams were laid upside down in the centre of the village. Small holes were then drilled in the two planks that comprized the V-shaped keel, with matching holes in the cross-beams. Fastenings of strong sinnet and the outer skin of rattan cane were passed through these holes and tightly fastened. The keel was then turned the right way up and two grooves were made on the upper sides of the planks. Upon these, planks forming the sides were carefully fitted edge to edge. Again, small holes were drilled along the seams and the planks fastened. The bow and stern fittings were constructed separately and when secured, they curved gracefully upward for, and aft to a height of twelve feet, giving the canoe the shape of an elongated crescent. It was fifty feet long, three feet deep, with a four-foot beam, and large enough to carry forty warriors.

Large quantities of pariniarium nut paste were prepared and every seam well caulked from the inside. When it dried it was as hard as cement. The outside of the canoe was then completely pitched in the same material, but before the outer coating was quite dry, mother-of-pearl and cowry shells were inlaid to create specific designs.

Throughout this two-month process, Renton worked particularly hard. Not only was he relieved to be free from the drudgery of catering for Kabou's stomach, but he also grasped the opportunity to display his knowledge of boat-building and woodwork. He was no Doorey, but years at sea had taught him many of the skills of the long-dead ship's carpenter and he was keen for this to become common knowledge. Over those weeks he earned a degree of respect that transformed his status. Yet despite this, no one was prepared to tell him the true purpose of the endeavour.

The launch of the canoe was to be Renton's first experience of the ritual inhumanity of these people. One afternoon he watched as scores of small canoes from those islands allied to Sulufou made their way towards the village. The women were dressed in newly woven croton thongs, their hair decorated with hibiscus and bougainvillaea, the naked men glistening in coconut oil, their limbs decorated in red and blue wood paints, their faces streaked with white lime. Some carried eight-foot-long spears, the lower shaft fashioned out of palm wood, the upper section and tip made from human shinbones. Over their shoulders each carried a three-foot-long fighting club, its shaft decorated with pearl shells. Everyone, residents and guests alike, assembled on the dancing ground beside the canoe sheds. In the centre of this open space stood the new canoe decked out in palm fronds, coloured feathers and flowers.

To the blowing of conch shells, the beat of wooden drums and an orchestra of panpipes, a column of men entered the arena with ankle rattles attached to their feet. Some knelt, beating their spears against their fighting clubs, the rest gathered round the canoe, whilst the crowd, with flowers waving, swayed and chanted. The men started to circle the canoe, faster and faster, their ankle rattles shaking in a frenzy of sound. The warriors circled first one way then another until quite suddenly, to the blast of a conch shell, a masked figure emerged from the crowd.

Renton watched in horror as the mood of the crowd instantly changed from exhilaration to fear. Half-man, half-fish, the figure prowled the perimeter of the now silent crowd. There was a palpable sense of anticipation as he paused – then moved on.

Each time he stopped there was an audible gasp. Finally he moved purposefully forward and placed a fin-like hand upon a female slave. Instantly the dancers set upon her and Kabou moved forward with a steel axe and decapitated her. At the moment of death, as her head rolled in the dust of the dancing ground, there were no gasps of shock, only a low moan, a great communal exhalation – some fainted, others were sick, some defecated. Drums and conch shells drowned out the terrible crying that followed. Then the chant changed; in high-pitched voices, men and women sang a song of sacrifice to Kosoko, the god of the sea. As the woman's corpse was carried to the canoe and its sides liberally daubed with her blood, Renton sought refuge in a deserted hut. He sat in a darkened corner and listened to the sounds outside as the chanting rose in volume and the rhythm quickened. Unseen by him, they had lifted the canoe onto the slipway, tied the slave's head to the prow and set off on a triumphal journey round the island.

That evening, he was summoned to the men's communal hut where Kabou sat flanked by representatives from the village and their allies from other islands. Oral history records:

> Kabou wanted to make him hard. He knew that killing was the way to make him hard and that if he killed then the people would respect him. Kabou told him that he had heard that the Maanaomba people had killed his shipmates a few weeks after he had left. Kabou said to him: 'You must kill three men from Maanaomba because it is our custom that if a man from your tribe is killed by a man from another tribe then you must kill that man.' It was a duty for him to avenge the death of his own people and that was why they had been preparing.

As he left Kabou's hut he must have been struck by how ineffectual had been his efforts to explain himself and the world he came from. Oral history records that, 'When he first learned to speak our language he used to draw things on a big flat wooden post made by the villagers. Sometimes he would draw things from his own world and the people would look at these things without understanding them. Other times he told stories of the white man's world, but no-one believed him.' For a people who looked out on the world beyond their lagoon and saw a line where the sky touched the water it was inconceivable that beyond the horizon lay lands so vast that they dwarfed their little world. To his hosts it was axiomatic that all people would be like them and that Renton, like Doorey before him, must come from communities much like their own – a people bound together by a siege mentality and a code of honour that demanded a communal response to any outrage committed against one of their number.

That night he made his escape.

5

Headhunting

———————— o ————————

IF the prospect of a headhunting expedition dedicated to
salvaging his honour had precipitated his flight, the decision
to find an escape route had been made months earlier – the
moment he realized that decades had elapsed between Doorey's
capture and his own. This contemplation of a lifetime without so
much as a sighting of his own people, forced him to redouble his
efforts to learn the language in the hope that, if he could understand what was happening around him, something or somebody
might provide some information or some clue that might link his
world to theirs. By the time he set off on the tree-felling expedition he was virtually fluent. Then he was handed an axe.

Finding a private space he sat down. Here, after months of
despair, was an emissary from his world that had made its way
somehow, from somewhere, to his lonely exile. Patiently he
sought out its provenance and learned that it was one of a small
number that had been acquired through trading with a nameless

island close by. 'I made myself acquainted as to every detail of that island, particularly in regard to its position, the distance and the chances of transit.' Mendana's Santa Isabel lay twenty-five miles north-west of Maanaomba island.

It was early evening when he decided to make his move. The village was still full of visitors gathered round the cooking fires of the post-launch celebrations and he decided to gamble on the hope that it would be a number of hours before his absence would be noticed. With a basket of coconuts, a flint and his warclub he made his way to Diudi's canoe. Diudi was an expert fisherman; his craft was speedy, light and manoeuvrable. It also carried a half a dozen spears and, although still a novice, his strike rate was considerably better than his clumsy efforts at fishing from the whaler.

He paddled all night through the calm waters of the lagoon making for the northernmost passage in the reef opposite the village of Maanaomba. As he remembered only too well from his capture at the end of the ordeal on the whaleboat the distance between the reef and the wide sandy beach of the village was only a matter of a few hundred yards. In daylight a canoe and its occupants would be easily recognizable from the shore. He knew his window of opportunity was narrow and that he had to be through the channel before first light. He paddled a course close to the reef, following the dim white ribbon of surf knowing that, although this was the quickest route to the passage, it also carried considerable risk, for at no time would he know where he was in relation to the shore.

At first light he found himself in the worst possible position, close to the reef, with the promontory of Maanaomba still to be negotiated. Worse still, the villagers, like his hosts, were early risers and there were already a number of canoes making their way from the shore in different directions. He paused for a moment, turned and, so as not to arouse suspicion, paddled slowly towards the dim outline of a mangrove swamp. Cursing himself for not having made the decision earlier, he decided to conceal himself there until nightfall. He had almost reached his hideout when he heard the blast of a conch shell and accelerated the last few yards, manoeuvring his canoe as far into the swamp as the tangle of roots and branches would allow.

Within half an hour the outline of a large war canoe loomed beyond the undergrowth. The occupants shouted to him to come out, adding that if he remained where he was they would kill him. (Later he was to learn that there were few more public statements of hostile intent than the rituals that surrounded the launch of Sulufou's new war canoe and that for a number of days the people of Maanaomba had posted lookouts the length of their territory.) He paddled out to meet his captors who grabbed him and, he assumed, clubbed him, for when he regained consciousness he found himself lying on the beach, trussed up like a pig and surrounded by the contents of his canoe. A crowd of fully armed warriors stood over him, a number of them still arguing as to whether they should kill him or ransom him. He sensed though, from the atmosphere of expectation, that they had decided upon the latter. After a few minutes the blast of a conch shell brought more armed men onto the beach as two fully manned war canoes appeared in the distance.

What followed was much shouting. Negotiations appeared to centre around where the representatives from each party were going to meet face-to-face. These exchanges were made more difficult by the visitors' understandable reluctance to come within range of the bowmen lined up on the beach. Eventually some agreement was reached and the occupants of one of the visiting canoes unloaded their arms into the other canoe and made their way north. A number of his captors immediately embarked in a small canoe and followed the visitors. For fifteen minutes both canoes stood off the reef before returning together. As they approached Renton recognized Kabou sitting in the stern of the visitor's canoe. He was hauled through the surf and dropped at Kabou's feet, whist Diudi's canoe was attached to the stern.

Still hog-tied and lying in the bottom of the canoe he looked up at Kabou's face. It betrayed nothing. He merely instructed the crew to rejoin the other canoe and to retrieve their weapons. The short journey proceeded in silence, punctuated, to Renton's surprise, by what sounded like suppressed giggles. A gentle bump heralded their arrival. Familiar faces looked down at him, smiling and laughing. His fetters were cut and, to a great cheer, Kabou hauled him up to sit beside him. The other canoe moved slowly past whilst young men grasped his hand and patted his face – even Diudi appeared delighted. Renton, on the other hand, was completely bewildered. Fortunately Kabou's impromptu speech gave him time to gather his wits.

The people of Maanaomba, Kabou announced, had twice spared this man. They wanted to point out that his shipmates had died as a result of their ordeal and that the village had been in no way responsible. With a dismissive gesture Kabou paused. The speech that followed was to alter the course of Renton's life amongst these people for the rest of his exile.

Kabou recounted the events of the previous day and how he

had informed Renton of the death of his companions. He then went on to describe how Renton, in the best traditions of all wronged people, planned his revenge. How, despite the dangers, he had decided to exact it personally. How he had set out alone, in a small canoe, armed only with his warclub and some spears. How he had clearly planned to conceal himself in Maanaomba territory and pick off his victims one by one. Kabou ended by saying that, despite agreeing to a ransom which he had no intention of paying, he was proud to sponsor such a brave young man, adding finally that as his charge was such a principled hot-head, then they had all better teach him to fight. Renton was speechless, but his silence amidst the cheers of the warriors was merely interpreted as modesty and only served to enhance his prestige.

In a culture where the primary purpose of a man's life was the acquisition of *mana* it was little surprise that, as one contemporary European commentator put it: 'these islanders have an insatiable taste for fighting and headhunting . . . it appears to be a perfect passion.' Evenings spent in the village had given Renton a clear picture of how early this process of indoctrination started. He had often observed the small boys sitting round the entrance to the men's hut listening to the telling and retelling of long past conflicts. These narratives were given an added sense of theatre by the presence of the hero under discussion. His decorated head was brought from his ancestral shrine and placed on a small plinth by the entrance to the hut. This also gave the whole ritual a sense of tension, for if one person faltered in the telling someone else would quickly pick up the narrative for fear that this failure might cause offence.

The stories were neither fragments, nor anecdotes but epic

narratives delivered in a declamatory style and in a language that was markedly different from the dialect that Renton had recently mastered. It was 'high speech', the language of ritual and myth, *tok blong tomate* – the language of ghosts. Each story was punctuated by a recital of rules and instructions, changeless, ancient obligations and responsibilities. Each narrative had at its core a parable designed to reinforce the sense of perpetuity of the ancestrally established order and its link to the descendants seated round the skull.

Prior to his attempted flight, Renton spent much of his time in the company of these boys and would often observe discreet debates about the previous night's tale during the following morning's short journey to the shore. Once on the beach he would be left with the sullen drawers of the short straws whilst the rest of the boys scampered into the bush to enjoy a morning's hunting. As he never saw the results of their forays, he became increasingly curious, however he was told that their favourite quarry was a large aggressive rat [*Mus Rex;* now extinct]. This rodent had claws, teeth strong enough to crack the hardest nuts and was able to climb trees – an ability that afforded the boys endless practice with their miniature spears and arrows.

After a number of weeks under their somewhat reluctant tutelage they decided that he had acquired enough of the language to be invited on a hunting party. Half a mile inland, off a well-trodden track, hidden behind a thicket of poison-leafed nalato bushes, stood a small leaf-house barely five feet high, an exact replica of the adult world. He crawled inside and sat down to be immediately confronted by their trophies. Hanging from the beams were dozens of smoked heads. Rats, iguanas and lizards eyed him vacantly. It was then that he decided to introduce Scotland's national sport and was gratified to notice, during the ensuing weeks, a progressive thinning of the morning war party as more and more of them joined him on a makeshift football pitch. This pleasant recreation had been brought to a halt by his attempted flight and the subsequent transformation of his status.

War parties were split into two cadres, spearmen and bowmen, although there did not appear to be any deliberate selection process. From a young age boys expressed a preference and were duly inducted as weapons carriers into their cadre of choice. Renton, due to his muscular build and his total lack of experience with bow and arrow, was to be trained as a spearman.

All warriors carried four-foot-high wooden shields which were stout enough to deflect spears or arrows. They were rectangular in shape and cut out of a hardwood called *fata*. In a fight a spearman would carry the shield, club and additional spears in his left hand while he brandished a spear in his right. A bowman advanced behind his shield setting it up and firing from its shelter.

Training involved mock battles with spears and arrowheads tipped with a cork-like bark to prevent injury. Prior to the start of these exercises he was required to learn a number of *hakas* common throughout the Pacific. These involved bounding, stamping, thigh slapping and scratching the ground with his feet whilst reciting a variety of chants, all of which, whilst invoking various ghosts and ancestors, contained the same message, namely his prowess as a killer whilst at the same time belittling and cursing the enemy. There was much dodging and ducking to escape being hit, which involved leaping from side to side whilst at the same time making sure the shield protected both head and torso. Hand-to-hand fighting involved much thrusting and parrying with the shield whilst the right hand wielded a club or a short-shafted spear.

Although Renton conscientiously applied himself, he was somewhat at a loss to understand how these training sessions applied in the field when it appeared to him that the major consideration in all these forays was to avoid a pitched battle at all costs. All the stories of previous headhunting raids contained one crucial element – surprise. In 1870, during Renton's time on Malaita, a European trader witnessed such a raid fifty miles away on the Florida Islands. At dawn he looked on unseen while a fleet of six war canoes, thirty men in each, paddled slowly towards a sleeping beachside village. The canoes were drawn up a couple of hundred yards from the village at a point masked by a low promontory.

Then they advanced in a line, fanning out to approach their prey on three sides. After a while a dog started barking, and with a terrible 'Wah-wah-wah' the warriors charged. A shower of spears hurtled into the midst of the long row of huts, piercing the bamboo-thatched roofs and hanging outwards at crazy angles, while the axemen streaked in behind.

The barely awakened villagers were mostly too paralysed to move. Clinging to one another in the darkness of their huts, they could only pray that the invaders would not come to burn them out. Some of the bravest, however, attempted to crawl out only to find two axemen stationed by the door. They struck swiftly with their steel axes, cleanly severing heads from shoulders in one blow. Ten minutes later they were away again with two or three women and half a dozen heads, bundling the lot into the canoes and paddling for their lives.

After three months of training, Renton was judged at least competent enough to protect himself but as the purpose of the coming raid on Maanaomba was entirely motivated by the need to redeem his honour and exact vengeance for the death of his companions, Kabou was not taking any chances. Renton was duly assigned three bodyguards as the loss of face that would have been incurred by the people of Sulufou if he were to be harmed would have been irreparable.

Predictably the attack was planned for first light and was preceded an elaborate night time ceremony of propitiatory offerings which Renton described in some detail:

On the eve of the raid a great fire was kindled within a sacred enclosure, and upon this the burnt offerings of pigs were so disposed. As every warrior feels it incumbent to present something, a curious provision is made beforehand. It frequently happens that out of a litter of pigs, one or more do not live. The priesthood faithfully preserves these stillborn beasts by drying which are then stored away for scared purposes.

When the solemn ceremony is in progress each worshipper brings to the officiating priest a tiny morsel of this dried pig, wrapped up in leaves. The priest receives the morsel from the worshipper and with many contortions and snorts, lays it before a deity. He proceeds then to invoke powers on behalf of the communicant. This he effects by a series of impressive gasps, keeping his mouth open and expelling the air forcibly from his lungs, so making a strange sound of an extremely sacred nature.

> The supplicant finds the greatest comfort in this ceremony and after presenting his offering he is prepared to cast fear to the winds. He believes himself invulnerable in the coming war, supported by the consciousness of the immunity from wound or harm granted by the gods.

Suitably emboldened, Renton's war party set out for Maanaomba in three war canoes each over fifty feet long and large enough to carry forty warriors. Except for the steersman who stood in the stern manoeuvring a large keel-shaped paddle with his hands and feet, he and the rest of his companions sat double-banked on twenty thwarts. To Renton's right he could pick out not just the detail of the other two canoes but the faces and torsos of their occupants. From stem to stern each canoe was decorated in an elaborate marquetry of silver nautilus shell, which, like the warriors, smeared in white lime, was easily distinguishable in the moonlight. The sepulchral effect was intensified by the pale ribbons of phosphorescence that trailed in the wake of each canoe as it cut through the still waters of the lagoon. Hanging from the prow of each was an ebony figure that advertised their intent. The stylized head and torso of a warrior held, in his cupped hands, a miniature human head.

His crew kept perfect time, the paddles rising and falling rhythmically to a chant that was sung in a high minor key. In the bow sat the stroke-maker, maintaining a stroke of about thirty to the minute but every so often singing out the opening phrase of a chant in a lower octave and faster tempo. This rapid spurt would continue for a few minutes before dropping back into regular time.

They travelled north for two hours, guided by the white ribbon of breakers that surged over the lagoon's coral sea wall. Quite suddenly the stroke-maker lifted his paddle above his head and the canoe drifted in silence. In front of them the dark outline of a spit of land jutted out from the undulating coastline and the lagoon narrowed to a channel less than three hundred yards wide. Following the steersman in the lead canoe the war party made for a small beach at the head of the spit where they disembarked, leaving half a dozen novices in each canoe to await their call.

A footpath led from the beach across the narrow finger of land that concealed their canoes and within a few minutes they stood on the opposite shore surveying their objective. Half a mile away a long strip of white sand interrupted the dark mass of mangrove swamp that ringed the wide bay. The village huts, set back in a clearing one hundred yards from the beach, were easily discernable in the moonlight, so too a collection of canoes drawn up on the beach.

They divided into two war parties, one group of twenty making directly for the beach to remove the villagers' only means of escape. The tide was low and the lagoon easily fordable and as they set off with their weapons held aloft, the main body of men disappeared into the bush. They moved inland in a wide arc keeping their distance from the village until their track bisected a pathway that led towards their objective. Here they stood in complete silence, waiting for first light. Then, according to Renton's *Courier* account:

> before a single sleeper had stirred, the whole body burst into the village. The unhappy wretches thus surprised had not a chance to resist or to escape. Their canoes had been cut adrift and removed just before the assault; as they rushed out of their huts they were clubbed, speared or

shot with arrows, and in a few minutes many of the adult males of the village were exterminated.

One man ran the gauntlet and dashed towards the water. He plunged in, emerging off the beach, standing up to his shoulders in the water, facing his enemy. Renton continues:

> So desperate was his aspect that although twenty pursuers had dashed into the water after him, he held them in defiance and stood at bay, none daring to attack him hand to hand and face to face.
>
> At last however, his fate came. A cunning warrior had, unobserved, swum out and now came silently behind him with a spear poised ready to strike. One moment he was glaring in bold defiance of the overwhelming array he faced; the next a blow had struck him where the head joins the neck; his head fell forward, his nostrils gurgled a moment under the water, and then his corpse floated on the sea and was triumphantly seized by two score eager hands. The slain was beheaded, and the gory spoils collected to grace the victor's triumphal return.

Renton was renowned as an excellent swimmer. Was he 'the cunning warrior'?

Renton was clearly in a very difficult position as he sat in Brisbane being cross-examined by the *Courier*'s eager journalists. The problems he faced are evident in a coda to the account of this first raid. Not surprisingly, he was questioned about the fate of the captured women and children of Maanaomba. The article comments: 'Renton was not explicit, and we did not press for particulars, which he seemed reluctant to give.' Bearing in mind the following testimony, it is not surprising that Renton was so reticent.

The incident occurred in June 1883 in a village on New Georgia, two hundred miles west of Malaita, and was observed by a European trader. The ritual involved the dedication of a newly constructed building to house war canoes.

The chief of the village was a man named Nono. The sacrifice in this instance was a male child and a female pig. It was necessary for the victims to be of opposite sexes. The child, a boy of about nine years old, had been brought with four other slaves, one of them his mother, from a village on the north side of Santa Isabel.

The house was of course near the sea, and the men of the village sat in a circle round the front of it, while the women and children stood in the background, among the latter being a slave child and its mother, the latter being aware of what was to come, but the child all unconscious. It was, however, crying, as it had been kept for two days without food.

I was invited to go inside the house, which was rather dark, as all canoe houses are; but when my eyes became accustomed to the dim light I saw three old men sitting against the posts of the house, and behind each was a cooked body tied upright to the post; the heads had been removed. Two of them were women who had been disembowelled; the third was a man.

I came out of the house again, and suddenly an old man appeared standing near the end of the house. He had worked himself into a frenzy, and stood glaring at the surrounding people. Nono, the chief, went up to the mother and seized the child by the hand. The woman managed some slight resistance, but it was feeble and the child was dragged reluctantly to the old man, who seized it by the legs with his two hands so that the child was sitting on his neck in a position that we call 'pick-a-back'. With a loud yell the old man began running round the house; this he did three times, and then ran into the sea.

When he had got above his waist he threw himself backwards, and repeated this operation two or three times, of course ducking the child, and then he ran out of the water again, the child meanwhile, somewhat exhausted and clutching his shoulders with his hands. Again he ran round the house and then into the sea, repeating the operation. This time, on coming out of the water, the child, now thoroughly exhausted, was hanging head downwards on his back.

He went up to the front of the house. Nono, the chief, now took a twelve-inch trade knife and with one gash across the child's throat, and then a chop, the head was off and the blood streaming from the neck.

The man, still carrying the child on his back, then ran round and round the house, scattering the blood on the house and ground till the body ceased to bleed. The pig, a small one, which was close by, with its four legs tied together, was brought and killed by being thumped and jumped on. Then the two were cooked together. They were afterwards eaten with the other bodies, and the child's head stuck up in the canoe house.

This was the world Renton inhabited yet his *Courier* account avoids any mention of the ritual inhumanity of his hosts or its slave-based culture. Throughout he chooses carefully what he is prepared to reveal about a civilization he had lived in for almost eight years – hardly surprising in view of the oral history of Sulufou:

> In the first fight, the Maanaomba fight, Renton went there and killed three men. And when they had all finished fighting Renton returned home first. Kabou asked him: 'What about the others, are they alive or dead?' Renton said 'All of them are alive and they are following me.' And then he said, 'I have killed three men.' Kabou was happy, he looked on Renton like his own son and he said to the people: 'If anyone harms this young man now, his backside will hang from my wall.
>
> Renton was a strong man, a warrior, a man of kustom. Kabou was proud of him and decorated him. He went on at least six raids and every time he killed men.
>
> When he killed he didn't take the heads. He said he didn't want them in his hut so he took the teeth of the dead men. He didn't cut, he knocked out the front teeth with his subi, them he took them home and the people made small holes in them and they hung them round his neck on a necklace . . . a tooth for every kill.[1]

*   *   *

It is clear from the *Rose and Thistle* incident, that took place early in the third year of Renton's exile, that knowledge of his existence had already spread to Santa Isabel. As Captain MacFarlane interrogated the temporizing chief of Maanaomba he was not to know how low the state of relations between that village and Sulufou had sunk. Not surprisingly his letter addressed 'to a white man' took two months to make its way down the chain of artificial islands to Sulufou.

Kabou showed Renton the letter. He was allowed to read it

but not allowed to keep it. He read it over and over again and never forgot it.

> It has been reported to me that there have been white men on this island. I have searched all over, but can find no traces at all. If any white man should find this, he should try to get across to Isabel, where vessels frequently call. In two months I shall return to Buccotta [Sigana] Island, and if a white man could make his way there by that time, I will give him passage to Sydney. I leave a pencil with this. [The pencil was gone].
>
> Captain MacFarlane, *Rose and Thistle*

It was now that Renton was to come face to face with the true extent of these people's attachment to him. He was no longer regarded as a valued member of the community but an indispensable one. Kabou absolutely refused to allow him to go to Buccotta Island. There was nothing he could do.

During the months that followed he came to understand that the only way he would have any chance of leaving was by enlisting support. In the early months of his exile he had excelled at the one activity that brought instant status, his nautical skills. However once he had mastered the language, he started to tell stories of his world which no one believed – except one man, Kwaisulia. Oral history records their burgeoning friendship.

> When Renton was with the children, one of Kabou's men was given the task of watching him, not because Kabou thought he would escape – Renton knew that if he ran away the bush people would not just kill him but eat him too! Kabou was just protecting his property for he had

plans for Renton. Kwaisulia was his escort's name. He would follow Renton when he was with the children, playing and learning and every evening go back with Renton and report to Kabou.

Later, when Renton was sent to do tasks by Kabou, like going to the market at Urate or Manibu or gathering food from his gardens, Kwaisulia would go with him and show him what to do. When Renton could speak the language he would listen to Renton's stories and ask him many questions about his world. They spent much time together and became friends.

It was a friendship that was to have a lifelong influence on the young native. In the nineteenth-century there were to be few Pacific Islanders who were able to straddle both cultures as successfully as Kwaisulia of Ada Gege. A trader who knew him well in later life described him as 'a strong dark brown man of powerful build. I suppose 5ft 10ins . . . different from others, a man of few words but with a character of authority; who thought deeply, made up his mind slowly but did not change it – very much respected and a great deal feared.' His father had been a bushman. Twenty years earlier he had brought a group of families out of the interior, formed an alliance with Sulufou and settled on Ada Gege, a deserted artificial island half a mile away from Sulufou. To cement the alliance, Kwaisulia's father had married a Sulufou woman, Kabou's aunt. His authority was reinforced by his considerable reputation as a fighting man and the *ramo* for both islands.

It was the *ramo* who led the community in war and blood vengeance. But unlike a town sheriff he was not an official office-holder, he was much more a gunslinger – a man defined by his deeds and the status those deeds conferred. To be recognized as a *ramo* a man had to club to death a number of men in personal combat. He had to establish a reputation for intimidating power. The more people he killed in combat, without injury to himself, the more this was taken as a sign of ancestral support. He became a man who not only dispensed justice but a man *'with the gods on his side'*. Once his reputation was established, a *ramo* seldom had to fight; disputes merely melted away before his intimidating presence.

Kwaisulia's father had been such a man and his son was expected to step into his shoes. It was to be Renton's good fortune that, having accidentally earned his entirely spurious reputation as a fighting man, it would fall to Kwaisulia to become his mentor and comrade-in-arms. Exactly the same age, height and build, they became inseparable. For Renton it had been a friendship forged by a most unlikely attribute – his friend's intellectual curiosity.

Prior to his accidental elevation to a man of status, Renton would occasionally attempt speculative conversations, particularly in relation to fighting, injury and possible death and although his informants always showed considerable courtesy and goodwill when he questioned them, these exchanges were invariably sterile exercises. As soon as he steered the conversation away from hard facts and into the realms of 'what ifs?' the replies were tautological or contradictory.

These were people who had no knowledge of abstract thought, for whom the analysis of human personality, motivation and the world of the subconscious was entirely foreign. They had no way of qualifying statements, expressing relativity or appreciating quandaries. Replies would contain no 'either' or no 'or' and would often be absolute but contradictory. When faced with exploring the solution to a dilemma a respondent would reply, 'He can, but cannot,' and a qualified response along the lines of, 'Theoretically he can, but in practice he never does, as it would make him unpopular', was entirely foreign. Only Kwaisulia appeared to be able to transcend the entirely concrete world of the lagoon.

When they were alone together Kwaisulia would often take him aside, hand him a plank of wood and some charcoal and ask him to explain in detail something that he had talked about the night before. Horses fascinated him. How had it been possible to teach such an animal to do a man's will? How was it trained? How did it behave? Since MacFarlane's letter the mystery of writing intrigued him. That a man's thoughts could be silently transmitted great distances seemed incredible. But he was even more bemused when he asked Renton questions that he couldn't answer. What were iron and steel? How were they made? Why does a bullet travel so fast? How exactly was calico made? The material world of Sulufou was understood by everyone and, to varying degrees, everyone could do everything. How was it possible, he asked Renton, that he could have lived in a world, much of which he could not explain and often had not even seen?

Above all, Kwaisulia wanted to learn Renton's language, which he perceived to be his knowledge. When Renton explained that language and knowledge were separate entities Kwaisulia was not convinced, so together they set about re-naming the world of Malaita in English. As Kwaisulia took his first faltering steps in that language he soon understood the distinction but he wasn't deterred and urged his friend to teach him more. Renton, for his part, had lost any sense of time, and with it any real hope that he might ever be rescued. After the MacFarlane episode he knew he had to find an ally if there was ever to be a chance of him escaping, so he redoubled his efforts to draw Kwaisulia into his world.

But there now followed a series of incidents that were to make that hope an impossibility. Rumours started to reach the lagoon dwellers from other coastal communities that the white man's ships were trying to trade in an altogether different commodity. They no longer wanted to trade their axes, calico and tobacco for food. These ships now wanted people.

6

'Grief, Terror and Rage'

B Y the 1860s the sandalwood supplies in the Pacific were almost exhausted and the ship-owners and men employed in the trade were looking for new opportunities. Landowners in Fiji and Queensland had taken advantage of the soaring price of cotton due to the American Civil War and set up small planta- tions, but just as cotton-growing had become profitable the war ended and the price dropped. As cotton shipped from Australia could no longer compete with the resurgent American industry, the plantations turned their land over to sugar cane.

Unlike King Cotton, sugar cane was a difficult crop to grow, taking longer to mature and requiring a messy, complicated and labour intensive process of manufacture before it could be turned into a marketable commodity. Cutting and processing had to be expertly timed and any delay, a strike at the mill or an absence of labour to cut it at the precise time, could ruin the crop. What was needed was a pliant labour force but when it became clear that the plantations were to be worked by 'native' labour, the *Brisbane Courier* grumbled: 'Are the industrious poor of the mother country together with their English ideas, English principles, English customs to be swamped by the barbarian?' But as no white man was willing to work for 'black' wages of £6 per annum the furore died down. A few Aboriginals were co-opted but no amount of inducements would persuade them to stay for more than a year and they simply wandered back to their own lands with their first pay packet. The plantation-owners now looked to Melanesia to provide a regular supply of labour and to the sandalwood ships and their crews to deliver them.

The sums they were offered were on a par with the money they had been making from logging sandalwood. Between £12-£15 was to be paid to the ship-owner for each recruit which, deducting a £3 government licence per man or woman, left him with a profit of about £10 per recruit. Most ships were between 80 and 140 tons with space for a minimum of one hundred recruits. Even allowing for the percentage in crew profit-share, an investor could expect to recoup the cost of a ship within three voyages.

For a fledgling industry looking for public support it was perhaps unfortunate that the first 'recruiter' they turned to was Ross Lewin but it was indicative of an attitude that was to pervade the whole business of what came to be known as 'black-birding'. Lewin had been one of the most successful of the sandalwooders and had earned his reputation through a complete disregard for the property rights on any of the islands that he had logged. Given the task of discovering whether there was any sandalwood on the New Hebridean island of Malekula he merely deployed a force of armed mercenaries in the south of the island and marched north, shooting his way through the opposition until he reached the northern coast.

In the spring of 1867 Lewin set up in business with the owner of the 120-ton *King Oscar* and published the following advertisement in Brisbane:

> Sugar planters. And others. Henry Ross Lewin, for many years engaged in trade in the South Sea islands and practically acquainted with the language and habits of the natives . . . begs to inform his friends and the public that he intends immediately visiting the South Seas and will be happy to receive orders for the importation of South Sea natives . . . Parties favouring H.R.L. with orders may rely on having the best and most serviceable natives to be had among the islands.

Lewin was rushed with orders, not only from plantation-owners, but pastoralists, town employers and ordinary households looking for female domestics. The problem now was how to catch them? The history of the first few years of this trade is almost a blank page. All maritime activity is dependent on a ship's log, not only to provide an hourly record of the location of the vessel but also the actions of its crew. Blackbirding was a business in which all the participants were involved in profit-share and it would profit none of them if the ship's log were to provide an accurate record of a recruiting voyage. As all the logs were doctored on a daily basis, it fell to those few European missionaries, resident on the islands, to record their activities.

On the New Hebridean island of Epi a missionary watched Lewin's tactics. A large party from the ship landed at first light some way down the coast from a sleeping village. They crept through the bush until they were behind it. Another group rowed the boats to the beach opposite the village. A bushfire was started close to the huts, then, with shouts and gunfire, the crew drove the panic-stricken villagers into the sea. Twenty men and women were scooped up into the waiting boats.

The *King Oscar* next visited Aniwa, a tiny island about fifteen miles from the larger island of Tanna. The resident missionary on Aniwa was an old enemy of Lewin's, so he anchored well away from the mission on the other side of the island. The conscientious missionary had been teaching the islanders English. After some discreet scouting, Lewin found one of them and discovered that some Aniwan canoes had recently gone to the nearby island of Tanna to trade. The *King Oscar* set off for the beach on Tanna and found the Aniwans ready to return. He persuaded them that he had been engaged by the missionary to take them home. On that first voyage, by terror and deception, the *King Oscar* is recorded as having brought 225 'recruits' back to Brisbane.

In that same year another boat, the *Syren*, dropped anchor at a recognized trading point off the island of Malekula in the New Hebrides. A group of natives, expecting to trade, swam out, pushing before them little rafts of bamboo bearing yams and coconuts. Others followed, their canoes full of produce. Twenty-one were hauled up over the gunwale to look at 'trade items'. According to the oral history of the island, when the wives of the kidnapped men saw the ship sail away, they swam after it for three miles calling for the *Syren* to return. As it sailed over the horizon, they wished for nothing more and sank beneath the waves.

Once kidnapped, the recruits had to endure a thousand-mile

journey back to Australia. According to the Queensland government regulations, each recruit was entitled to seventy-eight cubic
feet of air and five feet in which to exercise. By some oversight,
the regulations had omitted to consider the provisions below
decks and it was subsequently discovered that on one ship 'over
120 immigrants were crowded together, lying side by side, with
little if any space between each individual. People, not used to
natives, going down the hold, tasting the foul atmosphere, and
seeing the natives packed together like sardines, would no doubt
be disgusted'.

On the *Syren*, one of Lewin's competitors, half the islanders were
seriously seasick and unable to eat. Half of the rest, angry and terrified, started a hunger strike. The captain resorted to threats. He
stood over them and threatened to thrash the next man who
refused to eat. Inevitably, due to the situation below decks, dysentery developed, spreading quickly through the already undernour-
ished cargo. Twenty-four died before they were eventually allowed
to disembark in Brisbane. The *Syren* was quickly disinfected in
preparation for another voyage. This was a business where the law
of supply and demand overrode the few regulations designed to
ameliorate the worst excesses.

Lewin, aware of the esteem in which the missionaries were
generally held on those islands that had experienced the brutal
impact of the sandalwood trade, now exploited this fund of
goodwill. He would deliberately make for those islands where
there was a resident missionary, or an island nearby that knew of
his existence and had some experience of proselytizing. With a
ship's boat providing cover, members of his crew would take a
book each and land on a beach. There they would stand, singing
hymns. Lewin, meanwhile, dressed in a white mackintosh, white

bell topper, spectacles and umbrella, would descend from the ship and be rowed ashore. A reverential crowd would soon assemble and the white 'disciples' would hand round leaves torn from some magazine, explaining that they were religious tracts. The white apparition would land to a suitable display of obeisance from his 'disciples' who would then explain that he had just been made a bishop, or the governor of Sydney, or some other far fetched dignitary, and that he now wanted to honour them by inviting them aboard.

The *King Oscar*'s first two voyages netted 507 recruits. All were sold on at an average of £9 per head and the proceeds were shared by Lewin and his three partners, one of them a Queensland MP. It was almost inevitable that a trade, so profitable and so inadequately policed, would attract individuals with even fewer scruples than Lewin. James Murray [no relation to the Captain Murray of the *Bobtail Nag*, Renton's liberator] was clever, personable and energetic but a man with what could be described as a 'personality disorder'. That he was also a doctor could, in the circumstances, be viewed as a somewhat lethal cocktail. His first appointment after qualifying was as the surgeon attached to Otago Hospital in New Zealand. He was charming, apparently competent and, most importantly, idealized by his patients. Exactly how he exploited this idolization was never clear but stories started to circulate about his behaviour and, although none of the allegations was ever aired in court, Murray's father believed them and cut him off without a penny.

Murray moved to Australia and soon secured the post as resident superintendent at Melbourne's Benevolent Asylum. Feeling that his responsibilities were impinging on his social life, he devised a novel way of making sure he could enjoy an uninterrupted long weekend. A subsequent enquiry revealed:

> The day after his departure the authorities noticed the extraordinarily somnolent condition of many of the inmates. Most of the poor old folk were asleep and snoring the whole day long. On enquiry it transpired that Dr Murray had devised a way of keeping his charges quiet and comfortable during his holiday. He appears to have given a very large dose of morphia – in some cases as much as two grains – to each of the persons whom he thought might be at all troublesome in his absence.

When he returned he talked his way out of the scandal, ably supported by his charmed patients, and with no harm done to his reputation he moved on to become resident physician at Melbourne Hospital.

Murray, had already ingratiated himself into Melbourne society by volunteering to be a member of an expedition assembled to search for the explorers Burke and Wills whose disappearance in the Outback had already assumed mythic proportions. He had proved such an excellent travelling companion that he was the obvious choice to join another search party assembled this time to look for the remains of Leichhardt's 1848 expedition. After a seventy-five mile march into the Outback, the expedition's leader, finding no water at the designated map reference, decided to push on with an Aboriginal scout, leaving Murray in charge of the rest of the expedition. His job was to hold the little party together and preserve discipline until the leader returned.

Although capable of remarkable ingenuity when so minded,

Murray appeared to have no moral compass – it was to be the Melbourne Asylum all over again. No sooner had the expedition's leader and his scout disappeared over the horizon than with a yelp of delight Murray ripped open a couple of flour bags and triumphantly held aloft three large brandy bottles. Together with the three remaining members of the expedition, Murray settled down to drink his way through the cache. By nightfall they were all comatose and when they were woken late next morning by the searing heat it was to the realization that they were completely alone. Their horses had disappeared. Bereft of the means of portage they staggered back to civilization, abandoning £4,000-worth of equipment donated by the people of Melbourne. Murray, ever the arch-manipulator, concocted with his fellow inebriates an entirely plausible story. As the expedition's leader never returned, Murray once again escaped censure.

He was promoted to chief medical officer of the government sanatorium in Bendigo. For a brief moment this town had been the most famous in Australia, when a surface gold seam of quite extraordinary density yielded fortunes to many prospectors. Now, twenty years later, a gold-rich quartz reef had been discovered deep beneath the surface and the rush was on again. The febrile atmosphere of the town suited Murray perfectly. Rich prospectors, capable of financing access to the lode-bearing seams, flocked to the town and Murray built up a lucrative private practice as they threw money at the only 'establishment' doctor in the town.

It is a measure of the mercurial unpredictability of the man that, spurning the many offers of partnership in the current rush, he decided that his fortune lay thousands of miles away, not in gold but in blackbirding. With the considerable earnings from his private practice in Bendigo he returned to Melbourne and purchased the 250-ton *Carl*. The British administration in Fiji was offering tracts of land on long leases and at no cost in an effort to encourage white settlement. Exploiting what came to be known as 'Fiji Fever' Murray advertised for prospective pioneers. It was typical of his unblinking duplicity that he concealed the true nature of his intentions not only from his eleven passengers, but from all his crew.

The *Carl* was a week out of Melbourne when Murray brought up the subject of blackbirding to discover that most of the crew would have nothing to do with the idea. Undaunted, he bided his time and once the ship had docked in Fiji's Levuka harbour he unloaded the pioneers and paid off all the crew with the exception of the first mate, Armstrong, whom he promoted to captain. Then from the harbourside bars and cafes he crewed his ship with experienced blackbirders. For a man like Murray this enterprise provided a wonderful opportunity. With a crew and captain entirely beholden to him, he set out to hunt for a quarry, unfettered by any rules or regulations. This was to be the perfect playground for a psychopath.

As the *Carl* left Fiji, Murray still had four encumbrances on board wishing to buy land in the New Hebrides. Mr Bell was an invalid, Mr Grut, a married man with a wife and child. Arriving at the island of Tanna, the four were speedily unloaded on the nearest beach. Within a fortnight Bell and Grut had been killed and eaten; wife and child, however, were rescued by a missionary.

The *Carl* sailed on to Epi where Murray revealed that he had done his homework. At breakfast he announced: 'I'll tell you what is our best plan. This is a big ship, and we can make it pass for a missionary ship. If we disguise ourselves we can get some natives to come on board and put them down below.' What followed bore little resemblance to Lewin's polished performances. Armstrong, the captain, turned the mate's monkey jacket inside out, displaying a florid red lining. Another crew member wore a red overall, Chinese smoking cap, slippers and carried a Chinese umbrella, someone else was dressed in a tiger skin cloak. Most carried books and pieces of paper. A crowd of islanders gathered at a safe distance where they remained, all having witnessed the aftermath of far more convincing displays.

As the *Carl* continued northwards, Murray went back to the drawing board. It was clear that the natives were anxious to trade – all the experienced crew members had told him so – but only offshore. It was only at sea that they felt secure. If a ship hove to, they would meet it, their canoes loaded with produce, and mill about beside the hull. Murray now devised a strategy. Lumps of pig iron ballast were rolled in canvases attached to ropes and suspended over the ship's rail. As the canoes came alonside the ropes would be released and the furled pig iron dropped on the unsuspecting visitors. Once the damage was done the canvases would be hauled back into position ready for the next drop. The initial 'drop' off the coast of Malekula netted twelve 'recruits' and a number of fatalities as the overexuberant crew, responding to Murray's psychopathic urgings, forgot the object of the exercise.

Murray sailed on to the Solomon Islands where he discovered that his strategy was perfectly designed to garner large numbers of 'recruits'. Unlike the rest of Melanesia, where small outriggers manned by no more than two or three traders gathered round the ship's hull, the Solomon Islanders arrived in large six- to eight-man canoes designed for inter-island trading. News of the

Carl's progress filtered up the east coast of Malaita and Renton recorded:

> The natives first went out in their canoes, and the whites smashed the frail barks by dashing heavy pieces of iron through their hulls, careless whether, as frequently happened, some unfortunate might be in the way and have his limbs shattered by the missile. Sometimes the victims would resist; in which case a rifle would be used to shoot down the boldest and the strongest. Then the rest would be secured.
>
> By these practices the natives were swept off by the score in a very brief space. There was scarcely a coastal village but had to mourn the loss of its people. The inhabitants were convulsed in grief, terror and rage.

Renton and the lagoon-dwellers were protected by their barrier reef but halfway down the coast it petered out, giving way to a succession of coves and inlets that had become a popular anchorage for ships wishing to trade. The *Carl* made for a point close to the island of Leli where, within half an hour, it had successfully 'dropped' two trading canoes. The chief of Leli immediately dispatched three war canoes to attack the *Carl*. As they closed they were raked with volleys of musketry. Among those hit was the chief's son. As the rest of the natives jumped into the water and swam for their lives, two of the ship's boats, already gathering the victims from the initial drop, moved out and caught most of the swimmers. Those who resisted were clubbed or shot. Murray, having added sixteen Leli men to his haul, sailed northwards.

The *Carl* stopped briefly by the lagoon. Renton was on the

mainland with a group of men making his way down a bush path when he saw a twin-masted schooner moored just beyond the reef. He left his companions and rushed down to the shore but as it was high tide he had to swim across to Sulufou. He arrived to meet a number of canoes that had just returned from a visit to the now distant schooner. As soon as it had appeared they had put off with a supply of yams, coconuts and tortoise shell. The ship was very close to the reef and as they manoeuvred up to its hull some pipes were handed to them followed by persistent attempts to induce them on board. This urgency made the villagers suspicious and they immediately retreated back to the other side of the reef. It appeared to Renton that the only reason that their canoes had not been swamped was because they could have easily escaped by swimming among the reefs before they could have been caught.

On Leli next morning the body of the chief's son was found washed up on a beach near the main village. The grief-stricken father sought vengeance and offered the remarkable sum of four hundred porpoise teeth (enough to buy four war canoes) for the head of a white man. Everyone knew whom he meant, but it was also characteristic of Melanesian thinking that he should want the most powerful chief on the eastern coast to lose what he himself had lost – the favoured one. For Jack Renton, the doctor's actions presaged the worst year of his life on the island.

Renton was at a loss to explain what was happening. He assumed that a new source of guano had been discovered close by and that the ships needed labourers. The villagers dismissed this suggestion, for apart from Kwaisulia and a few others, everyone believed, as Renton put it:

That the whole human race lived under conditions little different from their own. Thus the white man presented himself as a nomadic race eternally roving about the sea in their big canoes. If the white man had any island at all it must be a very little one otherwise they would not require to leave it and come trading for yams and coconuts. They themselves traded for such things because they could not live without them and they assumed that the white man was governed by the same necessities.

Their theory about the recent captures was that the white man, having evidently been sailing about on the barren ocean, was under the necessity, from time to time, of obtaining fresh provisions, and when pressed by hunger, swooped down on some island and snapped up as many inhabitants as he could, thus obtaining a stock of fresh meat.

Murray moved on, scooping up twenty more from Isabel, then up into the northern Solomons. Murray now had sixty-two men from Malekula, Malaita and Isabel, but the *Carl* was a large ship and there was room for another eighty. In the Straits of Bougainville, off the island of Buka, lived a people who had had no experience of trading with the white man. They came out to meet the *Carl* in large numbers, as much out of curiosity as any desire to exchange goods. The *Carl*'s cook gave a vivid account of the events of the following three days:

> There were a great many canoes alongside. They were smashed just as usual, and the boats lowered. We were that busy that I can't tell you how many canoes or natives were got. As fast as we smashed one canoe, another would

come up before we could look round. The natives were very bruised when they came on board, and the bilge water from the two ship's boats was mixed with blood . . . We stood out at sea that night and came in again in the morning further round the coast. Canoes were smashed as usual. We were then about a mile from the shore, so far that the natives on land could not see what was going on. We took about forty that day.

We stood out to sea that night, and came in again next morning further down the coast. Three large canoes, containing from seven to sixteen men each, came alongside. The pig iron was got ready before they reached us. Dr Murray called out, 'Well boys, look sharp now. We want these natives. We want about thirty more.' Dr Murray gave the signal and the canoes were smashed in the usual way.

In all the *Carl* scooped up eighty-five Buka men before she set sail for Fiji. That evening chaos reigned below decks as panic-stricken men from Buka, Isabel, Malaita and Malekula, none speaking the other's language, veered between fighting each other and trying to break open the hatches. The desperation of this human cargo was made more acute by the shared conviction that the fate that awaited them was to be food for the white man. By dusk, with most of the crew the worse for drink, Murray started firing into the hold. The clamour below was briefly silenced, only to break out again, and as other members of the crew joined in. The cook recalled:

I went to the cabin after the first row had quietened. I saw Dr Murray loading a revolver. I asked where the captain was, and was told in the lazaret [storeroom], at the grog barrel. I went down and asked him why he was not on deck doing his duty like a man. There was firing on and off during the night. At 4 o'clock everything was quiet, and I went into the galley and served out some coffee to the men. While they were drinking coffee in the cabin, one of the crew ran aft and said, 'Why, there is not a man dead in the hold.' Dr Murray put down his coffee and went forward. He was absent about five minutes, and then returned and fetched his revolver. The second mate got an inch augur, and bored some holes in the bulkheads of the fore-cabin, through which Dr Murray fired. The first and second mates fired as well. After a bit Dr Murray came aft. Lewis, the second mate, said, 'What would people say to my killing twelve niggers before breakfast?' Dr Murray replied, 'My word, that's a proper way to pop them off'; meaning the holes in the bulkhead.

A ladder was lowered into the hold and the survivors told to come up. Those that could, climbed on deck, many bearing gunshot wounds in the arms, legs and chest. Then two natives who had decided to co-operate were sent down with ropes, which they tied to the seriously injured and hauled them up. Under Murray's direction the lightly wounded were separated from those who could not stand. He and three other members of the crew brought lengths of rope that they handed to the 'friendly' natives who were instructed to tie up the hands and feet of those lying on the deck. Another witness remembered an almost eerie silence during the massacre, of noises below deck but 'no cry of pain, no appeal for mercy or moaning from the wounded'. It was only when Murray ordered the two friendly natives to pick up the first of the wounded, a six-fingered child, and prepared to throw him overboard that:

> the men who had never cried out, uttered a protecting wail of anguish and terror at the treatment of the sacred body of one they reverenced as the favoured of the gods. He was held over the rail and Murray moved forward and pushed him overboard. At this, all the Bukamen who could do so, jumped overboard. All the dead men were then brought up on deck. The friendly natives went down, fixed a bowline round them and hauled them up. There were about thirty-five dead men hauled up and thrown overboard. It was over before noon.

Seventy natives had been killed outright or tossed, badly wounded, into the sea. This left a cargo of seventy-seven of whom twenty-five were men from Malaita. The hold of the ship was thoroughly cleansed and whitewashed before the *Carl* returned to Levuka harbour in Fiji. It was inspected by the crew of HMS *Rosario* who reported that the ship was 'beautifully clean and in first class order for carrying natives'. These were sold to a plantation-owner and Murray paid off the crew of the *Carl* at the rate of two shillings a head for the survivors.

On Sulufou Renton waited for the inevitable and, as oral history records:

> A *ramo* from Kwaio country made an agreement with the chief of Leli. He came to Sulufou. Many people knew he was coming. As he approached the village in a canoe the

110

villagers started to make a noise. Kabou was in his house and he came out and asked: 'Why are you making this noise?' Everyone was afraid and wouldn't speak. But one man, Ei, told him. He said that many people wanted Renton killed and that was why they were making all the noise.

Kabou walked back into his house and took out two of his holy spears and stood waiting for the *ramo*, who came with other men, including a cousin of Kabou's who was living in Leli. He said: 'Brother we have come here today to take your boy. We're going to take him to Leli and kill him.'

Kwaisulia then came up and stood beside Kabou. Kabou then said: 'Whoever wants to kill Renton will have to kill me first.' Then Kabou's wife walked forward into the area where they were standing which was a tabu area in which women were never allowed to enter. The *ramo* was very disturbed. She then pointed to her loincloth and said: 'Any man who wants to kill Renton will have to kill us first.' Then she took off her cloth and it was stained in blood [menstrual blood] and laid it on the ground between the *ramo* and Kabou. It had never happened. The Leli man left quickly.

For the next few months Renton lived in a continual state of anxiety. His presence on Sulufou was a constant source of tension and many in the village made little secret of their desire to be rid of him. Without the support of Kabou and Kwaisulia he would certainly have been sacrificed. Meanwhile, the chief of Leli bided his time and, after four months, his patience was rewarded.

One day a small vessel was sighted making its way towards Leli.

The natives waded out into the sea and laid their long-handled axes on the seabed. They then returned to sit under the palm trees until a boat full of white men put off from the ship and rowed towards the shore. The chief stood up and, walking towards the shoreline, beckoned to the boat. With a series of gestures the recruiters made it clear that they wanted to trade for food and water. Other natives then gathered round the chief and, producing bamboo water-carriers, indicated that they would deliver the fresh water first. A ship's boat was secured in the shallows, the crew disembarked and the empty kegs were handed over. Having filled them, the natives and the white crew formed a chain and started to ferry them back into the boat. Each member of the boat's crew had to walk a few feet to meet the next man in the line to pass on the kegs. The islanders, dragging their axes along the seabed with their toes, awaited the signal. The chief bent down, took up his axe and drove it into a white man's skull. The others acted in unison. In less than a minute it was finished.

The next day a number of war canoes approached Sulufou from the south. Renton records:

> They were shouting and yelling in the most extraordinary manner. The villagers at once concluded that what had long been expected was about to happen, and that they were going to be exposed to an attack in resentment for harbouring me.
>
> While some flew to arms others discussed the possibility of averting the attack and putting an end to the situation by surrendering me at once. But the closer the boats came the more obvious it was that their commotion had a different reason.

As they came close, I understood what had happened. The approaching natives were decked out in various articles of European clothing. They landed amidst tremendous uproar. Every one of them had some parts of the spoils of the ship. Some had wheels of the works of a clock suspended as ornaments from their ears and noses, sheets of paper from the ship's log, fragments of chronometers and telescopes, crockery, cabin fittings and a host of other articles.

The main reason for the visit was a formal acknowledgement that the chief of Leli had collected his blood bounty and that Kabou's boy was no longer in danger. Further discussions revealed that after slaughtering the crew, the villagers noticed two white men still on the boat, trying to manoeuvre it into the wind. They set out in canoes and caught up with it near a reef. The man at the helm they had killed with arrows, the other had been captured alive, but they were unable to prevent the boat drifting onto the reef where it had been looted before it sank.

Later that day, Renton approached the Leli islanders and asked to be allowed to see the man. He met with a flat refusal. Over the subsequent weeks he learned that the survivor had met Doorey's fate and was being kept, hog-tied, in a pigpen. Apparently the poor man displayed none of Doorey's skills and was being subjected to almost daily torments.

7

The Arms Race

———————— ○ ————————

BACK on the plantations it was becoming very clear that those taken by force were very difficult to manage, especially if they happened to be Solomon Islanders. They either tried to escape or simply refused to work. Fiji was now following Queensland's lead and large tracts of land were leased from their traditional owners and cleared for sugar cane. However, with the demand for labour outstripping supply, plantation-owners in the know regularly attempted to offload the most troublesome recruits onto newly established businesses on the remoter islands of the archipelago.

Within a few weeks of landing in Fiji, twenty of Murray's Buka men found themselves back in Levuka harbour, this time on the small cutter *Keva* which ran a regular business ferrying recruits to different islands. A few miles out to sea the three white owners, having no knowledge of the circumstances surrounding their cargo's enforced exile, went below to the galley leaving their four

Fijian crewmen in charge of the sullen Buka men squatting on deck. Within a few minutes the unwilling passengers had broken up into small groups and were lolling around the ship's rail. If the crew had been forewarned they may have noticed that these casual gatherings exactly matched their own number.

A splash and some stifled cries alerted the white men below, but as each emerged from the hatch they too were picked off one by one. A single Fijian survivor swam fifteen miles to shore with the news. The ship itself disappeared into the void of the Pacific – its passengers, although 'saltwater' people to the man, had no knowledge of sailing ships.

A short while later the *Peri* set out from Fiji's Suva harbour with yet more of Murray's rejects (including twenty-five Malaita men, sixteen of whom had been captured at Leli) bound for various islands where they were to be delivered to new owners. The ship was dangerously overcrowded with recruits from different islands, none speaking the other's language. And, despite their weeks in Fiji, none of the passengers had been made aware of the nature of their contract and were still tormented by their original misapprehension. To the men of Leli it appeared to be the *Carl* all over again. As one of them later recalled: 'As Leli men we talked together: "As for us, we are going to be killed as meat for a feast." So others said, "Suppose we kill the sailors as we have nothing to lose?"'

The spark that lit this tinderbox of apprehension occurred on the first morning at sea and involved their first meal which comprised a couple of spoonfuls of rice per recruit. Seeing the mood of their passengers, the outnumbered crew filled up another pot. Whilst it was simmering, one of the white men, who had not been party to this decision, emerged from the hold and rushed between the groups of squatting islanders. With a yell of 'You disgusting pigs!' he seized the pot and hurled it into the sea. That night the *Peri*'s crew shared the same fate as their counterparts on the *Keva* – except for one Fijian who was spared so that he could navigate the vessel. Unfortunately, as soon as an opportunity presented itself, the terrified man jumped overboard.

Given the mix of passengers and the multiplicity of languages, no situation could have been better designed to ferment the horror that was to follow. As the *Peri* drifted slowly westwards, life on board became a babel of incomprehension and suspicion as each group manoeuvred to lay claim to some small part of the boat, the smaller the group, the less favourable their territory. After three days the food ran out and within a week the starving passengers were chewing boards and packing cases. Then, as the water supply ran dry, the largest group – the sixteen men from Leli – made their move. To forestall any opposition they had already taken possession of all the ship's iron, now they forced the two smaller groups into the hold.

All the passengers were from coastal tribes with no tradition of cannibalism but, overwhelmed by hunger, 'it was agreed that we should eat some, as it was so uncertain how long we would have to endure before we would reach land. It was the commencement of eating human beings and that day we ate two women, one in the morning and one in the afternoon.' The culling continued for three weeks and as the days past their daily visits to the hold met with less and less resistance as 'those who remained wished that the ship would sink and that they would all be drowned.' Despite sharing the bodies of two humans a day between the sixteen of them, they continued to waste away. The problem was that the meat they were consuming from their skeletal victims contained no fatty tissue. No matter how much they consumed it was of negligible nutritional value.

After thirty days the hold was empty. It was at this moment that the Leli men's aversion to cannibalism reasserted itself with such force that even when one of their number died they could not bring themselves to touch the corpse: 'he was rolled up in a canvas, weighted with stones and thrown overboard. Then the second moon came and we sighted land. Some said: "It is the Solomons," but others: "It is a different country." That night heavy rain fell and we drank it. Had it not been for the rain we would all have perished. When the sun rose we knew we were in a strange land and later that day a ship drew near."

The ship was HMS *Basilisk*; the strange land, the coast of Queensland somewhere north of Townsville. It was 5 February 1872. In thirty-five days the *Peri* had drifted 1800 miles westwards through a sea infested with coral reefs, finally passing over a submerged part of the Great Barrier Reef or through one of its few narrow channels.

From a distance Captain Moresby of the *Basilisk* was puzzled 'by the slovenly set of her sails'. He hoisted an ensign and, having received no response from the *Peri*, made a cautious pass. 'There were signs of strange neglect and not a soul was moving on board: but just as we were thinking her abandoned, two wild-looking creatures rose up in the stern, and then we saw that others lay on the deck as if asleep.' One of the 'wild-looking creatures' was Aliverete, the author of the *Peri*'s account. 'When we saw boats coming towards us Laisenia said to me, "Alas for ourselves, we shall be killed." Then I said, "What about us? Get you ready and let us kill one of them and be slain ourselves afterward."'

118

As two of the *Basilisk*'s boats closed to within thirty yards, the sailors were dismayed to see the two wild-looking figures totter towards the ship's rail clutching muskets. But as they rowed hard to take evasive action the guns continued to point harmlessly in the same, fixed direction. Captain Moresby recorded: 'As our crews boarded, other half-dead wretches tottered to their feet, fumbling with rusty, lockless muskets, and our men gently disarmed them. But what men! They were living skeletons, creatures dazed with fear and mortal weakness. Wasted to the bone, some were barely alive, and the sleeping figures were dead bodies fast losing the shape of humanity, on a deck foul with blood.' Further examination revealed an empty, waterlogged hold and 'the ransacked cabin, the blood, the planking splintered and scored with axe strokes that told of tragedy'.

The voyage of the *Peri* was to become the focus of a campaign in Australia and Britain for a reform of the labour laws, but the facts presented at an official inquiry were exclusively drawn from naval sources. It was a testimony to the gulf that existed in language, culture and racial attitudes, that none of the survivors were ever asked to give evidence. It was to be twenty years before Aliverete, by then a Methodist minister living in Fiji, recorded the details of the voyage.

However, when it came to the facts surrounding the first part of their five-month odyssey, these emerged much sooner and from a most surprising source – James Murray himself. When the *Carl* delivered its catch to Fiji most of the crew signed off, happy to draw a veil over crimes in which Murray, in his own inimitable fashion, had made sure that everyone felt implicated. On the second voyage, with a new crew and only the ringleaders, Dowden, the captain, and Armstrong, the mate, still aboard, the atmosphere became poisonous. Within a fortnight both accused Murray of attempting to lace their food with arsenic. Then on the *Carl's* return to Fiji, after a considerably less successful second voyage, Murray became convinced that they were both trying to poison him!

One contemporary described him as 'cruel, treacherous, mean in money matters, a liar in word and a traitor in action, brutal in authority but a coward in danger, there seems but one palliation for his depravity. It is not quite certain whether he is not sometimes mad.' Mad or not, Murray sensed the game was up and decided to make the first move and, once the *Carl* docked in Fiji, the doctor went straight to the British Consul and told him everything. It was a confession of bewildered contrition: of a mere amateur who, finding himself out of his depth in a business he had no knowledge of and literally at sea, was drawn through weakness and inexperience into colluding in behaviour that he knew was wrong – it was a masterstroke. Armstrong and Dowden were immediately arrested and sent to Sydney by warship. Accompanying them, though not as a prisoner, was Murray with a safe conduct pass, having agreed to co-operate fully and turn Queen's Evidence.[1]

Meanwhile HMS *Basilisk* with the fifteen survivors from the *Peri*, anchored in Levuka harbour where the wretched survivors realized to their horror that they were virtually back where they had started. That night Aliverete and Laisenia clambered through the chain holes, slipped off the bows and swam ashore. Next morning, seeing the terrified faces of their remaining passengers, Moresby and the other officers set about scouring the port in a futile search for an interpreter. Finally it was decided that if the problem of communication was impossible to surmount then the men from Leli should at least be compensated for their ordeal. Boxes of trade goods, calico, tobacco, axes, knives, muskets and shot where hastily assembled and, as the *Basilisk* set sail for the east coast of Malaita, they were presented to the bewildered passengers. These were gifts that were to have profound repercussions.

*　*　*

Comparing the oral history to Renton's own account of his last three years on Sulufou it is clear that he airbrushed out of his narrative many of the most significant events. Descriptions of incidents either have no biographical or chronological context, or are deliberately misleading. His relationship with a woman named Borie provides a typical example. According to oral history:

> Renton had been here for a number of years and his friend Kwaisulia was married and it was thought that Renton should have a woman. There was a young girl, her name was Borie and she was a great-niece of Kabou's. Everybody knew that Borie loved Renton and she became Renton's woman – everyone in Sulufou knew this. They didn't marry, but Renton was her man. After a year everyone was happy as Borie was having a baby. Then she died in childbirth. The whole village mourned – Renton and Borie had loved each other.

Renton was unable to resist mentioning her during his interviews with the *Courier* and he constructed a neat piece of fiction that appealed to Victorian sentiments of self-abnegation and gave a clear signal to his readers of the limits to which he was prepared to 'go native'.

Renton was advised, after he had become fairly domesticated, to get a hut for himself, his friendly chief offering to buy a suitable partner for him. Renton was, however, of a prudent turn. Of these inartificial, fair ones of the village he speaks with some animation and one of these little beauties seems to have made an impression on his heart. She was the young and pretty sister of his protector. The language of the heart is everywhere the same and many a kind glance told the young Orkneyman that he would not be an unwelcome wooer; and for his own part he does not disguise that the name of the merry Borie sounds sweet in his ears yet.

How her mighty chieftain brother would have regarded the suit of an alien and dependent aspirant is more dubious, but Renton was inclined to think that his consent might have been won. But it was never asked. The young captive never ceased to long for a return to civilized life, and the desire for release so ruled his existence that he refrained from adding to the too numerous difficulties which stood in the way, being aware that in the eyes of his captor such circumstances would operate powerfully to prevent his release in the event of a vessel at any time visiting this secluded spot. Consequently he restrained his natural inclination, and saw in time his sweetheart share the hut of a mate of her own race. Poor Borie, and her first baby, within a year of her wifehood, shared the eternal sleep of her ancestors.

It is a curious epitaph. Borie, far from being a distant relative of Kabou's, is elevated to a Pocahontas-like status and Kabou is a young man (throughout the whole narrative Renton avoids mentioning that Kabou had a number of children who were older than he was). Finally Renton marries Borie off to someone of her own race. In fact the only event that squares with the oral history are the circumstances of her death.

If Renton was circumspect about the details of his personal life, he was even less forthcoming about the impact of Kabou's patronage on his own standing among the lagoon-dwellers. Only Slade's observation of their reaction to the news of his leaving, provide any clue. In fact Renton benefited from a rather more enlightened approach to the chiefly exercise of power and patronage than existed on the rest of the island. The artificial islands were a relatively recent creation and the chiefly families, bereft of the legitimacy of the ancestral 'Generations' of Malaita, mythologized their belligerence. Narratives of the deeds of warrior chiefs were handed down from generation to generation as a form of ancestor worship, which indirectly deified the chieftainship itself. However, these men were pragmatic enough not to be seduced by any ideas of a divine right to power and were under no illusions about their tenuous relationship with their subjects. Unlike the medieval baron, they encouraged a meritocracy and any man was guaranteed patronage if he demonstrated particular abilities. A canny chief would make a point of recruiting henchmen into his inner circle from outside the island and his immediate family – people who would be more dependent on his favour and less likely to ally themselves with disaffected groups on the island. Kabou was no exception and, having supported Renton through his year as a pariah, he installed him and Kwaisulia as his closest aides.

The last three years of Renton's exile saw an extension of Sulufou's power and influence in the lagoon and an expansion in its population. Abandoning their customary ties to kin and country, young men from distant villages made their way to the largest of the artificial islands, drawn by the glamour of Kabou's chieftainship. On Malaita the prestige of a village was dependent as much on its reputation of being a haven of peace and refuge as its reputation in war. There were various phrases used to describe what a particular chief stood for and what it was felt he had done for his people. Thus Kabou was said to be 'the root of the land', that he 'drew up' those who came to him for protection.

This expansion of Sulufou's power and influence was also due to Renton's presence. Four years after his arrival, stories of Kabou's white headhunter had spread throughout the coastal regions of Malaita and Isabel. Renton was later to acknowledge that feuding and warring in the region was almost continuous but, according to oral history, he played little or no part in the politics of the lagoon. Instead, he and Kwaisulia concentrated on persuading Kabou to adopt a different approach to hostilities and in particular the use of reliable intelligence and making sure that the element of surprise was not compromised by the widely advertised rituals that would precede a raid.

The first opportunity to put these principles into practice occurred when a group of men from the artificial island of Funaafou were killed during a trading expedition to Alite on the west coast of Malaita. With neither the resources in people or weapons to avenge this loss, the inhabitants of Funaafou had no option but to approach the most powerful island in the lagoon with the offer of blood money which Kabou accepted. Renton urged patience; Alite was a well-defended island over a hundred miles away. A small group of men was sent to the village of Arabala on the mainland, opposite the island of Alite. They had instructions to offer the chief of the village a valuable gift of porpoise teeth for any information about the movements of the villagers of Alite. In August 1872 information arrived that a large number of men, women and children had left the village and had moved north into Coleridge Bay where they had set up temporary dwellings near the beach whilst they harvested betel-nuts.

Renton's *Courier* account mentions only two raids, the first on Maanaomba; the second 'was round the other side of the island against a tribe who had made their habitations on the main island quite close to the beach'. Along the east coast of Malaita, coastal villages were all situated inland, on well-defended vantage points, and only temporary homes were ever situated on a beach. In the florid style of the popular journalism of the time, Renton's account continues:

The time of arrival of the scene had not been quite so judiciously arranged, and the threatened tribe saw the gallant warriors approaching and incontinently fled into the interior.

Balked of their prey, the invaders made the best use of their disappointment by setting fire to the abandoned dwellings, and, as is the manner of gallant warriors of all nations, in affecting a reasonable amount of loss and suffering when they are unable to murder. As they bustled about in their enjoyment of this occupation they were disagreeably interrupted by a sudden and rapid succession of arrows falling among them, discharged by a single hero, who, from the margin of the bush, thus resented their proceedings.

According to Renton, this solitary patriot was in a state

of mind much akin to the Malay amok; that is to say excited to the point approaching mania and utterly regardless of his own life. He continued to wildly shoot his arrows even when his enemies closed upon him, and was fitting another shaft to the string when a dozen weapons simultaneously crashed down on his skull or were plunged into his body.

A few moments more and his carcass was mangled in a fearful manner, every raw lad on his first war expedition was eager to flesh his maiden weapon in order that on his return he might boast in the village how he had struck a mighty man of war. Ultimately the carcass was heaved high in the air on the points of a score of spears and flung into the blazing fire of the hut.

Renton ends his account there but in the telling of the tale his interviewers noticed the mask slipping – 'Renton, so recently removed from native incidence and savage ideas, could not help warming up a bit, and his quickened utterances and flashing eyes showed that he had not yet disassociated these recollections.' Or perhaps it was his knowledge of the aftermath. It had been a famous and notorious raid with killing on a scale hitherto unknown on Malaita. The self-sacrifice of the lone defender had been a desperate attempt to buy time for the villagers of Alite, but as they fled into the bush they came face to face with a wall of precipitous rocks and were slaughtered where they stood. The intelligence from the people of Arabala had been worth the inducement and Renton and the Sulufou war party returned with the heads of over one hundred men, women and children.

In a stone-age culture where the head count from a successful raid seldom numbered more than a dozen, wars would usually splutter on for months and years as the victims sought to retaliate. Eventually when honour had been assuaged and the numbers of the dead approximately equalized, peace would be made. The scale of the killing of the Alite people was unprecedented and the oral history of the lagoon, although celebrating the number of kills, gives equal weight to a fact that clearly haunted these people – they did not capture any guns.

It had been almost a year since HMS *Basilisk* had dropped anchor off the island of Leli. The twelve survivors of the *Peri* had disembarked carrying with them the compensation for their ordeal – chests full of tobacco, calico, axes, knives and Snider rifles. The delighted chief had held a number of feasts and there was no community within a fifty-mile radius of Leli that had not been invited to witness demonstrations of the effect of European firearms. Kabou, Kwaisulia and Renton now realized that they had very little time. For the people of Alite, retaliation would either require the mobilizing of a large number of warriors or – and Renton thought this much more likely – they would pay blood money to another group on the island who had similarly benefited from European contact.

Although Sulufou's domination of the lagoon was founded on its size and its number of warriors, its ability to mobilize its economic power had long been its most potent weapon, based on the village's monopoly of the most valuable currency on Malaita, porpoise teeth, and strict control of the culling that provided them. Kabou decided that if they were to gain access to European technology they would have to buy it. He explained to the assembled priests that it was a matter of life and death and, as Kabou himself was a priest, they immediately agreed to the cull.

An armada of canoes set out through the passage in the reef and waited. This daylight vigil continued until, on the third day, a large school of porpoises appeared, gambolling about on the seaward side of the reef. A great cry went up: 'They come, they come!' The canoes closed in a line across the passage. Now close to the canoes, the porpoises cruised back and forth in front of the line. Then they disappeared. In the silence the occupants strained their eyes and some dived overboard to watch the school as it dived deep, nosing about the precipitous drop on the seaward side of the reef, looking for another opening.

After a couple of minutes a priest on one of the lead canoes shouted: 'Make way, the king of the west has come!' Suddenly a large male porpoise leapt into the air in front of the canoe and made for the passage, followed by the whole school. As the porpoises made for the shore the canoes followed, spreading out behind them across the lagoon, their occupants beating the water with hollow bamboos full of pebbles. Alarmed at these noises and the shouts of their pursuers, the porpoises retreated towards the shore, gradually driven on until they were in the shallows.

At this point the noise died down and the priest stepped out of his canoe. A large male porpoise drifted nearby. The priest approached him, stopped, turned and walked slowly towards the shore, closely followed by the animal. Other hunters now dropped into the shallows and walked beside the slowly moving school as they followed their leader towards the shore. With arms lifted and faces bent towards the water they sang softly to the passive animals coaxing them forwards.

Soon the animal's bellies were touching the sand but instead of turning away, they flapped and wriggled as if asking for help.

The men leaned forward embracing them and coaxing them over the sand ridges. On the shore, a line of woman and children sang softly, clapping their thighs with one hand whilst in the other they held knives and spears behind their backs.

The animals showed no signs of alarm and wriggled forward towards the coaxing and swaying of those lining the shore. The priest threw his hands in the air and shouted 'Lift!' Groups of men closed on the passive black shapes and half carried, half dragged them to the shoreline where they lay completely still. Suddenly there was a long scream from the priest that was immediately taken up by the waiting women and children as they descended on inert bodies with their weapons. Soon the shallows were crimson with blood as men, women and children screamed and danced around the twitching corpses.

A few days later Renton and Kwaisulia set out with the newly minted currency to buy arms. Rounding the northern end of Malaita they turned due south to the Floridas, a small group of islands on what they believed to be the main shipping lane between Malaita and Guadalcanal. Everywhere they were received with courtesy and everywhere they heard the same story – ships had attempted to recruit but no one was prepared to leave the island. It was only at the end of their third meeting in a large village that they understood the reason. Every discussion had been conducted in the formal setting of the *vaukolu*, the communal meetinghouse, with the male elders of a particular village. Behind them, however, sat a phalanx of women with whom they continually conferred. Renton initially thought that this was some exercise in democratic decision-making, quite unlike anything he had seen on Malaita, until it gradually dawned on him that the Floridas were a matriarchy and that the women had absolutely forbidden any of their men folk to be recruited.

They turned north-west into the strait that separated New Georgia from Santa Isabel, making for Isabel's shoreline. Thick bush extended down to the water's edge, and for mile after mile there was a total absence of clearings or tracks. Unlike the precipitous coast of their own island, here the land sloped gently upwards under an endless canopy of trees. The thin plumes of smoke that would have indicated an inland settlement were nowhere to be seen. For a day and a half they made their way along this deserted coastline then, as they entered a small bay, they noticed a large clearing on a hill surrounded by steep, almost perpendicular cliffs. They beached their canoe and followed a narrow pathway round the redoubt to a series of steps cut in the rock. Fearing an ambush, they made their way cautiously to the summit and as they crested the hill they were surprised to find themselves standing on the edge of a large clearing completely devoid of any evidence of human habitation. It was encircled by half a dozen hardwood trees, each over a hundred feet high. Nestling in the topmost forks of each tree was a large house.

The two men approached one of the trees and, craning their necks, they could see anxious faces peering down at them. Their yells of greeting were met with a shower of stones which, having been thrown from a considerable height, they evaded with ease. They retreated to the opposite side of the clearing, lay down their weapons and returned. For half an hour they sat in the middle of the clearing and waited whilst the occupants engaged in a series of shouted exchanges high above their heads. Eventually, slender rattan cane ladders were gingerly lowered and the villagers descended. As they moved cautiously forward to inspect their visitors, Renton and Kwaisulia were immediately struck by the absence of the young. The village appeared to be entirely populated by the middle-aged and the elderly.

Communication was painfully slow, despite the fact that over the centuries Solomon Islanders, with over eighty language groups, had developed a lingua franca based almost exclusively on signing. After much scratching in the earth the villagers grasped where the two men had come from and the purpose of their visit, at which point they were invited into a nearby tree. On reaching the top of the ladder they were surprised to find a large, well-built house. Renton estimated it to be over twenty-five feet in length with a ten-foot-high roof and a solid wooden floor covered in mats. At either end were spacious balconies piled with blocks of rock coral.

Fifteen years previously there had been an upsurge of head-hunting along the coast. War parties from Roviana appeared to have a special liking for the region's fair-haired women. In early 1865 matters reached crisis point when the nearby village of Mahaga was attacked. Apart from capturing a score of young women, the Rovianan's had left over a hundred headless corpses in their wake. The whole population of the region moved out of the villages and into tree houses situated on naturally defensive positions which they fortified with stone walls and stockades. Since then the villages had been occasionally visited by war parties, but their musket balls had been unable to penetrate the thick wooden floors and they had tired of being showered with arrows and rock coral.

To Renton's question about the absence of the young the villagers confessed that throughout the region the strain of living under the threat of constant attack had taken its toll. The young, in particular, had tired of their semi-arboreal existence and had emigrated to Mboula Point in the south-west corner of the island where they now lived under the protection of a man named Bera. The villagers added that, if they wanted to trade for weapons, they would find plenty there.

As they made their way south, the evidence of once thriving settlements beside every bay and beach they passed was still visible beneath the encroaching vegetation. The coastline was a wasteland, the people either dead or fled. Then, as they approached a rocky peninsula, they were suddenly confronted by the press of humanity. The shore and coastal shallows were full of canoes of different shapes and sizes. Three whaleboats, the first Renton had seen for six years, were making their way to a small offshore island. As they rounded the headland they came upon a collection of large houses built on piles, some positioned along the shoreline, others jutting out into the bay. Behind them smaller houses clung to the ledges of the promontory and at the top stood a fortress, its walls made of limestone and its roof of thatch; it reminded Renton of Orcadian farmhouses and seemed to him more out of place than the whaleboats below.

For a brief moment their arrival was greeted with suspicion. From a distance Renton's naked body was, by now, indistinguishable from the rest of the population. Only when they looked at his features did they recognize the identity of their visitor. Some shouted 'MacFarlane, MacFarlane!' – (clearly he had arrived three years too late) – others knew his name. He and Kwaisulia were escorted through the streets of the town towards the limestone fortress. For Renton it was a deeply dispiriting experience, as almost every man they passed was carrying a firearm. Clearly these were people who had had years of contact with Europeans and it was quite likely that porpoise teeth would be of no interest to them at all.

They were led through the gloomy corridors of the fortress to a large hall where they stood with their escorts and waited for Bera to make his entrance. Kwaisulia gasped audibly. The room was full of objects that he had only imagined from Renton's descriptions of his world. In one corner was a three piece suite of button-backed leather armchairs. In the middle of the hall stood a large refectory table surrounded by church pews. To one side, a kitchen dresser displayed a large collection of pewter ware – bowls, mugs, drinking cups, plates and tureens, together with a boxed set of stainless steel cutlery. The room was decorated with maritime ephemera. From the rafters hung flags, pennants and ship's bunting whilst, on rustic-looking shelves, lay a clutter of obsolete navigation instruments, compass housings, telescopes without lenses and dismantled barometers – Bera clearly had a liking for ship's brass.

He made his entrance from the far end of the room, followed by a small group of retainers who immediately drew up a large chair, which they placed a few feet in front of Renton and Kwaisulia. Bera eyed them for a moment and then sat down. He was a large man in his late forties. He wore a German naval jacket which, although of the correct cut for his shoulders and arms, was unable to accommodate his considerable girth. On his head sat an English stovepipe top hat which Renton remembered from his early childhood but which had gone out of fashion long before he had gone to sea. He was naked from the waist down except for a pair of ill-fitting spats, which merely exaggerated the size of his splayed toes.

Bera was keen to practise his English but had taken the precaution, much to his visitors' astonishment, of summoning a Malaitan interpreter who hovered nervously in the background. He said he expected to be addressed as 'King Berry', adding that all the Europeans he had so far encountered called him by that name. Thousands lived under his protection along the southern coast. He had drawn people not only from all parts of the island, but young men (and here he gestured to the redundant interpreter) from other islands as well.

He then escorted the two young men to a redoubt overlooking the bay and, waving at the expanse of water, announced that he had been dealing with European ships for so long and that his anchorage was so popular that they had named it Thousand Ships Bay. He alone was able to guarantee them recruits and so they came every month. Each man signed up for three years labour in Queensland at the end of which they were returned to their point of departure with a trade box full of European goods and a firearm.

As for himself, in return for each recruit the Europeans provided him with anything he desired. Thus his warriors were the best armed in the Solomon Islands. At this point Renton and Kwaisulia were ushered down a dimly lit passageway to Bera's armoury where they were shown their host's most recent gifts. He announced that, having acquired land on which no one lived, he had 'sold' it to the Europeans. In one section of the armoury lay the payment – 84 axes, 500 knives and 136 Tower muskets. In other parts of the armoury Renton estimated that there were over 200 Snider and Martini-Henry rifles, together with 50 revolvers and another 200 Tower muskets.

Bera then suggested to Renton that he stay at Mboula Point

until the next ship arrived. Renton, realizing that no one knew the purpose of their visit or what each of them carried in their shoulder bags, immediately thanked Bera for anticipating the purpose of his visit, pointing out that, as he had been living for so long in the lagoon, he would first have to return there to wind up his affairs but would return within a week. Secondly, he assured Bera that his rescue would not go unrewarded and that he could expect many gifts. For the first time their host smiled and pointed out that that was the reason he had made the offer.

During the years of their friendship Kwaisulia had learned enough English to understand exactly what had just taken place. They were faced with a market where traditional valuables were worthless; only one currency could purchase firearms – people. As the two men followed the interpreter back into the town, Renton murmured to him in English that their best chance lay with this man and that they should offer him not just their porpoise teeth but a cut of any down payment made by a recruiting ship of those it signed-on – if and when he was able to bring it to the lagoon.

That evening in a men's hut peopled with Bera's Malaitan mercenaries they discovered that they were pushing at an open door. Orianou was the interpreter's name and as they questioned him it became clear that most of Bera's overseas mercenaries, far from being lured by the promise of bounty, had joined his burgeoning army out of desperation – most were 'land poor'. In Orianou's case he had been born on a small island near Funaavou. Orphaned in infancy, his relatives had divided up his inheritance and, by his teenage years, he found himself an outcast. Sent as a crewman on a trading expedition to Isabel he had disappeared into the bush and made his way to Mboula.

Orianou paused, looked at the two men, and then asked if he could return with them to Sulufou. Renton reached into his basket, drew out the porpoise teeth and made the offer. The man looked down and shook his head. Renton glanced at Kwaisulia fearing all was lost. His friend was staring impassively at the bowed head, and after a moment he nodded. Renton looked back. Orianou was weeping, quietly he whispered his thanks, adding that for years he had dreamed of deliverance and promised them that he would bring a ship to Sulufou.

The two men decided to leave that night. Renton suspected that Bera had every intention of extracting the highest price for handing him over and that if he returned he could expect to be virtually ransomed. Clearly Bera felt that he was gullible and grateful enough to return, but what would happen if Bera changed his mind overnight?

They made their way along the coast to the open sea and then navigated due east by the stars. By first light they could see the mountains of their island silhouetted by the sunrise. Since they had left the fortress Kwaisulia had said very little. As they stroked their way across the thirty-mile strait with Renton sitting aft, he noticed that his friend would occasionally drop his head and mutter something to himself. At other times he would pause at the end of a stroke as if locked in some train of thought. He felt his friend was making a supreme effort to come to terms with a vision of the world that, until then, had only existed in imaginings fuelled by his own descriptions and some rough charcoal sketches.

After the years of acculturation that had permeated his consciousness Renton had been surprised by his own reaction to Bera's fortress. Perhaps it was speaking in English, but within a few minutes he had retrieved his past life and with it an objectivity and clarity – he was no longer living in a liminal state. He looked at his friend with different eyes. Like most lagoon-dwellers he had formidable upper body strength. The deltoid muscles that ran from his neck to his shoulder blades were overdeveloped from years of paddling, as were his biceps, triceps and forearms from the sheer physical effort of feeding, sheltering and fashioning an environment from tools of flint and stone. As they had stood together in Bera's fortress Renton had watched Kwaisulia's stone-age world crumble around him. From now on his physical attributes would matter very little in the world he had glimpsed in Mboula.

As they reached Basakana Island on the northernmost tip of Malaita, Kwaisulia turned to Renton and told him that he would come with him to Australia. With a pragmatism that even surprised himself, Renton suggested that it was, at least, a start. With Bera to the north and Leli to the south and the people of Alite looking for a champion, the recruits that would have to be signed up for Queensland would need to number dozens if Sulufou was to match the firepower of their neighbours. Sulufou and Ada Gege needed guns, as many and as soon as possible. Their first task would be to make Kabou understand that the world beyond the lagoon had changed forever. Clearly, given what followed, it appeared that they were unable to convince the ageing chief of the gravity of the threat that faced Sulufou or that Renton's plan provided the only solution.

His *Courier* narrative is characterized by a wealth of ethnographic detail about his hosts and an almost complete absence of information about his own actions during his seven years in exile. It is only in the telling of the story of his rescue and his flight that the author takes centre stage and it is only in his account of the final day on Sulufou that Kwaisulia is mentioned – though typically, and for reasons that became apparent later on, he is nameless.

Late one night in the men's hut which I shared with about thirty others, most of whom were asleep, I was just wrapping up the remnants of some pork and yams I had been eating and stowing them in the rafters above where I slept, when a group of people appeared with two men under escort. They were two villagers from Isabel. They told me that they had been transported with their canoe from the village by a recruiting ship that was lying off the reef. I told them to wait there, gave them my food and went to the next hut to awaken my particular friend and communicated the wonderful news.

He was different from the others and possessed more imagination. He, alone, used to take an interest in my descriptions of the white man's country and its marvels, and he had often said that if I was given the chance of returning, he would accompany me. I knew the man would be greatly interested in the subject of my release and sought his counsel. We went back to the hut and everyone was awake by now, all questioning the two messengers. We realized that without Kabou's blessing there was little we could do.

Kabou, hearing the incessant and excited discussion, came into the hut. We lit a fire. The two messengers then showed him the presents they had received. Kabou said nothing. He made no sign at all. I explained to him what this meant, that all our travels to other islands, all our efforts that had been in vain would now be realized – if he would release me. He looked completely unmoved and left the hut.

Then, at first light Kabou ordered a canoe to be prepared and told me to come with him and the twenty-man crew, to visit the vessel which was standing off the reef some way south of Sulufou. When he asked a priest to come with us I knew the issue was far from assured. The ancestors would have to be consulted. As we made our way, my companions chanted an invocation – a sign to signify whether they approved of my release. Soon the inexplicable happened and not for the first time I was confronted with an event for which I could find no satisfactory explanation. The canoe started rocking at each pause in the chant; not a gentle rocking but one so violent that we threatened to capsize. I assumed that my companions were the cause of the canoe's rocking but as it was happening they were all sitting perfectly passive and I couldn't see how else it was occurring.

This sign was considered by the priest as a good omen and we continued our journey with the two astonished messengers indicating the passage they had taken the night previously. It hove into view, my longed for refuge – a European schooner tacking to and fro to maintain its position.

At this point, far from making for the vessel, the canoe made for the shore and a friendly village, which I believed the captain of the vessel had mistaken for Sulufou. And there we stood, on the shore, whilst everyone looked on in apprehension. I could persuade none of my companions, not even my friend, to accompany me and clearly from Kabou's demeanour I was not going to be permitted to leave on my own, neither were the two messengers allowed to approach the schooner.

I was overwhelmed with apprehension and started to

imagine that every move of the schooner was a preparation for it to leave. I thought desperately about how I could convey to the ship some token of my presence? There was nothing – no paper, no article of European clothing. Then I saw, lying in the sand, a planed fragment of an old canoe. I then hurried to a fire that had been lit – for it was still early in the day. I wrote on the plank a message: 'John Renton. Please take me off to England. The chief of this island asks a present from you. Won [sic] of the ships crew come on shore that I can speak with them. Shipwrecked on this island about 5 years ago." [He had 'lost' two and a half years].

Two of my companions then agreed to go in a small canoe belonging to the village and hand the plank to the schooner. When they reached the vessel the captain was apparently very disappointed that they had brought no white man and thought that he was being deceived. He told me later that he had been scanning the shore and had seen no one who looked 'white'. After many years I was almost as brown as my companions. They, realizing that the captain had little inclination to believe their gestures, picked up the plank in the bottom of the canoe and handed it to him. At that point everything changed. The captain wrote a hasty note to me asking how much 'trade' would be required to secure my release. He gave the two messengers presents and the note, together with a pencil to hand to me.

When I saw the canoe returning, myself and my friend made our way out to meet it. Being low tide we were able to wade almost the whole distance across the lagoon to the reef's edge. However we were also accompanied by a number of fully armed companions, delegated by Kabou to make sure that I did not escape. As the canoe arrived and I read the note from Captain Murray I realized that he was in earnest for two boats had put off from the schooner and were making for our position. At the sight of boats leaving the ship others came wading towards me and, on Kabou's instructions, ordered me to come back.

The position was critical, the men were becoming excited and angry at my delay in obeying and I felt that, at any moment, they might let fly with arrows or remove me by force. A number had already surrounded me. However, astonished by the novelty of seeing myself and my friend composing a letter, they merely watched. As the leading boat made its way to the reef's edge from the seaward side, I slowly approached from the shore side. It came rapidly within hailing distance and the white man at the helm stood up and shouted to me in English, asking me what would be required to release me. He said he had axes in the boat.

I advanced to the very margin of the reef, closely attended by two large men who held me by the arms. I spoke to the white man rapidly, but he did not seem to understand me. I then realized that I was speaking in a tongue totally foreign to the man standing in the boat a few yards opposite me. I held up one hand with all fingers extended. The man opened a trade chest and pulled out five new, gleaming axes which he held aloft.

Though I knew them well, none of those restraining me dared venture forward, although the boat's bow was almost touching the reef. At this point the white man shouted that he had plenty of rifles in the boat and was prepared to use force if necessary as the captain was determined to rescue me. At that point I found my English tongue and entreated him to be patient.

I turned to my captors and reminded them of the

dangers we had shared and suggested that they should at this point trust me because I had never let them down in the past. One marched forward with a bold face to receive an axe. As he reached the boat he saw an arsenal of firearms lying in the bottom, he grabbed his axe and rushed back, telling me to get in the boat as quickly as possible otherwise we would all be killed. I rushed forward and scrambled into the boat, which immediately pulled off out of bow shot. Suddenly I was surrounded by people shaking my hand and speaking my mother tongue. I looked back to see my island prison becoming even more distant.

For some inexplicable reason his account ends there and he neglects to mention the object of the exercise. Oral history records:

He told the men in the two canoes to go back to the others. He said, 'You go now, but come back in the morning. I will stay here on the ship with these people.'

When Jack went on board he was naked like us. The crew washed him and then they cut his hair and they dressed him in clothes like a white man. That evening Jack said to the captain of the ship that Kabou and his people needed cargo from the ship. They needed lots of tinned food, a boiler [sic], tobacco, pipes, matches, tea and, above all, iron.

The next morning Kabou and the others came to the ship in canoes. Renton stood on deck and all the men looked up but they didn't recognize him in his clothes and his short hair. Kabou asked: 'Are you Jack?' And Renton said: 'It's me, father.' Kabou shook his head and said it couldn't be because he looked like some kind of devil. And Renton said again, 'It's me, it's Jack, your boy.'

All of the men were afraid. Renton looked down and he saw how Kabou stood in the canoe and held onto the side of the ship and that he was shaking. Renton lifted Kabou onto the ship and showed him round, explaining what everything was. Renton took out some tinned food, opened it up, and said: 'This is our white man's pig. It's in a tin.' Kabou looked at Renton's trousers and asked him what they were. Then he asked him about his boots and Renton said that they were what white men walk about in. Kabou said that they must make the feet very sore.

Others came on board and Renton brought out calico, tinned food, tobacco, biscuits, tea, matches and pipes. They thought the clay pipes looked like dried fish. Then Renton lit a match and they were amazed when they saw fire. He took out twelve pipes and gave them one each. They all tasted their first smoke. Later when they were leaving he gave them many gifts.

Kabou and Renton went to one side and they talked alone. Later Kabou let people join the ship and accompany Renton back to Australia. For each of these men Kabou received iron. Renton promised to return with some presents. Kabou said he would need more iron.

Behind all First Contact stories of awe-struck, grateful natives there usually lies a more prosaic interpretation. The Sulufou episode is no exception. Kabou was about to lose many of his best men, a situation that threatened to leave Sulufou vulnerable. Thus in characteristic Melanesian fashion the issue came down to compensation ('he needed iron'). No doubt Kabou thanked Captain Murray for the trade box full of biscuits, tinned food, calico and tobacco but pointed out that he had fed and cared for a white man for almost eight years and that he was not only about to lose him but many of his warriors, including Kwaisulia (who in later years recounted that he had 'begged' Renton to take him.) What Kabou needed was 'iron' – a euphemism that Captain Murray, who had dealt with Bera for years, understood only too well.

It was at this point that the chief, tutored by Renton, agreed to become an agent and to collect at least fifty recruits from the lagoon when the *Bobtail Nag* returned. The terms being that the ship return within three moons, that Renton be brought as interpreter and that he, Kabou, receive one rifle and ammunition for each recruit. The *Bobtail Nag*, now full to the gunwales with recruits from Isabel and Malaita, sailed for Brisbane. It is said on Sulufou that, from the day Jack Renton left, not a single flint or stone tool was ever put to use again.

8

Between Two Worlds

———————— ○ ————————

RENTON'S survival was a unique event. No white man had survived for such a length of time in a stone-age culture and no one had ever become so acculturated. Slade's article, published within a fortnight of the *Bobtail Nag*'s return, generated considerable public interest and, although Renton would not agree to expose himself to the ordeal of public speaking, he was happy to meet the colonial authorities and representatives from the Queensland parliament. Armed with his first-hand knowledge, he was constantly at pains to point out that, seen from his host's perspective, the bungling attempts at recruiting amounted to nothing more than kidnapping and that any retaliation was predictable and logical. He went on to argue that it would be perfectly possible to recruit natives as long as the operation was carried out with the co-operation of village chiefs, who would need to be properly compensated for the loss of manpower.

Knowing full well that he had already promised to return to Sulufou, he then offered to demonstrate this new approach, hoping, as he put it, to avoid the mistakes that seemed to have been made everywhere else. Before he left he suggested to the Colonial Office in Brisbane that it might be politic to make some gesture. The Colonial Treasurer provided him with trunks full of gifts for his hosts and, two months after his rescue, the *Bobtail Nag* set off once again for the Solomon Islands. As the voyage was to be a showpiece demonstration of Renton's widely advertised approach to the business of recruiting, it would fall to his travelling companion Kwaisulia to supervise the murkier aspects of the transaction that would not find their way into the official record.

They hove-to off the reef opposite Sulufou and immediately Renton and Kwaisulia set about the official business which was duly recorded:

> By reason of the mutual confidence engendered by Renton's ability to make them understand fully the reason for these presents being sent them, the ship was enabled to anchor in perfect safety. The natives principally showed their confidence by permitting their young men to recruit themselves in large numbers to go with us to Queensland.
>
> When the vessel reached Sulufou where the tidings of events had evidently preceded us, the fact of their late captor returning loaded with presents for them seemed almost beyond their comprehension. Canoes by the hundreds and natives by the thousands swarmed around the vessel as soon as she came to anchor near the village.
>
> After the vessel had anchored, Kabou stepped on

board and, following his example, the decks bade fair to be swarmed. Any idea conceived from an attempt to realize 'Bedlam let loose', must fall short of that scene of gesticulation and jabbering. Kabou preserved his equanimity, his usual stolid expression. At that point thirty-one volunteered to join the ship for Queensland at once, and we managed to get the ship clear of all the rest by sundown. Early the following morning, the principal presents were arranged in order of merit, or according to the degree of friendliness Renton had experienced in their hands. About a score received substantial parcels, of which the contents were axes, knives, fancy pipes, beads, fancy boxes of matches, tobacco and pieces of hoop iron.

Perfect quietness prevailed while the distribution was taking place, though hundreds of eyes watched the proceedings, and as the recipients came forward separately to take possession of their share of the windfall, each was in a state of nervous excitement, their trembling hands betraying their eagerness. After this ceremony, fourteen others joined us as recruits. During this time Kabou was absent inland. Renton thought it inadvisable to leave his gifts with any person until he had seen their contents. Then as there was a grindstone for the natives which it was necessary to show them how to fix, Captain Murray and Renton went off with this article to the village. As soon as the grindstone was adjusted they took a walk through the village and Renton distributed pocket-handkerchiefs, pieces of red cloth, beads and other trinkets as he went along, so that none of the women's huts on the island were left without a token of remembrance. Immense excitement attended his triumphal progress.

Eventually Kabou came alongside the ship in a large canoe accompanied by five elder men. Next day he accompanied us on a five-day cruise along the coast and back, he being friendly with all the tribes en route. At the end of the journey Kabou and the elders received their presents and we parted company on the best possible terms. It may be expected that the white man will henceforth occupy a very different aspect from that which their Fijian experiences had necessarily relegated them. [Clearly an oblique reference to Captain Murray's namesake and the voyage of the *Carl*]

The following testimonial was inscribed in a book and being duly interpreted, was handed to Kabou: 'The Government of Queensland sends these presents to Kabou, and others of his tribe, as a recompense for the protection afforded to John Renton, who lived with them upwards of eight years at the village of Sulufou on the north-east coast of the island of Malaita, and who was taken thence by the schooner *Bobtail Nag* on 8th August 1875. Signed Captain D. Murray. Queensland Government. Nov 19th 1875'.

During all this grandstanding, Kwaisulia handed over to Kabou a large quantity of smooth-bore Tower muskets, powder and percussion caps. This final transaction was not recorded in the ship's manifest and was to set a precedent for all future transactions between recruiters and headmen on the island of Malaita. Within a decade the coastal areas were awash with firearms as each of the returnees insisted that their trade box of purchases contained one. Thus for each recruit released to work in Queensland, the island acquired two firearms – one for the headman releasing him and one for the individual at the end of his contract.

Although Kabou had caught up in the arms race, the effect on the surrounding area was grievous. The possession of firearms meant that islanders often lost all sense of proportion. The weapon became an instant status symbol, the noise and smoke precipitated a stone-age people instantly into the modern world. The fact that they preferred to blast away from the hip rather than carefully choosing a target and taking deliberate aim mattered little; its mere possession gave the owner a feeling of invincibility. Even when the musket was superseded by the breech-loading Sniders and Martini-Henrys that Bera had accumulated, demand for the Tower musket continued unabated. It took a large charge and made a tremendous noise – if the firer was knocked flat on his back so much the better. In the next few years, unbeknown to Renton or Kwaisulia, life on Malaita changed.

The *Bobtail Nag* returned to Brisbane. Owing to Renton's status in the lagoon and the lack of any official record of the currency that had fuelled the transactions, the voyage had been meaningless as a demonstration of recruiting methods in general. However, the government and the ship's owners were happy as more recruits had been signed up in a shorter period than any vessel had managed in eight years of blackbirding. Renton's cut of the profits, together with his fees for the articles, provided the fare for his passage home to Scotland with a large amount left over. He would not need to look for employment for at least a year. Kwaisulia on the other hand had signed on for three years to work on a sugar plantation near Rockhampton, three hundred miles north of Brisbane. Bearing in mind that Kwaisulia spoke enough English to make himself understood, Renton may well have sighed with relief when the 140 Malaitans left the city and he said goodbye to the one man who knew his secrets. They were never to see each other again.

Fifty years later, whilst researching his short memoir, the local Orcadian historian, John Marwick, interviewed those few Stromnessians still alive who remembered Renton's home-coming. His youngest brother Joe had been ten years old at the time and travelled with his mother and father to meet the boat.

It was my first trip to Kirkwall, and I'll never forget it. The three of us walked down the Kirkwall Pier to meet the boat, and there was what appeared to me to be an awful crowd of folk on the pier. I stuck close by my mother, and we stood back a bit, just to watch for anyone like Jack to come ashore. A whole host of folk trooped off the streamer down the gangway and were met by their friends, but never anyone for us.

Father says to mother: 'I think he's missed the boat.' We stood on the pier for a while longer until it was almost clear. I noticed a man leaning over the steamer's rail, looking at us, but none of us paid any attention, for he appeared a total stranger.

After a while father says: 'I'll go aboard and see if they know anything about Johnnie.' So off he went, leaving mother and me standing on the quay. He passed a chap leaning over the rail, but father paid no attention, neither did the stranger. Father looked around, but he could see nobody that he recognized as Jack, and he passed the stranger two or three times without taking any notice of him. At last the stranger looked up and said: 'Don't you know me, father?' He was very sunburned – a sort of coppery colour – what we call 'hard grown'.

His father had arranged lunch at the Castle Hotel in Kirkwall and to Renton's dismay it appeared that there were few people on the island who did not know of his adventures. His little brother remembered:

> It had leaked out into the town about him being back and I tell you, there were never such a do in the Castle Hotel. Folk crowded in to see Jack, so much so, that Mrs Ross, the owner, said she would charge us nothing because she had had the busiest day in her life.

After a couple of hours and feeling that he would not be able to keep up appearances much longer, Renton suggested to his glowing father that, as the journey to Stromness would take a couple of hours, they should leave. His mother shepherded her exhausted son into a waiting carriage whilst her impervious husband fielded the last of the congratulations. When they reached Stromness his mother instructed the carriage to bypass the reception committee waiting outside the North End Hotel and drive straight to the house. Renton was taken upstairs and, to his intense relief, discovered that they had prepared a small room of his own in the attic. For three days he stayed indoors. His little brother remembered that 'he was most awful quiet and did not have much to say about himself or his strange experiences'.

He was eventually persuaded to accept an invitation from Mr Ritchie the Free Kirk minister. His little brother remembered that 'Jack was not sure about going but he did in the end, and was very pleased when he came back. He seemed more peaceable.' Ritchie was a small dapper man who, in his youth, had also gone to sea. To Renton's relief he made no attempt to ask him any questions about the previous eight years, instead he talked about a misunderstanding in the port of Goa that had led to his imprisonment for a number of days. Unlike almost all the men Renton had known, Ritchie did not make light of an unpleasant experience. He talked about being afraid, of his sense of confusion at being at the mercy of his Portuguese jailers and of not being able to make himself understood. Above all he talked about the nights in jail and his sense of panic and despair as he imagined his ship sailing off without him. It was all neatly put – abstracted, honest, yet inviting comment. Ritchie had marked out a neutral territory of emotions that they explored together. For Renton, although he talked in a code that Ritchie never challenged, the conversation alleviated some of his torment.

He started to go out and visit old friends but, as Marwick discovered fifty years later when he interviewed their diminishing number: 'They all had the same tale to tell, that he was very reticent about his life among the savages of the South Seas.' One remembered how 'he used to walk on Grey's Pier with the men who walked back and forth of an evening, and often he was at a loss to express himself, some words he seemed to have forgotten altogether.'

His father bought a small rowing boat, which he named the *Bobtail Nag* in memory of his son's deliverance, and Renton spent the summer days in Hoy Sound and Scapa Flow exploring the uninhabited islands that dotted their perimeters. On other occasions he would take his little brother Joe for long walks along the weather coasts of Hoy and South Ronaldsay. Above all Joe remembered how 'he used to bathe a lot in the sea, and I never saw anyone so much at home in the water. He could dive and stay under water for ever so long.' Others remarked upon his curious swimming style, how he lay flat in the water, face down and reached his arms out alternately in long sweeping stokes.[1]

In the evenings, depending on his mood, he made inconsistent efforts to mix with his peers but there were many occasions when his presence seemed to reduce other men to a ruminative silence. He was, after all, unprepared to talk about the one subject that his presence announced, his absence. One man, however, seemed impervious to this distance. Mr Spence, the local bank manager, sent a message to the house inviting him to lunch. His father insisted he accept. Being privy to all the community's financial secrets, Spence wielded more power than the Provost.

Lunch was at the bank and Renton found himself trapped in the man's office as his minions laid out the meal on the large expanse of his pedestal desk. Spence produced a sheaf of articles that he had written for various publications. From the diagrams and illustrations, most of them appeared to be about the numerous Neolithic sites that studded the islands. As Renton flicked through the articles, Spence made his offer. He had read the *Courier* account with great interest but sensed that, given its readership, Renton may have been put in the position of having to omit many of the more subtle and contentious aspects of his unique experience. He went on to suggest that, given more time, an account, tailored for a more educated constituency would have particular appeal. The scribes on the *Courier*, he was sure, had not done him justice. All Renton had to do was to meet him on a regular basis and merely go through a chronology that was clearly missing from the articles. Renton had to do nothing except tell his *own* story and he, Spence, would be his amanuensis, merely recording Renton's experiences. There was money to be made; it had been done before. Spence would find a publisher and they would split the royalties on an equal basis.

Renton, no doubt acutely aware of the danger, thanked his host for his interesting offer, which, as Spence had pointed out, would involve a considerable commitment. He would need to think about it and the meal passed without any undue alarms as the bank manager, keen to parade his knowledge of Renton's world, launched into a long account of his own interest in the ethnology of Oceania, inspired by his personal collection of Cook memorabilia

After Captain Cook's death on Hawaii in 1779, the returning *Resolution* and *Discovery* were forced by strong easterly winds to sail up the western coast of the British Isles and eventually seek an anchorage in Stromness harbour. Cook's replacement, Captain Gore, had none of the great navigator's talents, neither as a seaman nor as a manager of men and the crew despised him. In the words of one, he was 'nothing but a conceited and indolent old man'. As they sat in the port waiting for the wind to change, a number insisted on being paid off. For the ship's officers, aware of the recriminations surrounding Cook's death that they were due to face, the thought of arriving in Greenwich with a mutinous crew was embarrassing in the extreme. As there was no money to pay off the troublemakers the officers decided to auction many of the artefacts that the expedition had collected.

News of Cook's death had been widely reported long before his two ships limped into Stromness. Already a celebrity in ports throughout Britain, Cook was now a national hero and the auction attracted hundreds of Orcadians. Bidding was brisk and the money raised was more than enough to pay off the disaffected. A century later, many of these artefacts had been gathering dust in the attics, vestibules and outhouses of Stromness and Spence had purchased a considerable number. He added that he also had a large collection of literature relating to the Pacific and assured Renton that he would not find a more sympathetic, knowledgeable or enthusiastic collaborator.

Renton had to play for time, but he hoped not for very long. Within three weeks of his arrival in Stromness and unbeknown to his parents, he had written to Captain Murray asking him to approach the port authorities in Brisbane on his behalf and to offer his services as a recruiting agent. A month after his meeting with Spence, he received a reply offering him one of six newly established official posts to supervize the conduct of recruiting at a salary of £200 per annum, generous expenses and a pre-paid passage.

On the day before he left he visited Spence to convey his apologies. By way of recompense and knowing his interest in ethnology, he offered the bank manager a small collar, strung with human teeth, which he claimed to have received as a gift from the relative of a dead warrior.

In the foreword to Marwick's little book an account of the subsequent travels of this gift was provided by a fellow Renton enthusiast, Stromness's general practitioner, Dr Gunn. A number of years after Renton left the port, Spence sold the collar to another local collector of ethnography, Thomas Peace, the Provost of Kirkwall. When Peace died in 1892 his collection was sent for auction in Edinburgh. The collar was purchased by the National Museums of Scotland. At this point nothing was known about its history beyond the fact that it came from the Solomon Islands. Some years later, on a visit to the museum, the now retired bank manager Spence recognized the collar and provided the curator with the name of the original owner and the island from which it came. Having dealt with the issue of provenance, Dr Gunn then recorded his own impressions.

> The collar as now displayed must have formed a striking decoration for a dusky Malaitan warrior with no clothing to conceal it. Possibly it was also an advertisement for his prowess in war. It consists wholly of teeth, human incisor teeth. The fang or root is pierced transversely with a hole for the suspending chord, and between each tooth is a small perforated disc of shell to give the correct spacing.
>
> As to the original owners of these fine incisors one can only speculate. War and plunder are the usual outlet for high spirits among the islanders, and cannibal feasts to celebrate their victories. Whether the hostile incisors are then shared out equally among the victors or whether each warrior claims his own trophies, we do not know, but the latter plan is probable, and would make possession of such a collar highly desirable. In any case a white man can admire the trophy all the more fully since he knows that none of his own race have contributed to its formation. The white man's incisors are never perfect enough and never black enough to have any post-mortem decorative value.

Written in the late 1920s, Dr Gunn's musings reveal the paucity of ethnographic information about the island. There is no evidence that the islanders wore human teeth around their necks. As Renton observed, they collected heads. The only teeth worn were porpoise teeth, which were highly valued and only worn by priests or Big Men. It is likely that Renton's collar was an adaptation of the *lingomo*; a small wicker bag containing an incisor tooth from a warrior's first kill and was worn round the neck during a raid. In a recent examination of the collar carried out by David Whittaker, Professor of Forensic Dentistry at the University of Wales, he concluded that: 'The degree of wear on the teeth biting edges is similar and probably relates to about three decades of life . . . I believe the teeth are *not* from individuals of a great age, but of mature age.' Of the fifty-nine teeth on the collar, Professor Whittaker was able to identify fifty-seven 'with reasonable accuracy' and came to the conclusion that 'these are, therefore, teeth from a *minimum* of nine individuals.'[2]

Renton arrived in Brisbane believing that the new posts had been created as a result of his own demonstration of recruiting methods only to discover their creation was an administrative response to a supine judiciary and a corrupt executive.

Although the courts of the colony had full powers to try 'piracies, felonies, robberies, murders, and other offences of what nature soever committed . . . in any island situated in the Pacific', in practice the Crown's law officers simply refused to frame charges, knowing that however much the nature of the offence was watered down, from murder and kidnapping to simple assault and robbery of canoes, they had little chance of conviction. After all, as the juries rationalized, the islanders did not need the 'special protection of British Law'. The Europeans who were risking their lives every time they went near the islands should have 'unfettered discretion' to take whatever precautions necessary.

Queensland was also a small colony where the politics of cronyism were rampant. The recruiting trade was seen to be vital to the economic interests of the colony and those interests were in the hands of the politicians and plantation-owners. Even the sale of recruits was in the hands of the executive. The Brisbane firm of John Fenwick & Co. of Queens Street had branched out into the profitable business of placing recruits and by 1867 it had become a sizable part of their business. Robert Ramsey MacKenzie, one of the partners of Fenwicks, was Premier of Queensland at the time. Two other partners were prominent politicians. As for the recruiters themselves, techniques had advanced somewhat since the days of 'snatch – snatch' and 'kill – kill'. Now it was 'the tricks of the trade'.

Jemmy wore a Ku-Klux-Klan costume with a big waterproof bag under it. Sitting on the beach with the inevitable boat full of crew providing cover he would appear to drink vast quantities of salt water. The natives would watch as he got visibly fatter and fatter until he whipped the costume aside to reveal a large water-proof bag underneath. At other times he would arrive at a beach and start striking matches until he had gathered a crowd around him. Then he would conjure, or walk on his hands, or swim out to sea and pretend to drown. He never used armed force and he was very successful.

Captain One-Eye, Carlos Santini, used his glass eye to threaten chiefs. He would explain that if he did not recruit a particular number of men then he would cast a spell on every man on the island and one of their eyes would fall out. He would then demonstrate that this was indeed possible. This particular story used to be told on the sugar plantations of Queensland and is probably the origin of the well-known story of an owner leaving his glass eye sitting on a tree trunk to oversee his labourers. All went well until one had the idea of buying a hat from the company store. The white man noticed that the workforce seemed to be slacking. The following morning, having positioned his 'overseer', he retreated into the bush and watched. Half an hour into the shift he saw one of his natives creep up to his eye and cover it with the hat.

Timber-toes Proctor, a veteran of the American Civil War, had a wooden leg of the screw-on type and he always carried a supply on board his ship. A crew member left a record of one of Proctor's performances:

We were lying off the beach where a large crowd of natives had gathered, and Proctor started performing a few tricks of magic with his wooden leg. He put his foot up on the gunwale and told the natives to observe what he was about to do. Drawing his revolver, he put a bullet through the foot. The natives gasped, then chattered and looked for the blood that failed to appear. Proctor laughed and took a sheath-knife from his belt, and telling the natives to watch again, drove it clean through the place representing the calf of his leg. There was a space in the timber of the limb through which the knife could pass. While Proctor stood grinning at the boys with the sheath-knife stuck through his leg, a native who was behind him, thinking to verify for himself the white man's mysterious insensitivity to pain, stuck the small blade of a penknife into the seat of his pants. The effect was instantaneous. With a yell the magician leapt into the air, while four of the startled boat's crew fell overboard, and the natives on the beach beat all known records in reaching the scrub.

Deception and subterfuge may have taken the place of kidnapping but the issue of 'informed consent' still remained and far too many missionaries were sending accounts back to England for the Queensland government to remain complacent. They would have to be seen to be acting; otherwise the Colonial Office back in England would be forced to act over their heads.

In 1870 the government agreed to appoint agents to oversee recruiting on every ship that was employed in the trade. However, they were only paid £10 per month and their contracts lasted only for the duration of the voyage. In most cases this merely introduced another layer of investors in the enterprise, as the agents bought shares in the business. Those who were too poor were easily suborned with the promise of a commission for each recruit sold. Thus the 'tricks of the trade' often produced a ridiculous spectacle.

Once in sight of the Queensland coast the agent would explain to the recruits the purpose of their forthcoming interview with the port's supervising agent who was charged with asking them if they understood the terms of the contract and the name of their designated plantation. Armed with this information the recruits would probably then decide amongst themselves which planta-tion they wanted to go to and swap names accordingly. The supervising agent would then board and ask each recruit how many years he believed he was bound to serve. This always caused confusion as on most islands when an individual wished to indi-cate a number, rather than turning up the requisite number of fingers, he would turn them down. Once this confusion had been sorted out, most would be found turning down only one finger or two, trying to explain that they thought the period was for only one or two years or maybe only moons.

In an administrative system where everyone was in each

other's pockets, no one took any notice of the recruits, as the supervisor would probably be on a commission for the number he passed fit for work. The system was a dead letter, the ship-owners ignored it, the Immigration Office ignored it, as did the brokers and the planters. Writing about the situation in the *Brisbane Courier*, a correspondent quoted from a ship's manifest in the shipping columns: 'From Maryborough, 1 horse, 35 bags of sugar, 2 bars of iron, 1,500ft of pinewood, 13 labourers per Australian Joint Stock Bank, Townsville (Freight £27.12.6d).' Standing there on deck with tin labels round their necks indicating their destination, the recruits were just a job lot to be bought and sold like the rest of the cargo.

In the space of less than a year Renton had closed the door on two chapters in his life and was now faced with the problem of keeping the first one firmly closed. In his interview with the Board of Inspectors in Brisbane he made one condition – that he be excused from recruiting in the Solomon Islands. They may have found this surprising but as the bulk of the recruiting was still being carried out in the New Hebrides they probably did not ask too many questions, assuming no doubt that he was afraid he might be kidnapped again.

In retrospect it is not difficult to see why Renton would not want to return to the Solomons. From the evidence of the new addition to Spence's collection of artefacts Renton's presence in some parts of Malaita and the surrounding islands would have made the task of recruiting well nigh impossible. He was a young man with a reputation that stemmed partly from his prowess at killing. He would also have run the more serious risk of being recognized by returnees, who, having completed their three-year contracts, would be fluent in pidgin English and only too happy to recount to any member of the crew the exploits of the ship's government agent when he had been one of them.

In May 1876, when Renton boarded the schooner *Lucy and Adelaide* bound for the New Hebrides, this group of islands had already provided over twelve thousand recruits for Queensland – the problem was returning them. The 'time-expired' recruit had to be landed safely ashore at his own 'passage', or landing place, for the cycle of his recruitment to be complete. On recruitment, a ship was required to note on a track-chart the precise location of the 'passage'. However, as large numbers of recruits had either been snatched or duped three years previously, precise passage indicators were often non-existent. The description might simply read 'west coast of Aoba' and returnees themselves could not be relied upon to recognize a coastline that they may have only seen once from a ship's distance, three years previously. Land in the wrong community and the returnee would almost certainly be robbed of his trade box and might well be killed.

Writing in the 1930s of his time as a boatswain on a recruiting ship forty years earlier, Jock Cromer recounted just such an incident:

> I was standing on the deck of the *Forest King* off the island of Tongoa with a returnee when he pointed to a spot and told me of a dreadful happening that had occurred there. A Queensland ship called the *Ethel* had landed three young time-expired recruits there, and then gone on without anchoring. As soon as the vessel was out of sight, the lads were murdered and their possessions appropriated and divided. The bodies were

stripped of clothing and dragged along the stones to where a cooking oven existed. Just then another Queensland vessel happened to sail into the bay, where it anchored. Her captain, with field glasses in hand was watching the shore, and called to his crew: 'Hurry up with those boats, men, and see what those devils are after. There's something amiss on shore.'

As the boats neared the shore the natives left the bodies on the rocks and hurriedly disappeared into the scrub. The boat's crew landed and found the bodies, with leaves made ready for covering them, and the firewood cut for the cooking, though the entrails had not yet been removed.

On the year of Renton's first trip, five thousand recruits had already returned and on the basis of one gun for his 'sponsor' and one gun for the recruit there were ten thousand guns in the hands of natives living on the coast. These areas were 'recruited out' and ships were having to devise methods to attract natives from inland. Clearly written for official consumption, Renton's log contains extensive details of weather, ship's position and the number of natives recruited on each foray, but is completely silent about the basic methods of recruitment, which by now were standard practice throughout the New Hebrides and the Solomons.

A vessel would sail along the coastline and at selected intervals of about two miles the crew would throw overboard a bundle of sticks of dynamite; detonators placed in position and fuse torch lighted. The resulting explosion would echo through the hills and valleys inland. It was a recognized signal that a ship was ready to barter for labour and that on its return journey it would answer any smoke signal as being a sign that groups were ready to negotiate. It was during this short period that all the problems that recruiting presented to these small communities were thrown into sharp relief.

Like the Solomon Islands, New Hebridean societies were highly complex. Social advancement was based upon a network of obligation, debt and repayment, the currency being pigs. For a young man who wanted to marry, the bride price would be at least ten pigs. He would borrow pigs from his father and members of his group and the chief of his village might give him one. With the aid of his wife he would tend his crops and feed his pigs. But he still had to pay back the bride price. So he had to breed from them and, when they were small, lend them out to other people who needed them – people who would then be in his debt. He might cancel out some of his debt by trading with other communities who might give him one large pig for his smaller ones. He might also work at putting up club houses, stone works, carving wooden drums and many other services for which small pigs were paid by chiefs and rich men who needed these works done to confirm their importance.

A young man with energy and resource would be able pay off his debts in three to four years. Then he entered a new period and in a grade-taking society he would be welcomed with due ceremony into the first grade of manhood. Now free of debt he would start lending pigs to other people. He would lend as many as he could. When a neighbouring village wanted to make some sacrificial ceremony or a man wanted to make a chiefly rite, the young man would lend his pigs, the more the better. The pigs were being left to mature at another person's expense. There was always a demand and a shrewd man who could see ahead and who was so popular that people came to him for a loan, acquired more and more capital in terms of obligations, for in Melanesian society if a man gives you something, you must repay. If you do not you are a 'rubbish man'.

Pigs were progress, pigs were power and there would come a time when a man would call in most of his debts as he wanted to take another step up the ladder. It was for the next grade-taking ceremony he would have amassed his wealth. Everyone would be invited. Hundreds would come from the surrounding area bringing gifts to a celebration that would last all night. They would be saying goodbye to the person they knew for next day he would be reborn. That morning, as the exhausted guests stood in a long line, his wealth was lined up, tethered and squealing. The newly born man passed down the line killing them with his *subi*, one swinging blow straight between the eyes. He had destroyed his wealth, the result of years of effort. Now, as he divided the carcasses according to rules of reciprocity and kinship, he was reborn, free of all encumbrances and another stage removed from ordinary mortals and ready to resume his upward journey towards the next goal – the next grade-taking. But of course he was not without wealth. The distribution of his years of labour, his apparent largesse was nothing of the kind. In a society dominated by the rules of reciprocity, the hundreds who walked away with the carcasses of his wealth were bound to him. It was a ritual of a bank that lent all its money in one day.

This was a society where the purpose of living was constantly to strive to raise oneself in another's estimation and in a perverse and tragic way it was little different from the society that was beginning to overwhelm it. This was a clash of cultures that was driven by the same fundamental imperatives. And inevitably in such a society where power, rank and privilege were so sharply defined, where the effort of ascent was based upon a currency that only grew at a certain pace, it was not surprising that many young men welcomed the opportunity to acquire in three years, the prestige of a miraculous killing instrument and the wherewithal to revolutionize manual labour.

The unfolding drama of contact with blackbirders that must have replicated itself throughout Melanesia, found its way into the oral history of the island of Santo in the New Hebrides. Recorded in the 1930s, the historian speaks of events sixty years earlier:

I was a boy when a ship came, it was large and unlike our ships because it had no little one along one side. Many went out in canoes to see what this ship was. There were some black men and two white men on board, who blew smoke out of their mouths, no one knew how. The white men had pieces of what we now know is iron; but we could not see any good in it. But their fine beads were better than any we had made, larger and many colours and they gave some to us. These seemed to be a better sort of white men than the ones our fathers had talked to us about in stories.

Then all of a sudden they cut loose the several canoes tied to their ship and the people on board were stranded. Most of them jumped into the sea when they saw this but a boat belonging to the ship got between them and the land. It caught them, hitting them on their heads. Six were thus taken and one of them was my father, who was an important man with much pig business in the village and all about. No one knew why the ship had done this and many thought it was because they needed meat.

Two years after that another ship came. The brother of my father said: 'All right. It is now my time.' All said so. The white men came near the shore in a smaller boat, laughing and talking strangely and pointing with their hands. Many of our people were cold with hate that they came again so openly. They rushed and pulled them out onto the shore. They danced about and clubbed the white men with the large stone clubs that we have no more.

Some men on the ship fired guns at us: no one took any notice and they were far away. We thought it was only a noise then; only later did we learn that this was a new and wonderful way to kill a man. We ate these men and sent pieces to all the many villages. The white tasted sickly.

Then, one year later, the first ship came back again with my father and the others, except that one of them had died. And each of them had one of the guns that we had heard before, and all the things needed for it, and calico (very scarlet), axes, tobacco and such things as we had never told or heard before. Then we were sorry for having killed the other white men. For these were good people. Their things were things such as all men now wanted to have for themselves, for my father showed how an iron axe would cut twelve trees down, while [with] our stone or shell (such as we had always used) a man could not yet finish one tree. Many men now went until the ship could not take anymore people.

*   *   *

The older men deeply resented the undermining of centuries of village life but they were also aware that, as firearms became more and more commonplace on the islands, their own communities were locked into this arms race. Recruits would be released, but only at a price: one gun for the recruit and one for the chief and the community.

The effect on the ceremonial and spiritual life of the people was profound as groupings with access to western technology became immensely powerful. Tabus, which, by their very nature had held in check many of the more savage aspects of this world, were now challenged by men who needed to demonstrate that they were afraid of nothing. One dismal aspect of this was a reversion to cannibalism. In those areas of the Solomons and the New Hebrides where it was practised it retained a symbolic aspect, the idea of transubstantiation, that had been central to the practice and had even prompted one missionary to observe: 'Here in the Solomons we find an idea struggling thus repulsively – yet surely to our sight with wonderful pathos – to realize itself. A mouthful of flesh and blood is thought to convey some coveted power. In this act of cannibalism we seem to detect the germ of the Divine Truth.'

Now corpses were plentiful and many warriors would cannibalize their victims indiscriminately, precisely because it was tabu and would give them a reputation for fearlessness. In Malekula in the New Hebrides a chief killed and ate 120 men and hung their skulls outside his hut. In Fiji, one notorious chief made an alignment of 872 stones, one for each victim. The islanders' reaction to European trade and technology was, as one anthropologist has remarked: 'an intensification as they literally assimilated the competitive ideas of capitalism as a consuming passion' – a suitably Marxist interpretation. Yet where it is possible to examine the evidence, and this evidence is scattered and sparse, it is clear that the roots of this disintegration had been planted years earlier and were due to a cause entirely unrelated to recruiting.

9

'The Benighted People'

———— ○ ————

IN June 1844 the English whaleboat *John Bull*, pursuing a shoal of sperm whales through a narrow channel between Santa Isabel and San Jorge Island, found itself surrounded. The first mate, John Smith, recorded the ensuing confrontation: 'The natives kept coming off in their small and large canoes until there were two or three thousand of them.' They stood off, neither attempting to approach, nor 'exhibiting any signs of friendship'. This tactic, far from having the desired effect of forcing the *John Bull* to leave, merely unnerved the crew who 'perceiving their actions to be hostile, immediately got up arms.' The result was predictable. As the armada closed on the *nguanguao* (the 'disease-carrier'):

> the command of 'fire' was instantly obeyed by the discharge of six swivel guns, two cannon loaded with grape and canister shot and the discharge of thirty muskets. These discharges were followed by four more,

which overtook them before they could succeed in getting out of reach. The effect produced was tremendous; fifteen large war canoes were totally destroyed and most of their crew. The loss was estimated at two hundred men and as many drowned. Many others lost their paddles, and being so terrified by the unexpected roaring and destruction they did not know what to do or how to make their escape. In the confusion they paddled one against the other and some of them round and round having lost all their paddles on one side of the canoe. The scene produced was at once lamentable and laughable.

The islanders had good reason to maintain their cordon sanitaire. A couple of hundred islanders sacrificed in the heat of battle was a small price to pay when compared to the carnage that had been taking place elsewhere, ever since Cook's mapping of the Pacific in 1777–8.

The men aboard *Resolution* and *Discovery* were, in the opinion of Cook's deputy Captain Clerk, 'infernal and dissolute' and largely recruited from the dregs of British society. Though they may have been passed fit when they signed-on, these men were the infecting agents as well as the cultural representatives of a diseased society. Three-quarters of the population of Britain died from typhus, typhoid fever, measles, smallpox, bronchitis, whooping cough and a tuberculosis epidemic that was gathering in such intensity that, by the early years of the nineteenth century, nearly a third of all metropolitan deaths would be caused by 'the Great White Plague'.

So diseased were Cook's crew that during their stay in Hawaii their hosts offered them part of a *Heiau*, or place of worship, which was converted into a hospital for the sick and where,

Jack Renton aged twenty-seven – see page xvii.

THE AUSTRALASIAN SKETCHER

WITH PEN AND PENCIL

No. 35.—VOL. III.　　　MELBOURNE, SATURDAY, NOVEMBER 27, 1875.　　　PRICE 6d.

Renton fishes for a shark – see page 22.

Custom and practice. Two recruiting boats – one covering the other.

Sulufou, 2002.

The newly recruited on their way to Queensland.

On their return three years later.

Kwaisulia of Ada Gege in his late forties.

Ancestral head: the skull is overmodelled with parinarium nut paste, shell-inlaid eyes and decorated with curving bands of nautilus shell – see page 60.

Murray (centre) with Armstrong and Dowden and a group of 'friendly natives' from the *Carl*. Photo taken in Levuka, Fiji.

Levuka Harbour, Fiji, 1881.

Santa Isabel tree house – see page 130.

Cutting cane on a Queensland plantation, 1883.

Ingava of Roviana lagoon.

Nuzu Nuzu – These bodiless
figureheads were used to adorn
the prows of war canoes on
headhunting raids – see page 84.
They were regarded as emblems
to protect the canoe occupants
and a visually effective symbol
of headhunting. In their hands the
Nuzu Nuzu hold an unmistakable
replication of their intentions
– a miniature human head.

War canoes in full cry.

A fully manned war canoe from Roviana (in the stern sits Ingava).

HMS *Royalist* bombarding Ingava's headquarters, 1891 – see page 249.

Jock Cromer's recruiting ship the *Fearless* – see page 242.

A bush reliquary. In 1942 the invasion of Guadalcanal introduced to the Solomons a flood of GI's who took exception to being greeted in every village by a parade of skulls. In deference to their guests, the Solomon Islanders transported their ancestors and their victims to a more discreet location…where they remain to this day.

according to one of Cook's officers, 'they were treated exceeding well by the natives'. Thanks to Joseph Banks, this Pacific voyage is better known for hospitality of a more intimate nature but Cook's crew were so enfeebled by venereal disease that just before leaving Tahiti for Hawaii, Cook noted that 'there were scarce enough hands able to do duty on board'.

They stayed just two weeks in Hawaii before they left to explore the north-west coast of America. Returning ten months later, they found an epidemic of venereal disease spreading throughout the islands. Walter Ellis recorded that it was 'raging among these poor people in a violent degree, some of whom were affected most terribly; and it was the opinion of most, that us, in our former visit, had been the cause of this irreparable injury' – irreparable and trans-generational.

In 1786, eight years after Cook's ship had left the islands, the French frigate La Boussole arrived in Hawaii. The ship's surgeon recorded their greeting in Maui, an island where Cook had not even landed. They were met by people covered with 'buboes and scars which result from their suppurating warts, nodes, fistula, scrofulous swellings . . . atrophy of the eye, blindness and indo-lent swellings of the extremities and among the children, scald head, or a malignant ringworm, from which exudes a fetid and acrid matter. The greater part of these unhappy victims of sensu-ality, when arrived at the age of nine or ten were feeble and languid, exhausted by marasmus and rickets.'

Cook, Bougainville and Carteret all identified and acknowl-edged the source of these epidemics and, although the aetiology of many were imperfectly understood, they were understood enough for a policy of quarantining ships to have been part of international maritime policy in European and American ports throughout the seventeenth and eighteenth centuries. That a number of the Solomon Islands adjacent to Santa Isabel maintained a policy of total exclusion, speaks volumes for the potency of oral history and the memory of Mendana's *nguanguao* ship. It was a policy that worked well as the occasional whaleboat or surveying expedition had no interest in establishing a permanent presence. As each reported back on the depth and degree of the islander's hostility, the central and northern islands of the Solomons archipelago became a virtual no-go area. However, there was another group of white men who could not resist the lure of these uncontacted islands. They were not after sandalwood or whale oil – but human souls.

It seemed fitting to the Catholic Church that their work in the archipelago should start on the very island where, three hundred years earlier, Mendana had planted the Cross. It was an initiative blessed by the Pope and led by a bishop. In 1845 a mission ship made for the Ortega Channel at the southern end of Santa Isabel and an anchorage close to where the *John Bull* had decimated the islanders in such a 'lamentable and laughable' manner the previous year.

Assuming the ship to be the returning whaler, the surrounding population adopted a different tactic and withdrew to the high ground overlooking the channel. They watched as, with considerable difficulty, a small party of white men clambered over the ship's rail, their movements impeded by their ankle-length sky blue habits of the Society of Mary. The ship's lighter made its way to the small island of San Jorge and drew up to the beach opposite the deserted village of Midoru.

Led by Bishop Epalle, the little party of six gathered on the shore and waited, making the occasional conciliatory gesture in the general direction of the huts. After about ten minutes and seeing that their presence was eliciting no response, the bishop dispatched three of his party to investigate. They walked towards the village with arms outstretched. On reaching the first of the huts they knocked tentatively on the wooden lintel and peered inside. Having repeated this ritual on front of a few huts they appeared satisfied and returned quickly to the waiting bishop. The little party now stood its ground and waited.

From their vantage point half a mile away, overlooking the beach, the villagers of Midoru were also at a loss to know what to do next. These white men, their bodies completely covered in a material the colour of the sky, matched no previous description of the species. They found their gestures quite extraordinary, as if they were talking to some invisible presence. The absence of weapons was reassuring, but what if they were concealed underneath the folds of blue that covered their bodies? Eventually, after about an hour, curiosity won over discretion and the village headman, together with a group of elders and a party of young men armed with warclubs, made their way to the beach.

As the villagers approached the missionaries, Bishop Epalle extended his hand in greeting. The villagers stopped and looked at each other; this was a gesture entirely foreign to them. Then the village headman noticed the episcopal ring, glinting in the sunlight. All seemed clear now and the headmen walked forward to take the proffered hand but, as he attempted to extract the ring, it was immediately withdrawn. The headman retreated back to consult with the elders. One of the guards was dispatched to a nearby hut and returned carrying two lemons. The headman returned to the bishop, who again offered his hand. The headman offered the lemons and the bishop took them. The headman waited, the bishop smiled and, after handing the lemons to a companion, offered his hand again. The headman now grasped it with two hands and, with a wrench, attempted to extract his prize from the chubby forefinger. The bishop let out a yelp of pain but, undeterred, the headman persisted. The bishop's acolytes rallied to his defence. The waiting villagers, seeing their headman enveloped in a swirl of blue, rushed forward. If one action could have been designed to provoke complete panic amongst a party of celibate white men, it would the experience of being surrounded by a group of naked black men attempting to grasp at their nether regions in order to secure their concealed 'weapons'. Farce turned to tragedy as the mêlée turned into a fight and, as the Marists retreated to the waiting lighter, the bishop was felled with a blow from a warclub. By the time the party had reached the safety of their ship, Epalle was dead.

Seven years later the Marists made another attempt to establish a bridgehead on the Solomons. On the island of San Christobal, fifty miles south-east of Malaita, whaleboats had established a precarious understanding with a group of islanders in the sparsely populated bay of Makira. Here, in exchange for a considerable payment of axes, calico and tobacco, they were allowed to careen their ships. Six Marist missionaries were landed close to the whaling station. When the mission ship returned six months later they found two left, both prostrate with malaria. Three had been eaten and the other had died of blackwater fever. The mission was abandoned and for a while the Solomons were spared the attentions of the missionary movement.

The Anglicans and Presbyterians decided to adopt a different tactic from their Catholic competitors. By now it had become dramatically clear that on many islands the inhabitants made no distinction between seamen, traders, whalemen, sandalwooders, recruiters and themselves. If they were to be tarred with the same brush as the laity simply because of the colour of their skin, could not the bridgehead be secured by members of a different race – particularly as brave white Christians were no longer forth-coming? Fortunately for the Presbyterians they had an eager pool of recruits, groomed in the missionary tradition, living in Polynesia, 1,500 miles to the east. They might not be Melanesian but they were approximately the same colour and, indeed, some New Hebridean islands had Polynesian populations. Unfortu-nately it was not to them that the Samoan missionaries were sent, but to a string of Melanesian islands in the south of the archi-pelago. The mission ship returned six months later to a catalogue of disaster. On Tanna, all six had disappeared. On Efate and Fortuna, the majority had been murdered and the survivors were living under siege. On Erramango, the five Samoans had been captured and were rescued just as they were about to be eaten. However, on the southernmost island of Aneityum, all of the missionaries were found alive. They hadn't made any converts, but they had survived unmolested – clearly this was to be the bridgehead for the Great Commission.

In all physical respects the inhabitants of Aneityum were very like their more sanguinary cousins to the north, but they were quite different in character. Being at the southern end of the New Hebridean chain and having little or no contact with other island groups, there was less compulsion to compete. The Aneityumese were gentler, milder, less demanding people.

Inroads had already been made a decade earlier when John Paddon set up a sandalwood station and he, like the Samoans, had survived. It was clearly time for a white missionary to take up the reins.

John Geddie was a Nova Scotian, an old-style hard-bitten all-talking, no-dancing Presbyterian. He was intolerant, tough and completely inflexible. In 1848, on the way to the island, he broods in his diary: 'It's hard to realize the thought that I am really on my way to these beautiful realms where no Sabbath smiles on the benighted people, where no congregation assemble to engage in solemn services of religion, and where no preacher proclaims to them the good news of salvation, and warns them to flee from the wrath to come.' Given what was to happen to the islanders over the next twenty years the irony of this entry is painful.

Geddie's time on Aneityum, recorded in assiduous detail by himself and his assistant Inglis, provides a unique record of the impact of white contact on a small island community; unique in the sense that the material provided – censuses, conversions, records of births, and causes of death – makes it possible to build up an accurate epidemiological picture of the process of depopulation.

In 1859 Geddie and Inglis, after two censuses, estimated the population to be 3,500. During this initial stage of the ministry, the island was divided into six clan districts. Each of these clans had a public meeting place called the *intiplang* and there was, according to Geddie 'seldom familiar intercourse between people of one village and another as no one dared venture across the boundary into a hostile district'.

All this changed in 1861, by which time the majority of the

islanders had converted to Christianity. For Geddie and Inglis it was a triumph, twelve years of hard work had led to the first island in Melanesia turning to Christ. And their efforts and those of their respective wives had been prodigious. By this time the island could boast that virtually the whole population gathered in one or other of the fifty-six schoolhouses for an hour or more each week for religious instruction and literacy classes. This role model of dynamic evangelism attracted visitors so that, three or four times a year, these schools were visited by other missionaries, noviciates and lay evangelicals, parties that 'numbered sometimes fifty or one hundred persons'. On Sundays about five hundred people congregated morning and afternoon in each mission. In a very short period there had grown up a network of communication between people living in all parts of the island and the dozens of visitors who had come to admire Geddie's model Christian community.

In January 1861 the cruiser *L'Hirondelle* arrived with some of its crew infected with measles. As Geddie recorded: 'not half a dozen of persons on the island escaped the sickness and within three or four months more than one thousand Aneityumese were dead.' Thanks to Geddie's and Inglis' conscientiousness in recording the details of life on Aneityum it is possible to recon-struct exactly what took place and the island provides a template for a continent-wide tragedy that, over a 150-year period, over-whelmed almost every Pacific island.

It is only during the last fifty years that microbiologists have identified the many micro-organisms responsible for common diseases and determined their mode of transmission from person to person. Most acute infectious diseases which assume epidemic form are either what are loosely described as 'droplet infections' because of their mode of transmission, or those due to contamination of food and water by bacteria. In the benign South Pacific climate with its abundant rainfall, luxuriant vegetation, large varieties of fresh fruit, root crops and water teeming with fish, this second mode of transmission was probably responsible for very few epidemics. Contemporary white commentators accused the islanders of many things but lack of hygiene was not one of them.

'Droplet infections' include diseases such as measles, influenza, whooping cough and diphtheria, where the infecting agent is contained in droplets of saliva which are emitted when one sneezes or coughs, sings or speaks loudly. In confined spaces and the moisture-laden atmosphere of Pacific islands the smaller droplets remain suspended in the air to be inhaled by other people present and, although the larger ones may fall to the ground, the water from them evaporates and the 'droplet nuclei' become small enough to become airborne and inhaled. By early 1861 Geddie's Aneityum, with its regular regimented mass gatherings, had become the perfect environment for droplet infections. It would only have taken one worshipper infected by measles from L'Hirondelle attending these almost daily mass gatherings in an enclosed space for over an hour, reciting and singing, to have ignited the epidemic. The symptoms appear twelve to fourteen days after the person becomes infected and in a hot, humid atmosphere, with people moving freely and frequently round the island, to and from household to mission stations, this activity would have accelerated the transmissibility.

The effects were to be devastating across all age groups. By early April 1861 about one third of the people living around the harbour where *L'Hirondelle* had moored were dead. Geddie wrote that in other parts of the island the death rate was 'in some instances less, others more . . . [but] very few die of measles, it is severe dysentery which proves so fatal.' Everywhere on the island the mortality was 'greatest among persons in the prime of life, while many old and young were spared'. Physiologically it is understandable that a child's metabolism can accommodate higher body temperatures, but why the elderly of Aneityum suffered less is probably explained by a different cause. Quite simply most of them had resisted Geddie's evangelizing, so when they did become infected it was not in his schools or mission stations, but back in their villages, by which time the virus had lost some of its potency.

With the Presbyterians now established in the southern New Hebrides, their Anglican competitors started to make contact with the islands in the northern part of the archipelago with equally disastrous results. The harbinger was their mission ship *Southern Cross*, sailing back and forth from Australia and New Zealand bringing with it a whole raft of pulmonary diseases. Although it wasn't long before the islanders were making a connection between the ship and death, the Anglicans appeared completely impervious to cause and effect. Writing in June 1861, about a journey aboard the *Southern Cross*, Bishop Patterson observed:

By 4 or 5 p.m. I neared Aruas, in the bay on the west side of Vanua Lava . . . Somehow I did not much like the manner of the people; they did not at night come into the men's common eating or sleeping house, as before, and I overheard some few remarks which I did not quite like –

something about the unusual sickness being connected with this new teaching.

Summing up another voyage in August 1863, Patterson speaks of landing a mission party from New Zealand on the island of Mota where he 'found them all pretty well'. He then leaves for Malekula, returning two weeks later to 'find things lamentably changed. A great mortality was going on, dysentery and great prostration of strength from severe influenza . . . I spent two and a half days going round the island . . . During these days twenty-seven adults died, fifty-two in all, and many, many more were dying, emaciated, coughing, fainting.' To gather up a group of young men from New Zealand in the depths of winter and deposit them two weeks later on the shores of a South Pacific island and *not* expect one of them to be carrying the common cold, appeared the height of optimism.

Eight years later, in one of the last letters he wrote before he met his death in the southern Solomons, he describes visiting a small island in the New Hebrides. 'My afternoon ashore was one of the saddest for many a long day. I encountered in all about forty-eight people in the village whom of old three hundred would have been seen. Fighting going on and even cannibalism for the most part unchecked. They all have guns and will shoot at any white man. How to act upon these people I am altogether at a loss to imagine.' Like most missionaries who had been in Melanesia for over a decade he had a special affection for those people, often very young, who had converted to Christianity in the face of considerable disapproval. In his letter he mentions one such convert, Tivea, now in his late twenties whom he remembered as 'a laughing, sparkling-eyed youngster fired with the promise of the Great Commission'. Now he kept his distance from the welcoming party of missionaries, his eyes shifting hither and thither, terrified that he might give the impression that he approved of the visit. Patterson concluded: 'To see him as I saw him this afternoon is enough to break one's heart.' Tivea was in an impossible position. For the islanders the *Southern Cross* equalled death. The coincidences were too stark to ignore and any islander who appeared in any way complicit in the ship's arrival risked being blamed for any subsequent fatality. If Tivea had attempted to explain the danger he was in, would any European have believed him – even a good man like Patterson? It would have broken the bishop's heart to have had to face up to the fact that, in the process of bringing the Word to these benighted people, he was killing them in their thousands. No, better to ascribe the loss of eighty per cent of the population of one particular village to cannibalism and firearms – any alternative explanation was unthinkable.

Patterson's successor, Bishop Wilson, was concerned enough to consult the leading Victorian physician, Sir Patrick Mason. According to one of Wilson's missionaries, William Durrad, 'the doctor pooh-poohed the seriousness of the fact and said that the thing happens all over the world and that the natives simply have to get inured to the new conditions.' Durrad added that the problem for the Melanesian was that in the process of becoming 'inured' they were becoming extinct. Writing in 1920 from the comfort of his retirement in England he added two extraordinary afterthoughts:

> It has to be confessed that the *Southern Cross* is one of the chief agents in the distribution of pneumonia germs . . .

Among the many occasions I can recall severe illness
following the ship's visit none stands out so prominently
in my memory as an epidemic of pneumonia that raged
on Ticopia when I was put down there on one occasion
for a few weeks while the *Southern Cross* cruised among
the Solomons. The message of the Gospel was stultified
by the terrible sufferings of the people.

A few hundred miles to the south, a similar myopia appeared
to have taken hold amongst the Presbyterians.

After the assiduous recording of the details of the first
epidemic, Geddie and Inglis seemed to have become inured to
the gradual decimation of their flock and their records no
longer contain the wealth of information recorded during the
measles epidemic. In 1863 Geddie records that a 'severe
epidemic passed over the island . . . and swept off a large
number of natives'. In December 1864 there was an outbreak of
influenza which increased the number of deaths recorded for
that year. In May 1866 a disease 'which had all the symptoms of
diphtheria' appeared and within a month caused the deaths of
'probably not less than a hundred of the strongest and health-
iest natives . . . whilst those of advanced years were spared'.
Inglis records that 'for some reason the children entirely
escaped.' Not, however, in the following year when they were
the principal victims of an outbreak of whooping cough which
began in June 1867 and made 'something like a clean sweep of
the young children and told severely on half-grown boys and
girls, and weakly adults of all ages. No part of the island escaped
is ravages . . . Our island has now been visited by measles,
diphtheria and whooping cough in rapid succession. These

diseases have, in a short space of time, swept away one-half of the population.'

How did Geddie keep going? Fortunately he was a man with no imagination; an enormous asset in such work. Utterly preoccupied, driven, incapable of compromise, it would have required a quite exceptional determination of a kind that the placid, easygoing Aneityumese did not possess to hold out against a man like Geddie. Throughout the decade of disaster he never wavered in his belief that the decimation that surrounded him was part of His greater purpose, although this rationale was sometimes tested to the limit. 'It is remarkable,' he wrote after the first epidemic, 'that the deaths that have occurred for some months past have been amongst the Christian Party only. He, who doeth all things well, has wise, though mysterious, ends in view.'

Viewed in retrospect, the disasters that befell these passive islanders were the secret of Geddie's success. The island was a balkanized society with each chief having limited jurisdiction over a particular region – thus there was no chiefly plutocracy capable of mounting a unified resistance to Geddie's proselytizing. When the epidemics continued they fell upon all, without distinction, the chiefs, priests and the local gerontocracies that were masters of the native culture; its unities and certainties were swept away, sometimes in a matter of days. Who could the people turn to now for leadership, for some explanation for the calamity that had befallen them? Geddie became a new race of chief, schooled in the ways of major adversity, offering hope of salvation in this world and the next. And so he collected around his person and the vision he represented the failing hope of the island and, with it, a temporal power which he turned into a monument to the Great Commission during the last five years of his ministry.

During those years, the islanders of Aneityum toiled, in ever decreasing numbers, to demonstrate their commitment to Christ – in the vain hope that this demonstration would spare them further suffering. Work parties swarmed over the island, hewing out slabs of rock coral and felling trees, to build Geddie's monument to the first Christian community in Melanesia – a church of cathedral-like proportions, capable of seating over one thousand worshippers. By the time he left the island in 1872 it was completed. However, if the total population had ever gathered there, there would still have been space for three hundred more worshippers. Four years later a tsunami inundated the southern coast of Aneityum, destroyed his church and claimed two hundred lives; the only occasion when multiple deaths could be attributed to 'an act of God'. The remaining five hundred islanders gathered to witness the ruins of Geddie's monument and their years of devotional labour.

For decades this remorseless haemorrhaging of population continued in almost every corner of the Pacific. On Aneityum, there were 2,500 deaths over fifteen years; but it was all a question of proportionality – the larger the island, the greater the cull as the percentages remained constant. Thirty years after the first outbreak of measles on Aneityum, the virus arrived in Fiji aboard HMS *Dido*. On the former island it had killed one-third of the population, so too in Fiji. The people were estimated at the time to number 140,000 and it was recorded that 45,000 died in the epidemic in the space of four months. A Government Commission (by now the islands were a British Protectorate), reported:

Whole communities were stricken at one time, and there was no-one left to gather food or carry water, to attend to the necessary wants of their fellows, or even, in many cases, to bury the dead. Consequently many must have died of starvation and neglect... But the heavy mortality was also attributable in great measure to the people's dire ignorance, their blind unimpressiveness, their want of ordinary foresight, their apathy and despair. They became at once, overwhelmed, dismayed, cowed, abandoning all hope of self-preservation.

One looks in vain through 150 years of Pacific literature on this subject in search of even the faintest sign of empathy: regret, yes – empathy, no. It seemed that no one dared even imagine how these random, devastating and, for most, inexplicable visitations must have affected the populations. Their action, or more exactly, their inaction, is dutifully recorded, but little else. It is as if to recognize these people as fellow human beings with the same capacity for loyalty, love, humour or grief was too painful to contemplate. It was not as if this required a leap of imagination so much as the gift of empathy and that was a quality that appeared to be entirely lacking in even the most well intentioned Europeans. In the end it was a young anthropologist who, in a few letters written in the 1920s, described the human cost of these epidemics. Anthropology was a nascent science, fighting for academic respectability, but one that was attracting some remarkable young men and women.

When Bernard Deacon arrived in Malekula in 1926, its population had been in decline for over fifty years. He found himself in the middle of an epidemic of Spanish influenza. Aged twenty-four, recently down from Oxford and on his first fieldwork assignment, he faced up to the devastation that surrounded him and communicated from a small village in the bush something of his anguish and despair. In a letter to his fiancée Margaret Gardiner, he wrote:

> Margou – it is nightfall, and out above the trees and palms great black bars of clouds are gathering, still and oppressive. I am terribly overstrained, there seems nothing here but Death – a man was dead in the village this morning of dysentery – Jack, or Tevru. How many men I know have died! Paul & David & Kukan & Lagan & Manbogwr & Ailul, and Jota's father and many, many more, terribly many. My notes read like the last confessions of dying men. They die so simply, unassumingly, uncomprehendingly: all with this tragic swiftness. In one village of twenty, nine died in one week. Men have become carelessly ironic about death. It's not like death in war or crisis – it is the final death, the death of a people, and they know it more clearly than we do.
>
> There is an utterly weary irony about them – you cannot imagine how suicidal the gloom of working in it sometimes becomes. The sight of death numbs me, tears all the roots of meaning and fineness and possibility out of me. A stiff brown body, the flies fanned away from it, washed, covered in mats, already unpleasant in this vertical, tropical heat, and buried in a shallow grave in the house – it's absurd, again and again. One feels so utterly helpless and worse than useless by a dying man, he seems to be struggling with something far away that has nothing to do with you. Spanish influenza has wiped out whole villages in Santo, Pentecost & Malekula, one might say districts. I despair & despair again.

It is night, and I must stop and come back to my tiny little speck in the Pacific. Goodnight.

Three months later Bernard Deacon died of blackwater fever on the island of Malekula.

In a seventy-year period between 1860 and 1930 there was a stream of reports from missionaries, scientists, medical and colonial officers throughout the Pacific, all arriving at the same conclusion – Europeans were merely hastening that which was inevitable. In other words, they had only served to provide a favourable environment for the germs of death that were already there and 'an identifiable malaise in the stock itself'.

The year of Deacon's death saw the publication of Stephen Roberts's *Population Problems in the Pacific*, a summation of the 'decadent' theory. Yoking the Anglo-Saxon work ethic to Darwinism, he castigated the Polynesians – those one-time Argonauts of the Pacific:

> The voyage urge has gone and the natives luxuriated in enervating tropical islands, where life was too easy and nature too bountiful . . . [They] dawdled through a trance of mental and physical inertia, all was supine and nerveless and sorcery and superstition were in the ascendant. The race, denied the health-giving process of selection and of struggle, was giving way. This general lassitude perhaps explains why epidemic diseases were so terrible in their effects.

Roberts's comments were merely a preamble to a general attack on all Pacific cultures, listing a lack of hygiene, insanitary conditions, the abasement of women, cannibalism, war, abortion, infanticide and a 'general debauchery' to account for widespread depopulation before the arrival of the white man. He even asserts that: 'Epidemics occurred in Aneityum before the missionaries arrived' – a curious statement that appeared to imply that census-taking was alive and well even before Geddie and Inglis arrived. Then, turning to those recorded instances such as the *Novara*'s observations of the effect of a smallpox outbreak on Puynipet, Roberts observes: 'The native traditions, it is true, say that diseases are a result of the coming of ship-wrecked sailors, but it is difficult to argue from this, in view of the natural tendency of such born romanticists as are the Polynesians, to couple any unwanted plague or event with the advent of the strange man from overseas.'

His efforts to exculpate the white man from any responsibility for the dying out of civilizations reached a crescendo as he concluded: 'The Western imagination halts before consideration of such atrocities, and one shudders as if the mists had rolled back for a moment and let one glimpse into the abyss of sub-human existence. Little remorse or sympathy can be felt when such practices bring the inevitable retribution to the tribes concerned.' In short – they deserved everything they got.

Turning his attention to the lives of the islanders, post-contact, Roberts refers to a long list of reports compiled by colonial medical officers in the closing years of the nineteenth century, attributing population decline to wars, debauchery, drunken-ness, leprosy, syphilis, feticide, firearms and 'general enfeeble-ment'. Two, however, touched briefly upon a deeper reason. Leroy and Broca explained it as 'a sadness due to the neighbour-hood of the white – the impossibility for the native to support contact with civilization'. '*Le Kanaque s'ennuie – comme l'animal captif*', wrote a medical officer from New Caledonia, another described it as 'a kind of fatalism, an odd submission'. In 1874 Dr Litton Forbes, arguing from his experience as a medical officer in Fiji, even suggested that psychological despair was the main cause of depopulation, 'that great unsettling of the native mind, which almost eludes all accurate analysis'.

Throughout the nineteenth-century the northern Solomons maintained their opposition toward any incursion by the white man that was not on their terms. They may have been prepared to trade with ships for iron, firearms, calico – even hitch a tow in their search for heads, but he was not allowed to settle. As late as 1885 Hugh Romilly, after a voyage through the Solomons and noting what precautions they were attempting to enforce, concluded:

It is well known with what rapidity a disease from which they have hitherto been exempt runs through a native race. The epidemic of measles in Fiji, from which some forty thousand natives died, is one memorable case.

In many parts of the Solomons the natives have to thank the white man for a no less fatal disease. In one tribe in Bougainville, every infected man, woman and child was destroyed – a severe measure, but surely a sensible one, though one which could only be practised by a savage race. In most parts of the Solomon Islands this introduction of disease has produced a feeling of bitter hatred against the white man. To the native mind it appears a premeditated plot to destroy them. Is it, then, to be expected that they should welcome white men to their shores?

Our system of quarantine in the colonial ports is the

191

result of precisely the same reasoning; and we should have recourse to the same measures as those adopted in the Solomons: that is to say, we should certainly fire on any people we saw attempting to land from an infected ship. To the Solomon Islander all white men are infected.

Romilly's was a lone voice.

At the time Romilly compiled his report, epidemiology had been a respectable science for over fifty years, yet no one had attempted to undertake a survey on the worst affected islands. A selection of genealogical tables, randomly collected in any part of Melanesia would have provided a very accurate picture of population loss and its causes – after all, these were people who could recount these tables back for at least ten generations. Twenty-five years after Romilly had written his devastating report, a man arrived in the Solomons prepared to ask the right questions.

The anthropologist and psychiatrist W.H.R. Rivers stayed on two islands in the north-western Solomons in 1908 and again in 1914. He had been trained by the father of British anthropology, Maurice Haddon.

When in the Torres Straits with Dr Haddon twenty-five years ago, I discovered that the people preserve in the memories with great fidelity a full and accurate record of their descent and relationships. It was possible to collect pedigrees so ample in all collateral lines that they could serve as a source of statistical enquiry . . . In Melanesia this instrument shows conclusively that the fall in numbers is due quite as much to the decrease in birth-rate as the increase in death-rate.

On Simbo and Vella, Rivers collected a large number of genealogies for the previous three generations that had felt the full impact of white contact. He found a decreasing number of children per marriage and an increase in childless marriages. On Simbo, the first generation had produced 447 children from 207 marriages of which 19 per cent were childless. The current generation had produced 72 children from 110 marriages of which 52 per cent were childless. On Vella there was a similar decrease in fertility. On Simbo there had been no outbreaks of tuberculosis, dysentery, measles, smallpox, or influenza, and venereal diseases were unknown. The island had never seen a white missionary, had never heard of alcohol and, although they all had firearms, they never fought amongst themselves. The conclusion Rivers reached was revolutionary and, at the time, was met with incredulity.

By the time Rivers published his observations on the depopulation of Melanesia, he had embarked upon his second career as the distinguished neurologist and the leading light of the British psychoanalytical school. (His work at Craiglockhart Hospital amongst the shell-shocked victims of the First World War was to bring him immortality through his association with Sassoon, Owen and Graves.) He was quite clear about the reasons for depopulation. Between 1906 and 1909 the British Colonial authorities had abolished headhunting. These people were dying out from an absence of war.

This practice formed the centre of a social and religious institution which took an all-pervading part in the lives of the people. The heads sought in headhunting expeditions were needed in order to propitiate ancestral ghosts on

193

such occasions as building a new house for a chief, or making a new canoe, while they were also offered in sacrifice at the funeral of a chief. Moreover, headhunting was not only necessary for the due performance of the religious rites of the people, but it stood in closest relation to pursuits of an economic kind. The actual headhunting expedition only lasted a few weeks, and the actual fighting only a few hours, but this was only the culminating point of a process lasting over months or, sometimes, years.

It was a rule that new canoes should be made for an expedition to obtain heads, and the manufacture of these meant work of an interesting kind lasting certainly many months, probably for over a year. The process of canoe building was accompanied throughout by rites and feasts, which not only excited the liveliest interest but also acted as stimuli to the various activities of horticulture and pig breeding. As the date fixed for the expedition approached, other rites and feats were held, and these were still more frequent and on a larger scale after the return of a successful expedition.

In stopping the practice of headhunting, the rulers from an alien culture were abolishing an institution which had its roots in the religion of the people and spread its branches throughout every aspect of their culture. By this action they deprived the people of the greater part of their interest in life, while at the same time they undermine the religion of the people with no attempt to put another in its place.

No-one could be long on Simbo without recognizing how great is the people's lack of interest in life, and to what extent the zest has gone out of their lives.

From his original 1908 notes: 'The activities of the chiefs

mostly ceased with headhunting.' Njiruviri, his interpreter, complains:

> No-one is mighty now; they are all alike, they have no
> *mana*; they cannot go headhunting; they all do nothing.
> 'For generations the women here have practised effective
> forms of abortion and contraception. There is no doubt
> that this is [now] an active choice. The people say to them-
> selves: 'Why should we bring children into the world only
> to work for the white man?'

But that is exactly what they had done in ever increasing numbers since 1863 when Ross Lewin 'lifted off' the first batch of sixty recruits from the New Hebrides and delivered them to the cane fields of Townsville. Five years later 1,237 islanders were brought over, in 1873, 2,100 – recruiting had become big business. By the time Jack Renton took up his appointment as a government agent in 1876, there were 7,000 islanders working in Queensland. Nine years later this figure had increased to 11,700.There was not one corner of the New Hebrides or the Solomons that had not succumbed to the lure of the white man's world.

To attribute this eagerness to be recruited entirely to the desire to see the white man's world, to possess his goods or as a short-cut to kudos, is to ignore the effects of these random epidemics and the anomie they engendered in those communities still inca-pable of linking cause and effect. Comparing the populations of Malaita and its neighbouring island of San Cristobal, less then fifty miles away, between 1875 and 1900, brings the impact of this ignorance into sharp relief. Malaita, forewarned by the legacy of Mendana's visit three hundred years earlier, had imposed a cordon sanitaire with the result that its population remained virtually stable. During this same period San Cristobal opened up a large tract of land on its south-east coast to whaleboats and recruiters and saw its population decline from 43,000 to 4,000. Remorselessly exponential, these figures replicated themselves on the larger stage. In 1870 it was generally accepted that the population of the New Hebrides stood at 650,000. This figure had fallen to under 100,000 by the turn of the century.

For two generations the impact of such sudden, meaningless and random death was to have an effect, not only robbing the population of its people but leaching away at their certainties. Seen in this light it is not surprising that so many young men and women signed-on. They were attempting to escape from the disease and death that stalked their own backyard.

10

Sex and Death

———— ⚬ ————

WHEN Jack Renton took up his post as a government agent in the spring of 1877, he soon discovered that policing the conduct of the recruiting business would be well nigh impossible. There were thirty ships plying their trade and only himself and five other official agents employed by the government. The remaining twenty-four ships were manned by agents employed by their owners. If a captain found himself saddled with one of the official agents, everyone, owners, crew and captain were on their best behaviour with the inevitable result that most of the incidents of malfeasance that these six recorded were based on hearsay. A report would be written, a wrist slapped and the captain would set sail again. If he lost his command it would seldom be the result of a report by a government agent. He would only lose his command if the ship's owners judged that he had not delivered the goods. Results kept the crews in business, not their conduct or the quality of their seamanship.

Many crew members were off immigrant ships from Europe who, once they had arrived in Australia, had been discharged for incompetence. Others were deserters from windjammers, attracted by the shorter voyages and higher pay that was supplemented by backhanders and commission agreements based on results. With a human cargo in which everyone had a cash interest the dehumanizing results were inevitable. As one crewman recorded long after the trade finished: 'I have known the mate of a vessel go ashore at a friendly village, lie with a woman of an evening, and fire intentionally three shots from a Spencer rifle at an unoffending native from the same village in the morning.' A naval officer remarked that the masters of labour ships were mostly 'men of inferior character, generally drunkards, and not infrequently of the worst possible moral habits'.

In a letter to the *Melbourne Argus*, the missionary John Neilson wrote 'I knew of a native on board a ship who for some trifling act of insubordination was, on the captain's orders, tied up to the mast and tortured to death, and no one was punished for it . . . I knew well a captain in the island trade who used to maintain that natives had no souls, and that it was no more harm to take their lives than to take the life of a dog.' The captain of the *Heather Belle* was no exception.

It was a chaotic ship. A government agent once reported that the captain was known as a 'soaker' who 'in broad daylight, with fine weather, and himself at the wheel drunk and incapable, had run his ship ashore twice, once in the New Hebrides and once in the Solomons'. Back in the New Hebrides in October 1878, the *Heather Belle* returned six natives to Erramango Island and recruited six others to take their place. Among them were a young married couple, the wife being, as one member of the crew observed:

A very pleasant and good-looking girl. The pair seemed very devoted to one another, the boy taking care of the girl in a way that was charming to see.

On this trip, aware of the captain's reputation, the authorities had installed a government agent who the captain simply ignored. A quiet, apparently ineffectual man whom, for the time being, kept out of the captain's way.

The young couple had been on board barely a week when the captain discovered the young man could speak good English, having been recruited before. He took him to his cabin where he gave him a five-pound note and told to bring his wife and leave her there whenever the ship was at anchor (and the government agent ashore supervising recruiting). If he did this regularly, the captain told him, he would receive another five pounds at the end of the voyage. The young man took the money and showed it to his wife who told him to take it to the government agent.

We heard a violent altercation going on between the captain and the government agent. The young married couple were present, and the agent was holding up the five-pound note towards the captain.

'You dare touch that woman,' he said, 'while I'm on board, and by God you're for it. I shall give this note back to the boy in front of the authorities in Queensland.'

Then turning to the boy: 'That will do, my boy. Take your wife down below, and if you have anymore trouble with anyone, black or white, come and see me at once.'

Everybody on board had heard the wrangle and I was

somewhat surprised to find that I was the only one there who considered the government agent to be right. Most of the others said the captain was a fool to give the boy any money. He should have promised to give him a present, got the girl and then 'let the bloody nigger whistle for his money'.

The ship sailed for Aoba. Given the captain's predilections, it was hardly a surprising choice, for their women were reputed to be beautiful. Aoba was one of a small group of Polynesian islands in the middle of a Melanesian archipelago.

From Tahiti and its surrounding islands, since the dawn of the second millennium, the Polynesians had mastered the arts of seamanship and navigation that had eluded the Greeks, Romans and the Phoenicians. They had developed canoes seating up to one hundred people that could live in any sea. They had made wind and tide charts from grass blades and sticks and had developed a sextant made from a coconut. As one Maori scholar wrote:

> Columbus felt his way over the Western Ocean while his half-crazed crew whined for their gods to keep them from falling over the edge of the world; but the Polynesian voyager, the naked savage, shipless and metalless, hewed him out a log dug out with a sharpened stone, tied some planks to the side thereof with string, put his wife, children, some coconuts, and a pet pig on board, and sailed forth to settle on lone islands 2000 miles away . . . and did it.

From Taumotu to the Marquesas, and on to Samoa and Tahiti they pushed westwards, some driven to migrate by drought, war or over-population, others by a vague quest for a legendary homeland that lay to the west.

Once encountered by Europeans they exercised a fascination. In April 1768 Bougainville anchored off Tahiti and a myth was born. During his eighteen-day stay he strolled through shady palm groves, was entertained by hospitable families and admired the lush flora and brightly coloured birds. Above all, he was stunned by the people: 'I never saw men better made, and whose limbs were more proportionate; in order to paint Hercules or Mars, one could nowhere find such beautiful models . . . I thought I was transported to the Garden of Eden . . . everywhere we found hospitality, ease, innocent joy.'

A year later Captain Cook arrived and Joseph Banks rhapsodized: 'On the island of Tahiti where love is the chief occupation, the favourite, nay, the sole luxury of the inhabitants, both the bodies and souls of women are moulded into the utmost perfection . . . The breasts of the young women before they have children are very round and beautiful.'

In both the French and the English accounts there were allusions to the Polynesians casual attitude to pre-marital sex. By the 1830s over 150 whaling ships were 'resting up' in Tahiti at different times of the year. Syphilis had become endemic on the islands and the population of Tahiti and Moorea declined from 35,000 when Bougainville and Cook visited to around 8,000 sixty years later. However, the people of Aoba were spared the 'thorn in the rose' during these sixty years due to a fortunate misunderstanding. After his eighteen days in Tahiti, Bougainville sailed westwards to the New Hebrides. He claimed Aoba for the French, burying an oak plaque on shore to commemorate the event. As the ritual took place the inhabitants kept their distance, and when the French moved up the beach so the islanders retreated. They were shadowy people who appeared to be disfigured and discoloured. Bougainville soon came to the conclusion that these people were riddled with leprosy and beat a hasty retreat. He named the place Lepers Island.

Such unfortunates were bound to attract the attention of the burgeoning nineteenth-century missionary movement but when the first of them landed in 1840 they found not lepers but an island full of delicately tattooed Polynesian men and women. Word soon spread and Aoba became a favourite spot for 'rest and recreation'. As a crew member of one recruiting ship recalled:

The girls of the western end of Aoba island were perhaps the most winsome of all the islanders because of the gracefulness of their movements, the warm colour of their velvety skins, the clean cut regular features, and their gentle seductive voices. The delicate curves of their limbs and bodies were enhanced by exquisite tattooing. One could almost believe that the girls wore swimming costumes, so well and finely had the work been done upon their bodies. The tattoo marks started below the elbows, bands running up the arms and across the shoulders, thence down the front and curving up to a peak between the breasts. The pattern below extended over the greater part of the body, and finished just below the knees. It had all the appearance of clothing, yet the girls were as naked as they had been when they were born.'

Having supplied details of his own seduction and pointing out that the custom of 'free love' existed, he then mentioned that in his time [the 1870s] it was well known that venereal diseases were taking their toll. As he observed: 'The Aoban natives looked to the white man to cure their ills, and a man or woman who offered to recruit was to be suspected of carrying an infection, since the natives often wished to sign on only for the purpose of being ridded of their trouble.'

In fact recruiters did not visit Aoba until the late 1870s when they had little choice but to go after recruits wherever they could be found. Polynesians were not happy working on plantations with Melanesians. Polynesians were clannish, supercilious and had a reputation for having little compunction about cannibalizing those who were not their own. One agent recalled attempting to recruit on the southern New Hebridean island of Tanna. As he talked to the possible candidates they asked if there were any Aobans on his vessel as they were anxious to 'get at' any that he had. In the previous year a party of Tanna natives returning from Queensland had been lured from a recruiting ship anchored off Aoba. As the ship's crew attempted to recruit on the island, the Aobans persuaded the Tannamen to disembark by holding out the inducement of unlimited women, free of charge. The Tannese had disappeared and were said to have been killed and eaten by the Aobans. Now the Tannese were vowing vengeance on any Aoban they could find.

On 3 November 1878 the *Heather Belle* anchored off the north-west coast of Aoba opposite the village of Longana. The ship's boat went ashore to trade for provisions and to test their reception. Many natives came down to the shore, appearing friendly and bringing yams to the boat; they were paid in tobacco and beads. Significantly, women also appeared which was always regarded as a sign of friendly intentions. As a judicial enquiry later reported, one of the crew watching from the ship, Robert Young A.B. insisted on going ashore, 'with the expressed purpose of having connection with a woman'. Mr Nelson, the coxswain, told him he should not go and refused him permission but, as the ship's boat started to return to the *Heather Belle* laden with produce, Young ridiculed the danger, jumped overboard and swam towards the shore. The crew stopped rowing and watched Young disappear up the beach. About five minutes afterwards, without any cause, the natives opened fire on the boat which retreated post-haste back to the *Heather Belle*. The crew waited all day for Young to return, knowing full well that the gesture was hopeless. Next morning the ship sailed for Fiji.

Three weeks earlier Jack Renton had set out on his seventh journey as a government agent on the *Mystery*, leaving Port Mackay in Queensland with twenty-eight returnees bound for the New Hebrides. Through October they landed the men on Tanna Island in the south of the archipelago and, according to his log, they encountered the recruiting ship *Sybel* where he met a returnee bound for Malaita to whom he gave a present for Kabou. After landing another fourteen returnees on Malekula, the *Mystery* sailed on to Aoba.

On 4 November the boat lay off the north-west shore of the island. Renton's log records that he went ashore with a boat's crew and was met by several natives, two of whom were known to the crew as the ship had brought them back from Queensland the previous year. Although they were unable to be specific, the two men told Renton of an incident involving a white man and agreed to take the *Mystery* to Longana. Renton's log records:

Arriving there the natives were afraid to come near us, hiding themselves behind rocks, each armed with a musket, and bows and arrows. Sent one of the natives ashore to enquire about the incident. He returned and informed us that they had shot a white man immediately after he landed yesterday. 9 a.m. Returned on board the brig and informed Captain Daly concerning the man. On shore several times during this day; got two recruits, natives very friendly.'

For the next three days the *Mystery* made slow progress up and down the west coast of Aoba gathering recruits and trying unsuccessfully to obtain more information about the white man's death. On 9 November the ship anchored off Longana village for the second time. Billy Lifu was a member of the ship's crew. Ten years later he recounted what happened next. As was usual, two ship's boats set out for the beach. In the first boat sat the recruiter as it backed onto the beach. In the second, covering boat, sat the government agent, Jack Renton. Billy Lifu was steering.

A native asked the recruiter why the second boat didn't come ashore also, saying that it wasn't the custom here for one boat to stand off. The recruiter called to me to bring it to the beach. I called back, 'Don't you savvy, these men want a fight?' The recruiter said, 'Back in and don't be an old woman.' So I brought the boat up to the beach. I remember saying to another of the crew, a friend of mine, in our own language, 'You look out, George, I think these Aoba men want to make trouble for us. The master does not savvy them.' As we made towards the beach Mr Renton said nothing.

205

As soon as the boat touched the beach the Aoba men fell on us with axes and clubs, going for the white men first. I called for everyone to jump into the sea. George followed but left three fingers behind in the boat, severed by an axe blow as he gripped the gunwale while jumping. I went over the bows, but before I reached the water someone launched a tomahawk at me and as I dived, it stuck fast in my back.

George and I were good swimmers and we made for the *Mystery*; George without some of his fingers and me with an axe in my back. Presently we could see puffs of smoke from the beach, the Aobans had got the rifles from the ship's boats and were firing at us. Then two of them came after us in a canoe, armed with axes. As they came close, George and I formed a plan. As they reached us we dived, came up under the canoe and capsized it. The Aoba men were bad swimmers; we had them at a disadvantage. We throttled and bit them and held them under until they drowned. Then we righted the canoe, baled it out, picked up the paddles and made for the *Mystery*.

The axe was still in Billy Lifu's back when he arrived on board. When it was removed, the wound was found to be a clean one and it healed quickly. He kept the axe as a souvenir. Jack Renton, the mate, Thomas Muir, and three of the boat's crew were murdered. What then happened to their bodies provides a grotesque postscript but one that, given Renton's unique understanding of Pacific culture, would have come as no surprise to him.

By the late 1870s, those who had gone to Queensland returned to their villages with their trade goods and weaponry to find that their payment for three years labour in the cane fields was no longer a symbol of instant status – recruiters had now been active for over a decade. Crucially, those who returned had lost at least three years seniority in the grade-taking rat race. Aratunga, who had lured Renton and the others to the shore, was one such man. Short on pigs to sacrifice, he merely reverted to an earlier practice. With the killing and the forthcoming cannibalism of white men, Aratunga instantly transformed his status.

There was another powerful reason for this ritual, one that was present in many societies that practised cannibalism, namely the belief that by consuming enemy flesh one assimilates the *mana* of another individual's power into one's own. As an anthropologist who lived with the Liverpool River aborigines at the end of the nineteenth century observed:

> they did not kill men for food. They ate human flesh largely from superstitious beliefs. If they killed a worthy man in battle, they ate his heart believing they would inherit his valour and power. They ate his brain because they knew it represented the seat of his knowledge. If they killed a fast runner, they ate part of his legs, hoping whereby to acquire his speed.

On the evening of 9 November, a few hours after Renton and the others had been killed, word spread to the neighbouring villages. In Longana, beside the dancing ground, six large pits were dug, about five feet deep, eight feet long and four feet wide, then lined with fire-blackened stones. Nearby was a long narrow structure housing stone platforms – the tables used for the preparing and carving of pigs, but in this case being prepared to carve up 'long pig'.

In the gathering gloom, large groups of men and women arrived from along the coast and from inland paths, summoned by the incessant beating of great upright wooden drums that surrounded the dancing ground. The rhythm, beaten on seven drums, with an extraordinary complexity and speed, was taken up by all the villages within earshot until it seemed as if the whole island was overwhelmed by a tide of nerve-shaking sound. Then the men appeared, shining with coconut oil, and began to dance. One European witness to a ritual feast on nearby Malekula described it as 'not "a dance of death" but a dance of victory. Not a dance of "savage abandon" but vigorous aggressive movements repeated in one pattern over and over again, with chants improvized now by one, now by another, telling the story of the victory, down to the minute detail which only people without writing can attain.'

Some dancers began filling the pits with wood and soon six fires illuminated the dancing ground. Then the women joined in. With whoops of triumph they gathered piles of stones and timber and started throwing them into the roaring pits. Then as Aratunga walked into the middle of the dancing ground, the drums were silenced. He shouted an invocation and from the darkness emerged a procession of young men. Two by two they entered, each pair carrying a bamboo pole under which hung a body tied by its wrists and ankles. The arena remained silent as each was suspended by his legs upon crossbeams placed round the dancing ground between the drums.

When the hanging was complete, Aratunga stepped forward holding a sharp-edged hardwood club shaped like a paddle. He walked towards Renton's body and struck the ribcage. At that moment a roar went up, the drums started beating and the dancers re-emerged carrying clubs and sticks. As they danced round they struck the bodies to the roars and chants of the onlookers. Soon all the bones were broken. The dancing continued as the women came forward. They detached the bodies from the crossbeams and carried them to the hut where they laid them on the slabs.

The bodies were disembowelled and beheaded, then thoroughly cleaned and filled with breadfruit, bananas, yams and taro roots. The heart and liver were placed on the chest and the whole body was wrapped in banana leaves. Other women then removed the hot stones from the pits, using bamboo rakes and paddle-shaped shovels. As the dancing continued the covered corpses were lowered into the pits, together with pigs similarly prepared for those men who had never killed. To the roar of conch shells the hot stones were shovelled back into the pits. Then the women joined the dancing and, as they passed the pits, they threw the entrails of the victims into the flames.

The dancing continued as the bodies cooked – Renton, Muir, the three oarsmen from *Mystery* and Young from the *Heather Belle*. After a number of hours a group of women assembled around the pits and with huge brushes made from palm leaves, swept the smouldering embers off the stones. The top layer was then removed and the roasts lifted out with long curved poles and carried to the stone slabs in the cookhouse.

The charred banana leaf wrappings were removed, displaying the reddish brown, steaming bodies of 'long pig'. Under the supervision of Aratunga the bodies were cut up and, as each portion of the human body carried a ritual and hierarchical significance, considerable care was taken in the apportioning of cuts. Outside everyone stood in silence, their banana-leaf napkins poised. The women did the serving. The choice cuts, upper and lower forearms, were served to the assembled village chiefs; hearts, livers and cuts of thigh to warriors of the senior grades. The inner part of the thigh and the head, regarded as the greatest delicacies, were parcelled up ready to be taken back to the villages of the most senior guests.[1]

For the assembled guests a small helping was enough. Human meat is a very filling food and, however much a guest might dislike the taste, none would refuse as the meat carried transubstantive power and raised the donor ever higher on the graded ladder. And as with all activities related to grade-taking, those with choice cuts now had the duty to reciprocate or lose face. The impact of Aratunga's Aoban grade-taking was to be felt by both communities, black and white, for years to come.

The colonial authorities could not ignore the loss of a man who was regarded as one of their most diligent agents. HMS *Wolverine* under Commodore John Wilson was sent to investigate. With his guns trained on Longana and after much equivocation Aratunga gave himself up. For the local chiefs, obligated to him through his gifts of the choice cuts, the *nimangki*, this act merely increased their loss of face. For Wilson the question now arose of how to punish his prisoner and what punishment would be appropriate for the village. He had no idea of the intricacies of *kustom* life and Aratunga was in no mood to explain, merely stating that the killings were a revenge attack for ten men who had been kidnapped by recruiters years previously.

Wilson was not prepared to take responsibility and naively concluded that the village should be fined a certain number of pigs and that they themselves should be responsible for the formal execution of Aratunga. However, nature intervened and a monsoonal storm brewed up overnight, which prevented the *Wolverine* from landing their prisoner back on the island. Wilson was now forced to take the only other route open to him. He sailed to Fiji, the seat of British judicial authority in the Pacific.

After eighteen months in jail, Aratunga was brought before the High Commission Court. Judge Gorrie decided that as no single individual could be held responsible for a crime in which the whole community had participated it followed that the prisoner's position had been akin 'to that of a common soldier obeying orders from his superiors . . . I cannot therefore in such circumstances look upon the act of Aratunga who is not a chief . . . as separable from that of a hostile band . . . he must therefore be discharged.'

Back on Aoba, where none of the British authorities had attempted to inform the natives of Aratunga's incarceration, or the fact that he was awaiting trial, the assumption was that he had been executed. The loss of face for Aratunga's sponsors, Chiefs Sikiri and Ko-Wari, was considerable. They had accepted the choice cuts of the murdered white men and then allowed Aratunga to be surrendered up to the British. In an effort to shore up his authority, Sikiri led a war party to another part of the island and attacked a trading post, killing a white trader called Johnson while he slept. Johnson's partner, Chaffin, who was absent at the time, expected the British to take action and, in a letter to the Admiralty, indirectly blamed Commodore Wilson for the death: 'The reason they have for killing Johnson is on account of the man-of-war, taking Aratogo [sic] away, one of the murderers of the *Mystery* boat's crew. The Commodore failed to do what he must have known was his duty. He should have hung the murderers on Aoba.'

211

The British authorities now had to deal with the problem of avenging Johnson's murder. Happily, it was found that Johnson was an American subject and the question then arose as to 'whether we should take cognisance of the case or leave it to an American man-of-war'. They chose the latter and as the American Pacific naval station was two thousand miles to the north-east in Hawaii the matter was laid to rest.

Chaffin, an American citizen himself, was enraged by this supine attitude and decided to take matters in hand. Not being a British citizen he reasoned that he could hardly be arrested if he meted out his own justice. As the wheels of the colonial bureaucracy ground on another few months, Commodore Wilson received 'a private letter' from an anonymous correspondent:

> Mr Chaffin, seeing that nothing was being done to punish the natives for the murder of his partner, resolved to take the law into his own hands. He accordingly wound up his own business at Leper's Island [Aoba] where he had a trading station, and went on board his vessel to live. His object was, before leaving the place, to entice the chief who had murdered his partner on board, in which after some little time he was successful. One day the chief, accompanied by a party of natives, went unsuspectingly on board the vessel, and while talking to Mr Chaffin the latter took out a revolver, placed it to the chief's head and blew his brains out. The other natives at once jumped overboard, but Mr Chaffin quieted them by saying he would do no more, that he had avenged the death of his partner, which was all that he wanted.

Three years after Renton's death Aratunga was back in Aoba and, under the implacable rules of grade-taking, the major recipients of the choice cuts were bound to act. In August that year three of them organized the ambush of a ship's party from the recruiting vessel the *May Queen*. Nine crew members were massacred, including, unsurprisingly, its government agent. A report duly arrived on Commodore Wilson's desk expressing some mystification, as it appeared that the *May Queen* had done absolutely nothing to provoke the attack. McDonald, the government agent, had the reputation for being 'a quite inoffensive fellow'. Aratunga was duly presented with the choicest cuts.

The last two paragraphs of a missionary's letter to the *Melbourne Argus* must serve as a suitable envoi to the whole wretched affair, for Able Seaman Young and the victim of his stupidity, Jack Renton.

I have known a considerable number of white men who have been killed by natives whilst engaged in this trade, and while deploring their sad end, and regretting that they should have been cut down in the midst of their wickedness, I have in sober seriousness to express my decided conviction that most of them were men the cup of whose iniquity was full, and they suffered the due reward for their deeds.

Others, again, were men who had done no injury to the natives, but upon whom the natives took revenge for the evil deeds of their countrymen.

11

Beachcombers and Castaways

———— ⊐ ○ ⊏ ————

IN July 1879 a recruiting ship moored off the reef opposite the village of Sulufou. Island history takes up the story:

The captain was rowed to the village with an interpreter. When he landed he asked to see Kabou alone and was taken to his house. The people gathered round but no one was allowed to go inside. The captain told him that Jack Renton had been killed on Aoba. Kabou said nothing for a long time. Then he asked the captain if he could take him there with a few men so that they could pay their respects. Of course Kabou wanted to avenge the death of his boy and the captain probably guessed that. He told Kabou that Aoba was too far away and that anyway, he had orders to stay in the Solomons.

When the captain left, Kabou wept and wept. He was desperate to go to Aoba but everyone said it was too far – miles across the open sea, and that they would all die if they tried. Kabou mourned for many days. He allowed his hair to grow and refused to wash or eat. The other members of the family did the same. They did nothing but grieve, no eating, no fishing, no gardening – nothing.

For many days everyone in the village sat quietly and mourned for Renton. No one worked or fished, they ate pigs and taro and everyone was quiet and sorrowful. Other chiefs came, also men from along the coast and from inland and they sat with Kabou. He said it was as if his first-born son had died. All those who visited him pledged that they would not wash or cut their hair until he did.

Finally, after three weeks, Kabou led a procession of villagers into the bush where Jack Renton used to wash – it has always been known as 'Renton's Pool'. As he stepped in, a great shout of grief went up from all the people present and as he washed, he wept. The news spread to all the surrounding villages and that day thousands of men bathed and cut their hair. That evening, all came to Sulufou with offerings, and three hundred pigs were killed. The eating and the dancing and the telling stories of Renton's deeds went on for three days. But it is said that Kabou grieved for three years after the death of Jack Renton.

They made a memorial shrine, a tabu place, of the hut where Renton had lived. In it, they placed his fishing nets and taro sticks and the other possessions he had left behind. It remained standing until it was burned down in 1968.

Renton's own account not only mentioned no 'deeds' but also managed to erase any information about the last three years of his exile. Apart from his arrival and departure, there is only one other date that it is possible to confirm – the visit made by HMS *Basilisk* to Leli 'bringing back some natives, kidnapped by Fiji slavers' (the survivors of the *Carl*). The date was in March 1872. Two paragraphs later, 'about two months after the vessel left' the *Bobtail Nag* arrived – the date, June 1875. From the somewhat sketchy oral history of this period it is clear that his reputation rests upon his activities during these three 'lost' years.

In the 1890s the recruiter Jock Cromer befriended Kwaisulia and was shown many of the innovations Renton made in the design of war canoes and was told how, under his guidance, raiding changed from chaotic hit-and-run affairs to small groups fighting under a disciplined command co-ordinated by basic field signalling. His reputation was further enhanced not just because of his abilities as a killer but by the fact that he was never wounded. Believed to be blessed with an inviolable *mana*, oral history claims that he was initiated into the priesthood by Kabou. Innovator, warrior, strategist, counsellor; these were stories of a man so special that his hut was turned into a shrine.

Renton was one of the last in a long line of white men who, over the previous century, had found themselves in a corner of the world in which they had been forced to re-invent themselves in order to survive. For many of those who made a deliberate choice, these islands offered them status and opportunities undreamed of in the world they had left behind. In 1842 Herman Melville, himself recently rescued after his voluntary exile in the Typee valley in the Marquesas, met just such a man on a nearby island. As Melville's ship anchored in the bay, a canoe drew alongside, paddled by a group of young natives. Sitting in a regal chair in the stern was an Englishman, tattooed from head to foot. Melville, having recently toyed with the idea of never returning to civilization was both appalled and fascinated by a man who had gone more 'native' than he would ever have contemplated.

Liam Hardy explained that he had jumped ship ten years earlier and was the only white man on the island. Unlike the virtually bereft Jack Renton, Hardy had gone ashore with an insurance policy, a musket, a bag of powder and some shot. He discovered an island divided among several tribes, each confined to their own valley and constantly at war with their neighbours. Hardy seized his opportunity and placed himself at the service of the chief of the tribe who had found him. After a few months he was proficient in the language and set about training a war party. In a bold night attack, armed with his musket, they attacked two of the surrounding valleys. The opposition surrendered, stunned more by the noise than the effects of his firearm. During the following two days the rest of the island surrendered to his patron. His reward was the chief's daughter, four hundred pigs and ten houses. In England, he was an ordinary seaman, born and brought up in a workhouse. Here, he was warlord of the entire island. 'And for the most part', Melville wrote in *Omoo*, 'it is just this sort of man – so many of whom are found among sailors – uncared for by a single soul, without ties, reckless, and impatient of the restraints of civilization, who are occasionally found quite at home upon the savage islands of the Pacific. And, glancing at their hard lot in their own country, who can quibble at their choice?'

They were not missionaries, traders or the representatives of colonial powers, but a group of people who became known as beachcombers and later as castaways. Eighty years before Renton was washed up on Malaita the prerequisites for successful beachcombing had already been established. In 1783 the East India Company packet *Antelope* was wrecked in the Palau group between the Philippines and New Guinea, where her crew lived for several months. They established some basic rules: namely, they treated the islanders with friendship and respect as equals, their chiefs were afforded the courtesy due to their rank, they took great pains to avoid any conduct that might offend the local norms of behaviour and, perhaps crucially, they placed themselves and their firearms at the service of their hosts in a number of successful skirmishes. As a result they were treated with kindness and consideration and kept liberally supplied with all the provisions and luxuries that it was possible to provide.

When the *Antelope*'s crew finally sailed for China in a small vessel made from the wreck, several muskets were left behind to maintain the newly secured balance of power. Seven years later, the East India Company sent Captain McCluer to Palau to take presents to the islanders in return for their kindness to the castaways. The captain fell in love with the island and became the first of the gentlemen beachcombers. He remained on Palau for the rest of his life, maintaining a considerable retinue of women to look after his island-born children.

The establishment of a penal colony in the South-West Pacific led to an explosion in the population of voluntary beachcombers throughout the islands. Most escaped by seizing any craft that would float and, as early as 1790, a party of convicts on Norfolk Island, planning to form a settlement on Tahiti, seized the armed tender *Supply*. Over the next twenty years dozens of attempts were made, eleven of them successful.

However, it was the establishment, near Sydney, of the whaling station of Port Jackson to serve the growing American presence in the Pacific that provided the most opportunities, particularly as these ships had few inhibitions about assisting convicts to escape. Twenty years after the first transports had arrived, and still showing a lively interest in the colony he had been partially responsible for, Joseph Banks complained that 'the mischief the Americans have done by stealing convicts from Sydney is almost unbelievable.'

The American whaler *Otter* landed the first beachcombers on Tonga – seventeen convicts from Sydney. As a later commentator would point out, 'it would be naive to suppose that they could all secrete themselves in such a boat without the captain's connivance.' Two years later the *General Oats* took another ten to Tahiti with the captain's active assistance. Back in Sydney, attempts at prevention included a pass for all convicts working on ships in the harbour, regular searches and, with the consent of the captain [which was seldom granted], smoking the holds before departure. Many were caught but others succeeded and, once clear of land, few captains were going to turn back simply because a stowaway had been discovered on board. American anti-colonial feeling ran high and once the stowaway had been discovered he became part of the community below decks. One English convict, Joseph Harris, remained hidden on the American whaler *Caroline* for three months before the captain discovered him.

Cook's deputy Captain Clerk may have fulminated against their crews for being 'infernal and dissolute' but, compared with those that were to follow, at least they were experienced seamen. By the 1830s whaling dominated Pacific maritime activity and by 1840 the American whaling fleet alone numbered 652 ships. The average voyage lasted forty months and shipboard conditions were dreadful. The seamen endured appalling food, cramped, rat-infested living quarters and a shipboard regime of calculated brutality. Unpaid until the end of the voyage, each crew member contracted for a 'lay', a fractional share of the proceeds of the voyage. The owners, almost without exception, would grossly undervalue the cargo of the returning ship, while at the same time overcharging the crew for any purchases made from the ship's stores. A green seaman shipping out on his first voyage might be put down for as little as one two-hundredth of a share, with his compensation averaging out at $300 for three to four years labour at sea. Not surprisingly, most sailors shipping out on these whalers were green, as few professional seamen would accept such pay and conditions. The result of low pay and miserable working conditions was that by the 1840s, of the 18,000 men in the Pacific whaling fleet, one half were greenhorns and more than two-thirds of them deserted every voyage. Many, like Melville and his shipmate Tobias Green, took their chances far from the shores of civilization.

The numbers were augmented by others like Renton, shanghaied or pressed into service against their will, or those like the crew member of the *Delta* who found himself dumped, fever-ridden and moribund on some alien shore. Still more were the victims of shipboard disputes summarily abandoned on a beach like the unfortunate Thomas Aaron, 'with a bag of bread and a pistol without a lock to it'.

North-east from Sydney to New Caledonia, then two thousand miles due east to Fiji and Samoa, north-east again through the Society Islands and Tahiti, then due north through Taumotu and the Marquesas and onwards for another two thousand miles to Hawaii – by the 1830s a population of over fifteen hundred beachcombers were exerting an influence on every aspect of the islanders' lives. For centuries these communities had been highly receptive to the assimilation of immigrants. The island world had never been a closed one and, long before the arrival of the white man, canoes had brought visitors to all but the most remote islands; some by accident, others by design and on each island there existed a succession of rituals that acknowledged the individual's developing integration into their adopted community. It was only in the Solomons and the non-Polynesian islands of the New Hebrides, where all strangers were regarded either as fresh meat or as disease-carriers, that the beachcomber stood little chance of survival. It is probably no accident that the only recorded instance of a beachcomber surviving on the Solomon Islands should be in a village that had had prior experience of the very practical advantages of having a white man living in their midst. Jack Renton had a lot to thank Doorey for.

The inhabitants of these islands quickly realized that the white man was not some supernatural being but a human like himself. If they had harboured any illusions these were soon disabused by the behaviour of the average ship's crew, which suggested, certainly to the Tahitians, a shortage of women in their home country, particularly as it was apparent that there were none on board their ships. At first this race, clearly superior in material goods, was apt to be treated like some exotic curiosity and the status symbol of the local chief. Much to John Jackson's embarrassment he became the *manu manu* or the 'pet bird' of a Hawaiian chief who took him on tour, exhibiting his new possession like some bearded woman or two-headed calf.

Others, in accounts very similar to Renton's early days, found themselves co-opted as retainers whose primary purpose was to confer prestige on their protector. John Twyning was a steersman on a whaler wrecked on a reef in the Tonga group in 1830 where he was 'adopted' by a local chief. 'If he went out to hunt or shoot, I accompanied him, and I was employed to cater for his every need.' One task involved shaving his master – a hazardous undertaking owing to the risks involved in shedding blood. For the beachcomber life was precarious until he had, by some means or other, earned himself immunity by demonstrating his indispensability.

However, it wasn't long before the white man came to be valued for more practical reasons – his ability to look after and repair the numerous European articles that were beginning to find their way onto the islands. The nails, spikes and hoop iron of the early encounters needed fashioning into tools, while the hardware that took its place – the axes, knives, files, hoes, scissors, pots and pans – needed constant sharpening and repairing. In this rush towards the iron age, chiefs would go to considerable lengths to secure the services of ship's artisans by using their most potent inducement – sex. Captain Turnbull, on a cruise through the Hawaiian Islands in 1802, complained that 'nothing can withstand the seduction and artifices of the southern islanders; women, and a life of indolence, are too powerful for the sense of duty in the minds of our seamen. Had we relaxed our efforts for a single moment, the ship would have been deserted.' Even so, one Hawaiian chief managed to smuggle the ship's carpenter on shore where he joined a burgeoning colony of masons, blacksmiths, brick-makers, shipwrights and sailmakers already in his service.

These beachcombers performed a service that was of greater value to the islanders than any offered by subsequent visitors.

Most of them had learned their trade through apprenticeship and they warmed instinctively to the task of passing on their skills. They left a legacy of innumerable native craftsmen, able to turn their hands to anything from boat-building to mending a flintlock. As Renton was remembered for improvements he made to the islanders' own technologies, so too were other beachcombers remembered for introducing better tactics in warfare, new techniques for sailing canoes into the wind, the introduction of wooden bailing pumps for canoes, and new techniques for plaiting pandanus leaves.

'It is astonishing', wrote a ship's captain of the Hawaiians as early as 1808, 'how soon they acquire the useful arts from their visitors. Many of the natives are employed as carpenters, coopers, blacksmiths and tailors, and do their work as perfectly as the Europeans. In the king's force there are none but native blacksmiths; they had been taught by the armourer of a ship who quitted the island while I was there.'

There were some, however, that balked at giving too much away, fearing that they would make themselves redundant. The head carpenter of a Hawaiian chief refused to make a loom. Another protested at plans to teach his employer's brother to read, fearing that 'they will soon know more than ourselves.' However, William Mariner, advisor and confidant of the Tongan chief Finau, found that a demonstration of the advantages of literacy elicited a completely different response. Asked by his employer to write on a piece of paper, Mariner accordingly wrote the word 'Finau'. Then, ordering Mariner to turn his back, the chief took the piece of paper to another beachcomber and asked him what it said. The man glanced at it and replied, 'Finau.' The chief was astonished. He snatched the paper back, inspected it closely, and after turning it round and round, announced: 'This is neither like myself or anybody else! Where are my legs? How do you know it to be me?' After further demonstrations the penny gradually dropped. After some considerable thought, Finau decided that such an innovation had little to recommend it. 'Besides,' he announced, 'there would be nothing but disturbance and conspiracies, and I could not be sure of my life for another month.'

If the material culture and the white man's communication techniques were a source of fascination to the islanders, the white man's economic system completely baffled them. As the crew of the wrecked *Matilda* struggled ashore on Tahiti, to replace the recently arrested *Bounty* mutineers, they were relieved of all their possessions, including the most precious – a bag of dollars. Despite the *Bounty*'s visit, communication between the two parties was still very basic, though it was clear to the Tahitians from the behaviour of the new arrivals that they attached enormous importance to this bag. Noticing this, they duly attempted to convert the dollars into fish-hooks and earrings but, to the despair of their visitors, having eventually pronounced the objects to be absolutely useless, played ducks and drakes with them on the surface of Matavi Bay.

If money was regarded as an irrelevance, the same cannot be said of the islanders' reaction to firearms. This weapon changed everything. As James Beaglehole commented: 'The rise of pocket-Napoleons was implicit in the first sight of a musket on an island shore', and the reasons were the same everywhere. For centuries the islanders had lived in a cultural isolation in which a balance had been struck between the means of offence and defence. Total victory was a technological impossibility and, as a result, no one group could dominate the political landscape. Now there was a new offensive weapon against which there was no adequate defence and ambitious men dreamed of domination. But, as they soon discovered, these weapons were of little use without people schooled in their use and maintenance. In Fiji, evidence of the destructive power of this new technology became apparent when the schooner *Argo* was wrecked in 1800 on a voyage from China to Port Jackson. The natives salvaged a barrel containing a powdered substance, which they mixed with water and applied as body paint. When they attempted to dry themselves beside a fire the result was carnage.

If Renton's achievement was unique, in that his power and prestige were earned by using the tools and weapons of an already existing culture, the careers of other beachcombers were based almost entirely on their identification with this new technology. William Mariner's four-year exile on Tonga had spectacular and lasting effects.

These islanders had had a very early demonstration of the capacity for destruction that the Europeans were capable of. In the 1770s Cook had been captivated by the generosity of the islanders. Showered with gifts of food, handed over in formal presentations and accompanied by spectacular ritual, Cook was particularly taken by the beaming smiles of the avuncular and portly aristocracy. Reciprocal shipboard hospitality had included a demonstration of firearms and cannon that had been greeted with many smiles and compliments. Cook was so delighted that he named his discovery the Friendly Islands and visited there on three occasions. On the final night of his last visit, as he and his officers were enjoying a Tongan feast, a dozen chiefs were conspiring to murder them and seize the ship. The plan was only thwarted by their inability to muster a large enough war party before Cook left and he sailed away to the smiles and pledges of eternal friendship without ever suspecting how close he had come to death. The Friendly Islanders bided their time.

Twenty years later, their 'gift from the gods' limped into the same bay. She seemed huge – a 500-ton, three-masted British square-rigger, crewed by eighty-five men and carrying twenty-four cannons and eight carronades. The captain of the *Port au Prince* was desperate. Through Hawaiian interpreters he explained that he was shipping water at the rate of nineteen feet a day and needed to beach his vessel as soon as possible to caulk its seams. Cook's appellation appeared to be immediately confirmed as Captain Brown welcomed on board several chiefs and warriors bearing gifts of a large barbecued hog, cooked yams, fresh fruits and a retinue of young women to serve the crew. Finau, chief of Livuka, was introduced and assured the captain that he would find only hospitable people and an abundance of all that the crew would wish for. Finau and his party then departed, leaving Brown without an answer to his urgent request but having assured him that they would return next day.

The following morning the Tongans watched from various points around the bay as the ship's crew started to melt away in anticipation of the promised delights ashore. The Hawaiian interpreters lead the exodus, though for a rather different reason, having been advised by the Tongans that they would be much safer if they spent the next few days as their guests. By midday, shore-based calculations put the number of ship's crew still on board the *Port au Prince* at less than thirty. From the beaches and inlets surrounding the bay, an armada of canoes made their way slowly towards the stricken ship. Three hundred armed Tongans crowded on board. Brown was escorted ashore by a group of chiefs to discuss the details of his request, still convinced of their goodwill. He had been so wedded to Cook's impressions of these people that prior to the previous evening's shipboard feast, he had ordered all the muskets and boarding spikes to be stored below.

As he walked up the beach, the welcoming party clubbed him to death. As soon as the first warclub was raised the Tongans aboard the *Port au Prince* set about the remaining crew members. It was all over in less than two minutes. The Tongans went below to inspect their prize. As they entered the captain's cabin an unarmed figure walked slowly forward to face them off – it was a fifteen-year-old boy. As he was hauled up on deck William Mariner recalled: 'Upon the companionway a short squat naked figure was seated, with a seaman's jacket soaked in blood, thrown over his shoulder; on the other rested his iron-wood club, spattered with blood and brains. On the deck there lay twenty-two bodies, perfectly naked, and arranged side by side in regular order, but so dreadfully bruised and battered about their heads that only two could be recognized.'

On the beach, beside the bodies of Captain Brown and three other sailors, he was stripped of his clothes then marched to the far end of the island. As he passed through one village a woman came forward and, out of pity, gave him an apron of leaves to hide his nakedness. In the late afternoon he was taken into Finau's compound – 'As I entered the place, the women who sat at the other end of the room, beholding my deplorable condition, let out a cry of pity.' It was the start of a remarkable friendship as 'Finau had taken an extraordinary liking for me from the first moment he had seen me aboard the *Port au Prince* the night before. He thought I was the Captain's son, or at least a young chief of some consequence in my own country.'

The son of a wealthy London shipowner, Mariner had persuaded his father to allow him to spend a 'gap year' at sea prior to going on to higher education. Certainly by Regency standards, Mariner was a young man 'of some consequence' – and it probably showed. If the impression of dignity and poise were the most obvious factors in his favour (two qualities that the Tongans held in high esteem), fate also played a large part. Finau's first-born son had died when he was Mariner's age and Finau virtually adopted the young man, giving him the same name as his dead son – 'Iron Axe'. Finally, like all successful nineteenth-century leaders in the South Pacific, Finau was a pragmatist and needed an educated and pliant European to help him realize his ambitions.

The process of grooming Mariner proceeded apace as Finau appointed one of his wives to be the boy's Tongan mother. This remarkable woman tutored him in all aspects of Tongan society and culture and within a few months he was fluent in its language, customs and manners. This father-son relationship was remarkably similar to Kabou and Renton's, though due to the ordnance on board the *Port au Prince*, its impact on the surrounding islands was to be considerably more explosive.

In the aftermath of the seizing of the ship, most of the survivors were transported to other islands. The rest, who numbered about half a dozen, were housed in a separate compound and barred from court life. They were happy to defer to Mariner, seeing his status as an insurance policy. He, despite his age, was enough of a realist to understand the predicament that faced them all. 'The oven,' he recalled, 'was a great persuader.'

Their first task, together with the Hawaiian interpreters who had emerged somewhat shamefacedly after the killing was over, was to sail the *Port au Prince* through a reef and beach her. For the next few days the Tongans swarmed over the ship, stripping her of iron. Finau's prize, the ordnance, was left to the Europeans to salvage, although he insisted that he wanted the cannons. Mariner prevaricated and attempted to point out the obvious but Finau would have none of it. However, after they had hoisted one of them onto the shore where it lay like a beached seal, Finau grasped the problem and settled for the shorter, lighter carronades. Then, in a series of spectacular explosions, the Tongans torched the ship and set about salvaging the nails.

Invited on a rat-hunting expedition to a nearby island, Mariner watched and listened as Finau, with much arm waving and rudimentary sign language, outlined his ambitions to subdue his neighbours and unite them under his rule. Mariner was to take responsibility for the Europeans and the weaponry. Six months later a dozen Europeans, led by Mariner, found themselves part of an armada of 170 war canoes carrying five thousand warriors. Finau had decided to invade the island of Tongatapu, seventy miles to the north-east. Sitting on the brow of a hill overlooking the sea, the vast moated fortress of Nuku'alofa was virtually impregnable. For decades, the traditional Tongan siege methods, which involved little more than successive frontal assaults, had ended in failure.

Mariner had the carronades, shot and powder brought ashore. After a predictably inconclusive initial skirmish involving a few hundred of Finau's warriors, he ordered Mariner to show what he could do. The carronades pounded away leaving neat circular holes in the bamboo lattice surrounding the main redoubt. Finau, expecting a conflagration on the scale of the *Port au Prince*, was appalled. Mariner attempted to convince him that there would be carnage inside but Finau was not convinced. The cannonade continued until there was no shot left.

As Finau's army advanced, they met little resistance and took the outer defences with ease. Torches were lit and flung over the wall of the inner compound where the flames spread quickly from building to building. A breach was made in the flimsy latticework and Finau's men poured through. The most formidable fortress in all the islands had fallen in a few hours. When he entered the battle area, Finau was stunned by the carnage that Mariner's weapons had inflicted. Heads, arms and legs littered the compound, almost four hundred defenders had been killed by the cannonade and an equal number of wounded were now being dispatched by Finau's victorious warriors.

That evening, a victory celebration was held. Numerous captives were clubbed to death, their bodies quartered, washed in salted water, wrapped in banana leaves then cooked in a long line of earth ovens. Much to Finau's embarrassment, the Europeans refused all his entreaties to share in the victory feast. Whilst they fasted, canoes were dispatched to Livuka to bring acceptable provisions for the architects of the victory, a round trip that took three days.

The campaign moved on to the northern island of Vava'u. Word had spread and hastily constructed clay embankments now surrounded the fort at Feletoa. But, as Mariner set up the carronades, he was astonished to see the enemy massing *in front* of the embankments. To his frustration, Finau refused to allow him to fire upon the enemy until they had retreated behind their fortifications, contending, in Mariner's words: 'that these guns gave him too great an advantage, such as he scorned to take; that it was more honourable to fight them man to man than to use against them arms that were rather fitted for the hostilities of spirits than of man.'

The point, however, had been made. The sight of cannons, muskets, a platoon of Europeans and the reports of the blood-bath in Tongatapu were enough to convince the defenders to sue for peace. Finau, now recognized as the supreme chief of the Tongan Islands, granted Mariner large estates on the island of Vava'u and a personal retinue of fourteen men and eight women. The teenager's final year in the islands was relatively uneventful; he travelled widely and bided his time. A ship eventually appeared and his escape was every bit as dramatic as Jack Renton's – and for exactly the same reason, a marked reluctance on the part of his hosts to let him go.

Back in London he returned seamlessly to his old life, working in his father's firm as a commodity broker. Then, six years after he had been rescued, London booksellers began displaying a two-volume set with the lengthy title, *An Account of the Natives of the Tonga Islands in the South Pacific with an Original Grammar and Vocabulary of Their Language.* By the standards of 1816 it was a bestseller, running to several editions and remains a classic not simply because of the account of his adventures, remarkable though they were, but because the second volume is the first piece of ethnography written in the English language. It is a little gem, an epitome of pre-contact Tongan society. Wide-ranging and non-judgemental, it describes the social structure, material culture, the economy, religion, customary observances and contains a grammar and dictionary of the language. Mariner's curiosity had been insatiable; he had gathered up a mass of facts, retained them and interpreted them. Being a teenager, he had assimilated Tongan culture as naturally as he would his own and it is unlikely that any other European in the Pacific islands achieved the equivalent degree of identification and acceptance within a host culture – apart from Renton. As acceptance was, more often than not, dependent upon an outsider's capacity to engage in the primary activity of men, namely warfare, Mariner was fortunate that he could earn his spurs as a killer using a method acceptable to nineteenth-century readers. Jack Renton was in a rather more difficult position.

Mariner's book is the prime example of a genre – the beach-comber memoir. They were accounts by people who had spent months and often years with their hosts, people, who had been adopted into island families, often married native wives, were fluent in the language and had fully participated in island life. Five of these books contain the first grammars and vocabularies of island languages and all paint a vivid and intimate picture of island life at a time when they were virtually untouched by western society. Explorers may have passed through, and a number write perceptively about their encounters, but their visits were brief, communication was difficult and they describe societies in the throes of an earth-shattering event, namely their arrival. Subsequent accounts by missionaries, naval officers and traders are invariably Eurocentric, devoid of information about numerous aspects of native life to which they were never privy and all are informed by the bias of their particular purposes.

The beachcomber memoirs are not just unique testimony to societies soon to disappear under the tidal wave of white contact, but are written in the spirit of genuine affection and respect for the people with whom the authors lived. Those that were to follow would bring with them tensions, conflicts, exile and death as they interfered with island economies, destroyed their religions, demanded their labour and stole their lands. Only the beachcomber afforded the islanders the respect that they were due and wished to change nothing.

There is one other feature that all these accounts have in common; an absence of any hinterland, any sense of what the experience must have been like for the authors personally. This is not a failure of style for, apart from Melville, none even attempted to convey their own feelings of fear, alienation, doubt, loss, acceptance or transformation as they gradually reinvented themselves. This absence is most keenly felt in Jack Renton's account. He, after all, had further to travel than his any of his predecessors. In a part of the world that even the convicts from Australia had given a wide berth and that had become synony-mous with cannibalism, headhunting and ritual sacrifice, Renton attempted to redress the balance. His account of Malaitan life is a unique, detailed and, as was later confirmed, a substantially accurate depiction of a Pacific island culture prior to white contact. And Renton himself spent the rest of his life attempting to mitigate the worst excesses of the process of contact that was, by then, unstoppable.

Whereas the oral history of Renton's time on the island places relationships at the centre of the narrative, in Renton's account, not only are they almost entirely absent but Kwaisulia does not exist. The only explanation for this was, paradoxically, his friend's proximity during the time of his interviews with the *Brisbane Courier*. In the most sensational chapter in the narrative, involving detailed descriptions of headhunting raids, Renton paints himself as the astonished onlooker as his companions set about the enemy. It would have been potentially disastrous for him to mention to his interviewers that one of these young men was a close friend, currently staying in Brisbane and waiting to return with him to Sulufou, particularly as Renton had equipped his friend with the rudiments of English.

Renton was remarkably adept at covering his tracks and confided in no one. He also, one suspects, believed that the real truth about his activities and his status within Malaitan society was so fantastic that even if rumours had started to circulate, no one would have believed them. How else to explain his attachment to the one piece of forensic evidence that could link him to his 'crime'? It is only after a few months in the mundane world of Stromness that he finally divests himself of these symbols of the past. To his unsuspecting family he gave his killing club and ceremonial staff and to the bank manager, his collar – the material evidence of his prowess as a killer.

Because of the sense of a life lived beyond the pale, it is tempting to make comparisons with the central character in one of the most widely read novels in the English language, Conrad's *Heart of Darkness*. But Kurtz does not go native, he does his killing from behind the sights of European weaponry and sets himself up as a god – the god of racial superiority and colonial power. Renton is an altogether different animal. Inexorably, over the years, he is drawn into a nightmare from which he is always desperate to escape and when he colludes, he does so to survive.

It is only in the style of the telling that Renton's life mirrors Kurtz's fictional one. In neither is there a feeling that the story has been fully told. Kurtz is only seen through someone else's eyes and Marlow's narrative continually gives us second-hand glimpses of the central character. There is no exploration of motive, no analysis of cause, no denouement. Kurtz, quite simply 'is' – a story told to Marlow by other people. As with Renton, there is a great silence at the heart of the story. We yearn to know what it was like for Renton but he never gives any clue, except three brief sentences in a letter to his father after he was rescued: 'Every day fighting goes on between different tribes, and they cut off each other's heads. I had to go with them. I saw dreadful sights.' He gives us no clue to 'the horror, the horror' – if, indeed, he even felt it. As the narrative unfolds he moves further and further away from us.

Kwaisulia, on the other hand, offers a completely different picture. After he meets Renton, his life is one of accelerating acculturation. He moves remorselessly into a world that becomes increasingly familiar to the reader as his story takes on all the characteristics of the protagonist in a Trollope novel, played out in an exotic location. This is the tale of a robber baron, dedicated to the accretion of wealth, power and influence, ruthlessly exploiting that bedrock of Victorian capitalism – the laws of supply and demand.

12

Kwaisulia of Ada Gege

—————— ○ ——————

EQUIPPED with passable English and fascinated with the idea of the world that Renton had described in their years together on Malaita, Kwaisulia had returned with his friend to Australia. Later he was to describe Brisbane as being 'beyond his imagination' and that nothing that Renton had told him had prepared him 'for the size of the buildings and the speed of life'. Any doubts he may have had about his future course of action were quickly dispelled during the few weeks he spent in Brisbane as the *Bobtail Nag* prepared to return to Sulufou. The more he learned of the extent of the activities of recruiting ships throughout Melanesia, the more he understood that the demands of the nascent sugar industry were about to transform his world. If his people were not to become victims of the upheavals that were already threatening, someone would have to learn about the white man's world and bring that knowledge home. When the *Bobtail Nag* returned from its official voyage,

Kwaisulia joined the ninety recruits bound for the cane fields of Rockhampton.

Life on a sugar cane plantation was a seasonal one. During the cutting and milling season labourers worked a ten-hour day. In the evenings there were songs and dances accompanied by concertinas, Jew's harps and tin whistles. Leisure time was spent tending private gardens, hunting, fishing, going to race meetings or visiting fellow islanders on other plantations nearby. On Saturday evenings many labourers walked miles to the nearest town, where, with money earned from moonlighting during the growing season, they drank, gambled and patronized the numerous brothels.

Although they succumbed to many of the blandishments of the white man's world, the lagoon recruits appear to have been completely impervious to the appeals of his religion. Kustom tabus were strictly observed, ancestral gods invoked and traditional rituals performed, however when it came to plantation work, they proved themselves to be particularly well suited to the demands of their white employers. They were alert, aggressive, more sensitive to personal honour than other islanders and particularly clannish but they were also well organized and used to unremitting labour. Under Kwaisulia's direction this capacity for organization came to the fore.

By the late 1870s cane cutting and processing required a high degree of organization and teamwork. During this period the central mill swarmed with labourers unloading carts, carrying heavy bundles into the millhouse and raking up the macass – the mangled stalks that had been squeezed of their sugar and were now to be used as fuel for the steam engines that crushed the cane. Central to this mechanized production were the elite gangs of cane cutters whose rate of output could be estimated in advance

Kwaisulia and his recruits earned a reputation for cutting cane to the precise volumes that the process required and at the end of their three years the plantation-owners offered to extend their contracts at an increased annual salary. Almost all refused. With a single-mindedness that mystified their white employers, their three years labour had been entirely devoted to obtaining one particular item from the white man's world and as they started the long walk back to their port of entry they carried with them the few pounds necessary to purchase the means that would transform their status, an object they had talked about and dreamed of for three years – a Tower musket.

Kwaisulia travelled with them, but only as far as the port. His command of English had made him aware of the laws of supply and demand and the indispensability of a skilled and disciplined labour force. Now he needed to understand the mechanics and the economics of labour recruiting; the rules and regulations, the strategies that captains and shipowners used to circumvent them, in short, how exactly the white man made money from this enterprise. As a 'time expired' boy he was able to travel freely and for two years he worked as an interpreter for various port authorities. It was during this time that he made contact with recruiters who, having become aware of the demand for Malaitans in the cane fields, were keen to enter into agreements – if Kwaisulia could deliver.

Kwaisulia's return to Malaita was to transform the climate and the conduct of recruiting along its north-east coast. The word quickly spread amongst the ships that here, at last, was an acculturated, English-speaking islander with a detailed knowledge of the business, someone who understood the febrile climate in which they operated and was prepared to deliver recruits on a contractual basis and free them from the constant atmosphere of insecurity and random violence that had become the norm.[1] Inevitably there were those white men who found the experience of having to deal with an articulate and intelligent black man more than they could stomach. They were particularly discomforted by his acuteness, his capacity to second-guess their motives and the anecdotes about his experiences of working for the various port authorities that revealed his knowledge of the deceit and dishonesty that underlay the whole enterprise. But by the end of the year even those whose racism made it impossible for them to deal with Kwaisulia on his terms were forced to reconsider their position.

In Sepember of 1880 the *Borealis*, at anchor near Leli Island, thirty miles south of Sulufou, was boarded early one morning and the crew massacred. It had only been seven years since the *Leli* men had returned on HMS *Basilisk* with their appalling stories of their time on the *Carl* and the *Peri*. Further afield the crew of the *Esperanza* were murdered in the Western Solomons and to round off a grim year for the labour trade, fifty miles from Maliata in the Florida Islands HMS *Sandfly* lost five of their ship's crew, including their captain.

At the beginning of the 1881 recruiting season Kwaisulia had secured alliances with a large number of inland villages who had watched with envy the coastal people displaying the benefits of the axe, the knife and the hoe. Kwaisulia promised these potential recruits complete protection as long as they dealt with 'his' ships. For the recruiters, after the bloodletting of the previous year, to have one man with authority speak for a large area was the safest and most efficient way to organize the trade. It meant that the business of recruiting could be carried out in safety throughout the year and with no risk that a native trading partner might suddenly be supplanted by some less friendly and unpredictable group.

For the recruiting ships the area of the lagoon dominated by Sulufou and Ada Gege became known as the Urassi Passage and on the beach opposite the two islands a number of footpaths from the interior converged. It was from here that over the coming years a steady stream of recruits took ship for Queensland. In return, Kwaisulia and Kabou were supplied not only with arms and ammunition but a number of items that give a good indication of Kwaisulia's acculturation – dynamite, kerosene, medicines, axes, crowbars, barbed wire, iron spikes, looking glasses, cloth, guard dogs and a range of specific building materials.

But Kwaisulia's influence was not due simply to the possession of European things or the prestige he acquired through his association with the providers, but also to the extent to which he was able to combine these new enterprises and to put them to the service of more traditional forms of power. What he learned from Renton and from his time in Queensland was now synthesized into traditional empire-building.

Faced with the monopoly of the Urassi Passage and fearful of Kabou and Kwaisulia, the rest of the lagoon agreed to tributary status in return for being allowed to provide a yearly number of recruits. Ironically, Maanaomba, the island in the north of the lagoon that had murdered Renton's three companions, was the first to accede. The following account by a recruiter from the *Fearless* gives a clear picture of Kwaisulia's way of doing business [and also of his relationship with Kabou]. The year was 1883.

Off the northern end of Malaita lay the island of Maanaomba, which was inhabited by people who appeared to have an abundance of differences in their own internal affairs, but all agreed in their detesting Kwaisulia and his chief, to whom they paid tribute.

At the time the *Fearless* was at Urassi, Kwaisulia accompanied me in my boat as interpreter and guide, and used the opportunity to remind the Maanaombans of their tributary liability. The chiefs could come and interview Kwaisulia in my boat, as it was neutral ground, which ensured the safety of both parties. Had he proceeded otherwise to Maanaomba, he would have taken with him a bodyguard of some hundred of his warriors.

I picked up Kwaisulia in the morning. The chief [Kabou] handed Kwaisulia a small bag, and we began the ten-mile pull to Maanaomba. On our arrival there the natives, seeing whom I had with me, would not approach the boats, but sent for their chiefs who in a little while made their appearance on the beach. Each of them made a speech that lasted for about twenty minutes, and I was becoming inexpressibly bored when Kwaisulia whispered to me 'Watch them shake now.'

Opening the bag he drew forth a kind of cloak . . . it was the most elaborate piece of regalia, which he fitted round his neck . . . It was the chief's own insignia, and its wearer carried all the authority of the chief.

The demeanour of Kwaisulia when he donned the garment was regal indeed, and his gifts of oratory and histrionic gesture were manifest when he began to speak. The natives listened spellbound for an hour, and when he ceased, and removed the regalia and returned it to its bag, he had unquestionably won the day. He had spoken with such purpose that I got five recruits.

If the recruiter had not been so blinded by Kwaisulia's theatrics, the author of this account might have considered the effect of his own presence, for viewed from a Melanesian perspective the most lethal member of their society was 'the white man's friend'.

Kwaisulia, after his years in Queensland, understood this symbiotic relationship perfectly and on every occasion was at pains to impress the real seat of power. He was to enjoy this reputation as a 'friend of the white man' for almost thirty years. In 1901, a Sydney journalist watched Kwaisulia's and his theatrics in the presence a white man.

> I have in my time heard many orators but never one more effective. I did not know a word of what he said, but so eloquent were his manners and gestures that I easily comprehended his meaning. He arrested attention with a few declamatory remarks and immediately the babel of tongues ceased. Then he stated a number of acknowledged facts dispassionately. Next he entreated, and finally he threatened.

His years in Australia had taught him how to exploit the white man's preconceptions of his own race. Faced as he was, during the last years of his life, with yet another missionary paying a 'short call', Kwaisulia appeared in a spotlessly clean drill suit, sun helmet and sash. Knowing that his guest spoke nothing but English he presented him to the assembled crowd and embarked upon a speech in his own langauge whilst his son Kaiviti hovered close to the missionary's ear providing a prearranged commentary that bore little relation to the oration. The missionary was suitably impressed by Kwaisulia's 'wonderful command of strong language and gestures' and left under the misconception that he had made an impression upon his host. Within a few weeks Kwaisulia received a report from one of his minions that the man had returned and wished to remonstrate with him over 'his trade in boys'. Ever mindful of the missionary tendency to view the islanders as wayward children, Kwaisulia realized that the theatrics surrounding the man's previous visit had been a mistake. This time 'he walked in, stark naked without any ornaments and with a very angry face'. To the missionary's astonishment he found himself the recipient of an immaculately articulated lecture in his own tongue on the economic and social benefits of the labour trade and its contribution to the economy of Queensland. Kwaisulia pointed out that as both parties, black and white, benefited from wealth creation the missionary would be better advised to take his objections back to Australia and place them before the legislators, plantation-owners and shipping syndicates.

In 1886 Kabou died and, as with most of the coastal communities in the Solomon Islands, succession was not based on any strict hereditary principal but on ability, performance and reputation. Kwaisulia was the *ramo* of the community (a title he had acquired during his head hunting days with Renton), with a name that translated as 'Cut Bits Off' and a man whose sponsor had been the dead chief. There was no one to challenge his claim to the succession in both Sulufou and Ada Gege and he immediately set about widening his power base in the manner of all Solomon Island 'big men'.

A big man was a scaled-up version of the man who loaned and manipulated his wealth in pursuit of a network of obligations. In a society where affluence by hoarding was impossible because few items of value ever lasted, the only negotiable currency was obligation or, as Finau had announced to Mariner, 'If provisions are the principal property of men, as they ought to be, being the most useful and necessary, he cannot store it up because it will spoil and he is obliged to exchange it away for something useful'. Thus a big man would manipulate those resources over which he had control in order to create surpluses which would be dispensed on the basis of reciprocity – be they pigs, crops, feast-giving, financing bride payments, funeral offerings. All drew the recipient into a web of obligation and loyalty. For Kwaisulia, who also had control of the valuable traditional currency of porpoise teeth, his capacity to distribute largesse extended beyond those valuables that decayed over time. This wealth also made possible the financing of the most important communal rituals in Solomon Island life – the dedication or rededication of ancestral shrines, the building of communal houses and, most importantly for Kwaisulia, the building and launching of war canoes.

Kwaisulia gathered around him, not just people but also an aura, the special supernatural power of mana and the feeling in the eyes of his acolytes that ancestral spirits protected him. Now armed with the wealth of European cargo and at the centre of a huge spider's web of obligations spun from recruiting, his fiefdom spread to the whole of the northern part of the island and touched every aspect of traditional life. He involved himself in the provision of human sacrifices required for the settling of feuds, he monopolized and directed the porpoise drives and the minting of traditional money. Finally he set up a system of arranged marriages between the lagoon-dwellers and the Kwaio bush people which spawned a network of alliances with inland villages. For the first time his people, who for centuries had been reliant on bartering their fish for produce, had access to arable land.

His first crisis occurred the year after Kabou's death. A new act, passed by the Queensland government to regulate the trade, declared it unlawful to offer firearms to any of the islanders, either in exchange for recruits or to the time expired who were returning home. The Queensland recruits dried up. In 1885, the year after the the regulation was enforced, the number of recruits signing-on from the Solomons and the New Hebrides dropped from 2,300 to 900. However, as no colonial power had staked a claim, the islands were effectively autonomous and Kwaisulia immediately saw a business opportunity and opened up a new avenue of commerce with the French, German and freelance ships active in the region. The time expired recruits returning to the islands with cash they had been unable to exchange for firearms in Australia now purchased them from foreign vessels who had stocked up with supplies to meet this demand.

After the disastrous 1885 recruiting season, the British ships could no longer ignore the loss of their trade and reverted to the system the *Bobtail Nag* had used when Renton and Kwaisulia had undertaken their official voyage. Arrangements were made with Kwaisulia, the passage master, for access to the teeming human resources of the interior. In return, firearms, ammunition and dynamite were packed into cases usually manifested as containing trade goods and sold to the time-expired – through Kwaisulia. His own demands became more and more specific: clothes, clocks, tinned goods, furniture, white paint and tobacco leaf – as long at it had not been purchased in Malaita. As one recruiter said: 'He was far too cautious to smoke any Malaita tobacco on account of the likelihood of poison being introduced into it. There was not the least doubt that his enemies, of whom he had plenty would have brought about his death in that way, had he given them a chance to do so.'

In 1887 Kwaisulia felt himself powerful enough to embark on a campaign of empire building and he set about destroying the only opposition to his power in the thirty-mile stretch of the Lau lagoon. Funaa Vao was Sulufou's oldest and bitterest enemy and, during the last decade, offered the only alternative passage for recruiting ships. It was a testimony to his sphere of influence that when the war party set out it included war canoes from the area of Port Adam, a hundred miles to the south.

Kwaisulia led the strike force that headed the main assault. Ten years previously it would have been unthinkable for a chief of Kwaisulia's prestige to expose himself to danger. The risk of losing the chief would have been too great for the attackers to contemplate but Kwaisulia did not bother with tradition; he led the attack on Funaa Vao and oral history records that his generalship proved decisive. The island was overwhelmed, many of the villagers were killed and the survivors fled to the mainland. Kwaisulia took possession of the island, garrisoned it and installed as chief his eldest son, Jack, named after Jack Renton and born whilst he was living on Sulufou.

This act was a complete break with Melanesian tradition. Land was sacred; it could not 'belong' to any other group. A people may be defeated in battle but their chiefs remained the people's leaders even if they were now subservient to the victor. Kwaisulia's creation of vassal states was a new departure – and very European.

As recruiters looked for regular and guaranteed sources of labour it was inevitable that the laws of supply and demand would throw up monopolies. Bera had led the way though the accidents of geography and conflict. Thousand Ships Bay was the best protected deep-water anchorage in the Solomons but it would have counted for very little if it had not been for the legions of displaced men and women that peopled its shores, eager for the opportunities that recruiting offered. Kwaisulia's brief acquaintance with the opulence of Bera's court ten years earlier had fuelled a particular ambition. As he and Renton had made their way back from the fortress his expressed wish to 'go to Australia' had nothing to do with what the white man could teach him about their civilization. In true Melanesian fashion he sensed an opportunity for self-aggrandisement and intended to discover how to translate white greed into black power. The last twenty years of the nineteenth-century saw the emergence of men like Bera and Kwaisulia who understood this greed and who could back up their bargaining positions with displays of wealth and manpower.

Chief Gorai of the Shortland Islands would receive recruiting agents and ship's officers resplendent in a naval belt, sword, silk top hat and a seaman's jumper. His guests would be invited into his large wooden house to discuss business over a meal served European-style and eaten around a huge refectory table with damask tablecloth and a full set of silver cutlery. Over the port which was rather the worse for its travels halfway round the world, one ship's captain reported a particular misunderstanding. By now, forward contracts were standard and men like Gorai would undertake to deliver a certain number of men and women in return for a specific shopping list of European items. As items were offered and their use explained, Gorai showed no interest at all. Spurred on by his indifference his guests offered more and more exotic items. Eventually Gorai started to laugh and waving a dismissive hand explained that it wasn't a cargo he wanted to purchase but a ship and its crew. He went on to explain that he intended to arm it with his surplus cannon and sail round his territory gathering up men and women.

If European trappings were Gorai's particular predilection, Chief Ingava of Roviana had more traditional tastes. He was prepared to provide recruits in exchange for heads, although he made it clear that he did not expect his customers to provide them. All he required was some assistance and he would do the rest.Thus by the simple expedient of having his war canoes towed behind a recruiting boat until it hove-to opposite some unsuspecting village, Ingava had, by the 1890s, accumulated such a large collection of skulls that the British could no longer ignore him, particularly as thirty of them were decapitated Europeans.

In 1891 Commander Davis of HMS *Royalist* ransacked and burned Ingava's headquarters in Roviana Lagoon and destroyed his accumulation of skulls. As a result Ingava simply spent the next decade replenishing his stock. Not surprisingly, he had exhausted his regular hunting and slaving grounds so he launched a full-scale attack on northern Isabel, collecting over two hundred heads. Commander Davis's, action had managed to stimulate the very activity he had sought to end.

On Isabel, following Bera's death in 1884, there had been an intensification of headhunting as Soga, the most aggressive of his four sons, asserted the authority he had inherited. Within two years he had extended his father's territory along both coasts, deep into the interior, and had wiped out the population of San Jorge Island that lay off the south-eastern coast.

Basakana Island lies off the north-eastern coast of Malaita, facing Isabel. An island with no permanent settlements, it was used as an entrepot for much of the trade that flowed between the two islands. Here, on this neutral territory, fishing, trading and feast-giving involving the two islands had continued for centuries. When a trading party returned to Isabel with news of a large gathering of Lau people preparing for a feast, Soga could not resist the kudos of a foreign conquest.

The expedition was split in two. A war party landed at night some way down the coast and made its way next morning to positions surrounding the makeshift settlement, whilst a fishing party approached from across the strait. Nets were set some way offshore but within sight of the feasting party. The attack was made with a prearranged signal to the war party as soon as the Lau males were all engaged in a dance, their weapons stowed away in the huts. As the survivors fled into the shallows, the fishermen took up their concealed rifles and advanced on them. All were shot and beheaded – men, women and children.

Kwaisulia bided his time. He could not afford to risk attempting to attack Soga anywhere on dry land, he was too well armed. What he needed above all, as he had learned from Renton and the Alite raid, was accurate intelligence. Oral history relates that Kwaisulia himself went to the Gau region of Isabel, contacted groups of Soga's disaffected subjects and paid them to discover the one piece of crucial information he needed, namely, how many war canoes could Soga put to sea?

Within a couple of months Kwaisulia had gathered a fleet of war canoes from the length of the eastern seaboard of Malaita and concealed them in the narrow channel between Basakana Island and the mainland. Then, taking his distinctive white war canoe across the strait, he laid up in the lee of San Jorge Island, just ten miles from Soga's fortress overlooking Thousand Ships Bay. There he waited for the darkness.

Drawn up in the cove below Mboula Point were a dozen of Soga's war canoes. Kwaisulia dymanited three of them, making sure that he left at a pace leisurely enough for his own craft to be recognized. The next day, off the coast of Isabel, an engagement took place involving over two thousand men. In some ways it resembled the great Polynesian sea battles of the seventeenth and eighteenth centuries but with one crucial difference. Both sides were armed with hundreds of British and German-made rifles.

Kwaisulia had developed a particular strategy for this encounter. His canoes were urged to avoid broadside manoeuvres and to seek to engage the enemy head-on, then at the last moment veer across the bows of the oncoming canoe and fire. The strategy of crossing the T meant that, whereas Kwaisulia's canoes could fire into the massed ranks of the oncoming enemy, Soga's men would have to drop their paddles and pick up their rifles, only to find that the men in front obscured their line-of-sight. Kwaisulia's lagoon-dwellers were considerably more skilful boat-handlers than Soga's disparate collection of mercenaries, many of whom had been bush people. The result was a massacre. On the way home the victorious fleet landed at Basakana Island, which Kwaisulia then claimed by right of his victory.

His style was that of a modern nation-builder who, having united his people and conquered various dissident elements, was now ready to negotiate on their behalf with the outside world. Over the next twenty years, along eighty miles of the Malaitan coast and inland, all trade with the white man passed through Kwaisulia and his vassals. Even as late as 1907 there is a newspaper report of a group of Lau people, repatriated from Queensland to Sinalanggu Harbour, sixty miles south of Sulufou, refusing to land at their homes and electing to go to a mission station 'where they would be safe'.

Kwaisulia attempted to introduce a new order, not just to enrich himself but also to meet the presence of the white man. In this clash of cultures it was a project that was doomed, for the engine that drove the creeping cultural hegemony was not money, or arms, or native western acculturation, or even the birth of the British Solomon Island Protectorate in the 1890s – but Christianity.

13

The Last Resort

KWAISULIA had always been in the company of his European business partners when the subject of the missionary presence had come up and his attitude had been fashioned by their dismissiveness. His own view of the white man's world as being entirely profit-driven lulled him into an assumption that the missionaries were of no account and that if they continued to confront the commercial interests of planters and ship-owners there could only be one outcome. As the years passed and the missionaries' opposition became more vociferous he was forced to consider the nature of their power. Clearly if his business partners were unable to see off these remorseless critics and had expressly forbidden him to take any action, he would have to accommodate their presence or, at least, make himself available when they visited.

After his years in Australia he was familiar with the basic tenets of their religion but now as he listened to these men who appeared impervious to the pursuit of profit or self-interest he realized that he had failed to grasp its implications. He was far too politic to argue with them, preferring instead to encourage them to lay out their vision of the future. With a mixture of condescension and conviction they would warm to their task as they described a future that forecast the destruction of the moral and social order of his world. He soon concluded that Christianity was not a religion but a revolution and he was outraged.

Malaitan society was a stable society, well ordered and change-less. Everyone understood the limits of initiative and personal expression. Nothing was permitted to challenge the ancestrally ordained authority which placed the ties of kinship and the prin-ciple of communality at the centre of people's lives. Whether building a house, clearing ground for a new garden, preparing a feast or aiding others in times of trouble, all undertakings required the assistance of one's kin and as everyone claimed kinship with everyone else it was the cement that held society together.

Now he was told that all Christians were equal in the eyes of their god, that they were autonomous beings, free to choose their own course in life. He was told that to acquire prestige by the giving of feasts pandered to the sin of vanity and encouraged rivalry. Above all, feasting was a waste of people's time that could be better spent working individually to the benefit of each family's own economic interests. Feasting, Kwaisulia was informed, encouraged the sin of gluttony and besides when people ate too much they became ill.

His visitors then turned to the institution of marriage and the abolition of bride price. Every person should be able to marry whom they chose and economic impediments were not only primitive but also a heresy. Marriage, they maintained, was an extension of the principle of free will, a private matter between individuals. When the discussion turned to the question of adultery and divorce his visitors floundered briefly but he was left with the clear impression that, although neither was approved of, it was inevitable that some marriages would fail. However they maintained that it was a private matter and that public condemnation was not only irrelevant but also positively unhelpful.

At the end of each visit he drew breath and marvelled at his restraint. Every man on Malaita aspired to marriage and, in the process, the repayment of debt. Bride price created obligations that drove the aspirant into economic endeavour that would enrich his immediate family and his kin. These Christians now advocated a system of marriage based upon the whims of transitory emotion and a vague commitment that appeared to have more to do with a shared belief than a rigorous striving to meet one's economic, familial and wider social obligations. But the idea of sanctioning divorce was even more outrageous. Men and women on Malaita remained chaste until marriage. Thereafter fidelity was unconditional and everyone knew that adultery was punishable by death at the hands of a *ramo*. It was the way society had always been and everyone lived with the presence of the moral policeman. Moreover, being a communal society, it placed the responsibility for moral conduct not only upon the individual but also upon their family. If a *ramo* was unable to kill the perpetrator of a moral crime he would merely choose one of their kin, be it brother, father or cousin.

Not content with their proposals to abolish feasting, dancing, ancestor worship, bride price and fidelity, the Christians now set about attempting to undermine people like himself. He received a visitor from the island of Sa'a, one hundred miles to the south and the site of the only Christian enclave on Malaita. Literate and English-speaking, Fianawa was the son of Kwaisulia's allay Foulanger, the big man of Port Adam who had assisted him in the destruction of Soga's fleet two years previously. Knowing Fianawa spoke English, the missionaries offered him employment as a translator and his father, sensing the opportunity to gather information, urged him to accept. His task was to help in the translation of the New Testament into the Lau language. He showed Kwaisulia some of his work and then turned to Mark 10:25 and the reason for his visit. His translation of 'it is easier for a camel to pass through the eye of a needle, than for a rich man to enter the kingdom of heaven' had been changed by his employers. '*Ngwane ne rikii*' ('a rich man') had been altered to '*ngwane inoto*' ('a big man'). When he had questioned the missionaries as to why they had edited his translation he had been told that both meant the same thing. His father had sent him to ask Kwaisulia how he should respond. Kwaisulia urged caution, pointing out that at least there was a place where all Foulanger's troublemakers could be effectively isolated, whereas he, Kwaisulia, had spent a number of years and a considerable amount of manpower tracking down disparate returnees fired with this belief and removing them from his territory. He urged Fianawa to tell his father to make sure that no Christians gained a foothold on his territory. The young man observed that it wasn't the newly converted that were the problem – it was the white missionaries. If they decided to settle on the mainland there would be nothing a big man could do. Kwaisulia dismissed Fianawa's fears, pointing out that it would be a simple matter to discourage contact between one's own people and the white interloper. The young man replied that it wasn't contact with ordinary people that was the problem. Then he dropped his bombshell – Soga had converted to Christianity.

The story had started fifteen years earlier when Bera had been alive. In an attempt to further ingratiate himself with his white partners he had allowed the Melanesian Mission to establish a foothold in a remote inland village. This initiative had netted a number of young men who were taken to New Zealand for instruction. The following year the *Southern Cross* had returned carrying the same young men, now fully fledged missionaries. Bera reasoned that as they were from Isabel they would be easy to control, even though they now dressed like white men. Unfortunately, the leader of the little group, fired up by the new faith, made little secret of his contempt for *kustom* beliefs. Relations between the Mission and Bera deteriorated and he banned all proselytizing. He reinforced his displeasure by destroying the two canoes that provided the Mission's only means of transport. To forestall any more drastic action, Bishop Selwyn and his assistant the Reverend Penny sent the *Southern Cross* to rescue the acolytes.

High in the mountain forests on the site of the original mission station, Ino, the local big man, was proving much more receptive to Selwyn and Penny's blandishments and both he and a small group of native missionaries set about exploiting the chronic insecurities that had been generated by decades of head-hunting. Ino's heavily fortified village of Tega became a welcome alternative to the only other sanctuary on offer, Bera's feudal mini-state.

Ino soon came to appreciate the considerable benefits that his new status of protector conferred and he allowed the Mission to establish a school on his territory. By the early 1880s, Tega had a congregation of over a hundred converts. As a mark of gratitude Ino was invited on a specially arranged journey on the *Southern Cross* to witness ten of his villagers take holy orders in New Zealand. For the Melanesian Mission this paid dividends. On a visit to Tega, Bishop Selwyn reported: 'the safety of the place attracts people from the inland to it, and while I was there a large party, some seventy souls, came to take up their abode in the district. In this way it is a very important spot for our purposes.' A few months later, Ino, keen to further ingratiate himself with his new sponsors, agreed to provide sanctuary to one hundred bushmen who arrived en masse – as long as they were prepared to give up cannibalism.

On the coast, matters were still at an impasse. Bera was prepared to tolerate the Melanesian Mission's activities as long as they came nowhere near his territory. His stance was reinforced by the frequently voiced antagonism of his white trading partners towards the Mission's activities. There was nothing Selwyn or Penny could do. Then in 1884 Bera died. Penny reflected in his diary: 'it seems too good to be true' – it was.

Soga, although displaying none of his father's visceral antagonism, refused all the Mission's requests to be allowed to establish a school on his territory. Then, two years later, following his defeat by Kwaisulia, the inevitable happened. One of the trading ships imported the influenza virus and an epidemic swept through southern Isabel, killing hundreds. When the *Southern Cross* arrived in Thousand Ships Bay Selwyn found the young chief close to death. He was taken on board, treated and recovered.

As he sat on deck convalescing he could not escape the conclusion that it was the rituals around his sickbed that had spared his life rather than the efficacy of their treatments. Twice daily a group of men, black and white, had knelt together and, led by Selwyn, prayed for his recovery. As he looked across the bay towards the grieving households of his subjects, Soga was clear in his mind that it had been the white man's god that had spared him. It was not a belief that Selwyn did anything to disabuse and by the time he had returned to his fortress Soga had willingly agreed to the establishment of a Mission school in the bay.

Within a few weeks the opportunity arose for him to demonstrate his own loyalty to Selwyn when a war party from New Georgia arrived at Mboula and offered to buy heads from Soga. He immediately sent for Selwyn to come and back him in his refusal. It was to be the first act of an alliance between the young chief and the Mission that was to continue until his death. The following year he became a monogamist and started to attend the Mission school. In 1889 he was learning to read and write and was baptized with sixty of his followers.

For Kwaisulia this was a totally unexpected development and one that, given his own troubles, merely increased his sense of isolation. Foulanger may have found the missionary presence an irritant but, as the converts had their own Christian enclave on Sa'a Island, at least he could be assured that they were unlikely to settle in his territory. Kwaisulia, on the other hand, had to exercise constant vigilance, particularly as the lagoon had become the target not simply of the converted but of native missionaries. Soon he found himself forced to resort to the desperate measure of discreet assassination. His first victim was Aliverete Amasia, survivor and chronicler of the voyage of the *Peri*.

Aliverete had led the escape from the *Basilisk* whilst it was anchored in Fiji that had precipitated the fruitless search for an interpreter and the subsequent gifts of arms and ammunition to the remaining passengers. He and two other fugitives had taken to the bush where the headman of a Christian community found them. All were eventually baptized and given scriptural or English names. Aliverete (now Alfred) became a Wesleyan preacher. Fifteen years after his escape he decided to take the Word back to his pagan roots and settled on a small ancestral island near Leli. On a site beside his landing stage he put up a sign that advertised not his faith but his abstemiousness: '*Sa tabu na yangona kei na tovako*' – 'Alcohol and tobacco are forbidden'. As a subsequent enquiry by his church recorded: 'It puzzled the unsophisticated people around him, who decided that it was some foreign or strange form of witchcraft and that he was a dangerous neighbour.' When the report reached Kwaisulia he immediately put up blood money and the deed was duly done.

Peter Amboufa had been recruited through Kwaisulia in 1889. Two years later he was baptized and sent for training at the Queensland Kanaka Mission School in Bundaberg. He was regarded as their star pupil, a man of exceptional piety and strength of character – just the man to attempt to establish the first outpost in Kwaisulia's pagan state. Arrangements were made to launch Amboufa on his mission with a certain amount of ceremony. He departed in the recruiting ship *William Manson* with the Principal of the Mission, members of parliament, representatives of the Immigration Department and members of the press.

Joseph Vos, the captain, was distinctly nervous. He had been dealing successfully with Kwaisulia for many years and did his best to point out the likely outcome. The ship's owners would have none of it and the *William Manson* duly arrived at Urassi. As it came within sight of Ada Gege a canoe came out to meet the ship and Vos, recognizing Kwaisulia, quickly hove-to. He received his old friend on the gangway and took him to the privacy of his cabin. Vos pretended that he had only called to land some returnees to which Kwaisulia pointed out that recruits would be hard to come by as it was the planting season. It was only later in the day that Vos broached the real reason for his presence. Kwaisulia asked to see the cargo and Vos produced Amboufa and his two assistants, Billy Try, and Koby. Kwaisulia took them aside and spoke to them briefly in Lau and then, according to Vos, turned on him in a fury, exclaiming: 'I don't want those bloody black missionaries here. Soon there'll be a time when they are bigger than I am!'

To his considerable embarrassment and to the vociferous condemnations of the official party, Vos returned to Australia with his putative missionaries. Undaunted, Amboufa was on board the next recruiting ship bound for Malaita, where he was reluctantly allowed to land by one of his distant relatives in the north of the lagoon. On Kwaisulia's instructions he was given a place to live underneath a hut with the village pigs. After a while the villagers tired of his efforts to proselytize and told him to go.

For a man who regarded himself not simply as a follower of Christ but as someone divinely appointed to carry the Word to his people this was a small setback. He moved further north to another set of relatives in Malu, a large village adjoining Kwaisulia's territory. They allowed him to erect a small hut on a patch of land beside the beach. A few yards from his humble dwelling he put up a sign that announced his presence. Unlike

the unfortunate Aliverete, it was not a statement of abstemiousness but of faith: 'John 3:13 – For God so loved the world . . .'
more a source of comfort for the lonely occupant than a clarion
call to his illiterate neighbours.

For a while he had no success at all. Day after day he used to
go to the beach markets and point out to those assembled there
that although they worked hard to provide sacrifices to the spirits
it was by no means guaranteed that their *mana* would be
enhanced, either in this world or the next. If they became
Christians, he told them, they would be relieved of the necessity
of making further sacrifices and, in addition, be assured of life
after death. To this the gathered would always make one reply.
How did he know anything about this future life? Who from
Malaita had died and returned? When he urged them that surely
the white man, who obviously knew so much, could not be
wrong, his audience merely laughed.

But by the mid 1890s the white men were increasingly in
evidence. There were three trading stations on Guadalcanal, two
on Isabel, and in the Floridas the beginnings of a European town
to house the recently created British Solomon Islands
Protectorate. Not only were there Mission stations on these islands
but three in the south of Malaita. Everywhere he went the white
man flouted the most deeply held native beliefs. He blundered into
sacred shrines, picked up tabu objects, washed himself in spirit-
haunted streams, walked alone at night – time after time he broke
tabus that had always brought sickness and death in their wake.

Missionaries encouraged this iconoclasm. One in New
Georgia wrote:

We stood in a circle and solemnly committed these

people to Christ's safe keeping; for we could not mini-
mize the danger they were in, nor deny the power of their
old masters. But we could tell them with joy of 'the
Stronger than He'. Then taking down some more charms
from the eaves of a nearby house where they had long
brooded over the destinies of the people, we solemnly
made our way back to the river, taking the relics with us
to be thrown into the sea.

As the old certainties crumbled the people turned to the
priests to exert their supernatural powers. But the white man
seemed completely impervious to the anger of their gods.

Yet the conversions that followed were in no sense
Damascene. Melanesians are intensely practical people and their
beliefs primarily a tool for self-advancement. What they saw
when they looked at the white man's religion was something very
similar but immensely more potent – a religion that appeared to
be inextricably linked to his cargo.

Julia Blackburn in her book *The White Men* captures the
intimations of the arrival of a millennial power:

the white man sits in the shade and sweats. He eats his
own food and makes strange signs on white paper and
gives orders. He demands obedience and his power sits
on him like an invisible cloak. Goods are sent to him in
wooden boxes, in shining tins, in crates unloaded from
ships. Things are sent to him that do not belong to this
world, which could never have been made in this world;
matches, newspapers, corned beef, umbrellas and guns.
And yet what have they done to obtain it? They have not
hunted or prepared the soil or worked in any way. They

have simply waited, written signs on pieces of paper, given orders and waited some more. Miraculously all that they desire appears before them.

The white man says that they come from a distant land where the cargo is made. This land often seems indistinguishable from the place inhabited by their god. What is the source of this power, this presumption? The white man has his money and his god. A god that is obviously stronger than other known gods, and is pleased with his white people.

At this point many islanders abandoned their own customs and beliefs. They learned new songs and built new meeting houses to the missionary's design. They sat and listened to him, learned from his book and sang his songs, waiting for the moment when their period of initiation would be over and they would be told the secret which would reward them with as much power and as many possessions as the white man. Yet, having followed everything as instructed, they remained unregarded and unrewarded. No cargo landed on the beach by their village.

These were a people for whom all-important endeavours were accomplished with the aid of magic. It was assumed that as long as the ritual was correctly performed the relevant deity had no option but to grant success. Failure was not regarded as the fault of a god but attributed to the incorrect ritual. Their religion was viewed as a technology to be used to maintain their place in the cosmic order. It did far more than reflect social values; it governed intellectual life. They accepted their ancestral myths as the sole and unquestioned source of all-important truths.

All the most valued aspects of their cultures were believed to have been invented by the deities/ancestors, who taught people both the secular and ritual procedures for exploiting them. The 'living' dead appeared in dreams, showing them how to plant crops or make artefacts. Even when a man composed a new song or dance, it was authenticated with the claim that it came from a deity rather than from inside his own head. At first this might appear mystical but, in fact, people's thinking was extremely pragmatic – know the ritual (know the secret) and all would be granted.[1]

Clearly, the white man was in full control of his rituals, for all that he wished for appeared when needed. And when the white man said that it came from hard work they knew that it was not the truth because the white man never worked. Soon it was believed that the white man was hiding the secret of his magic, as he had made it abundantly clear in the numerous meetings that the people had attended in the house that the bible was his guide and inspiration. Throughout much of Melanesia people began to suspect that the white man was hiding this secret and the only conclusion was that he had torn it out of his book before he had given it to them.

But now any attempt to turn back the tide had been undermined by their betrayal of their dead ancestors and the time-honoured roles and obligations within their community that had provided the continuity that had given every individual a sense of place. This betrayal had invalidated the past. It no longer lived.

Twenty-five years after contact with the white man, an anthropologist visited a group of islanders off the coast of New Guinea and witnessed the anguish of ancestral betrayal.

The villagers took me to a small hut. It was painted in lurid washes, but very dilapidated. The floorboards were rotten. A young man brought for my inspection, first, a wand of hardwood, about seven feet long with a spray of very dirty, dusty, and tattered cassowary plumes bound to one end; second, a stone axe blade, well made and polished; third, a carved wooden statuette of the human form about five inches high, rudely executed, dusty, with smears of red and white chalk on it; fourth, a broad circlet of decorated turtleshell, battered and apparently very old. This, they told me, had been their 'book'.

It seemed to me as I handled these objects that they were from a former age when the people of Manem were renowned in the region as sailors, traders and fierce fighters.

I had just finished looking at these objects when one of Irakau's sisters pressed forward and begged me to shake hands with her. I did so. She burst into tears.

The others round me, men and women, also started to weep. Not the conventional wailing on a death or parting, but deep uncontrollable sobs with tears coursing down their faces.

For the Malaitamen, thousands of whom had been exposed to three years of white culture, the secret did not reside in the undisclosed pages of the white man's book, but in a new inducement. Four years of patient work in Malu had eventually yielded converts and now Peter Amboufa and his Mission were offering free education to prospective converts at no cost. The ever-practical Malaitans saw great advantages. Firstly they realized that it would be very convenient to write letters and to keep a record of loans, secondly that anyone who was literate could find employment within the burgeoning British administration or on a trading schooner and earn higher wages than Queensland offered. Education took on a mystical power.

One visitor quoted his cook, a heathen who went in his spare time to mission school:

> You white men are like us, you have only two eyes, two hands and two feet. How are you different? Because you can read books. That is why you can buy axes, knives, clothing and ships. You buy a passage on a steamer and visit places of which we have only heard, where people live in stone houses one on top of the other. You do not work hard; you pay us little money and we work for you, carrying heavy boxes on our backs. All this we know comes from books. If we understood books we could be like you. If we could read your books we would have money and possessions.

The problem was that these were mission schools. Basic literacy was the extent of the educational effort, a Gradgrind rote-learning regime based on one text, the bible. In the end the young men gave up trying. As one commentator observed: 'they continue to believe that they could have what they want if they were better trained. The youngsters, however, with pathetic optimism, eagerly take up the places of those who leave.' Even well into the twentieth-century a distinguished Christian academic, surveying the Mission schools in the Solomon Islands, was still defending this cruel deception: 'A mission school does not exist as an end in itself, or to give a diploma. It is supported by missionary contributions from overseas to carry out the Great Commission.'

Kwaisulia, ever aware that he relied on Europeans and their

steady stream of trade goods to retain his following, turned his attention to courting the British administration. Even before the creation of the Protectorate he had made representations to the governor general in Suva requesting that the Lau people be placed under the protection of Great Britain by being annexed to Fiji. When news of the creation of the Protectorate reached him, he placed himself and his warriors at the service of the new governor. 'Quaisulia [sic] can put a large force of fighting men into the field', the newly appointed Charles Woodford wrote in 1896, 'and if he proves to be what I expect he might be ready to arrange to keep the coast under order.'

The following year, much to his bemusement, he was awarded the Jubilee Medal by the fledgling administration. Yet this was the man who, in the same year, approached the recruiting agent on the *Fearless*, with whom he had done business for many years, with a curious request. 'Jack Renton's death still upset him very much, and he was anxious to know if it would be possible for us to take him and fifty or a hundred men to Aoba Island to avenge the murder. I had to tell him that such a thing was quite impossible, and that he must put it from his mind.' Blood vengeance was a never-ending cycle. Kwaisulia would have done better to have turned his attention to events in Australia for his income was about to dry up.

The wealth of the state of Queensland had been built on one commodity, cheap imported labour – Chinese, Japanese, Javanese, Malays, Indians, Philippinos and, above all, South Sea Islanders. Now a backlash was starting and 'coloureds' of whatever hue were being represented as a virus that threatened to overwhelm the white population. Newspapers such as *The Bulletin* in Sydney and *The Boomerang* in Brisbane fulminated against the 'Chows', 'Japs', 'Niggers', 'Fuzzy Wuzzies' and 'Tommy Tannas' and all other 'mongrelized races'. The idea of White Australia was becoming a national obsession.

In 1896 the parliament of New South Wales passed a bill explicitly designed to exclude 'all persons belonging to any coloured race inhabiting the Continent of Asia, or the Continent of Africa or any island in the Pacific or Indian oceans' and, with Queensland due to join the Commonwealth of Australian states in 1900, recruiting dried up. In the elections that followed the architects of this policy, the Labour Party, won a sweeping victory, carrying North Queensland in a landslide. The following year the new government twisted the economic screw by slapping an excise of £3 per ton for manufactured sugar and a rebate of £2 for cane grown and cut by white labour.

As preparations for deportation were made it was to the credit of the Queensland political old guard that they extracted a few concessions from Sydney. The aged and infirm, holders of freehold land and those islanders who had lived in Australia for over twenty years were exempt, but the rest had to go. Immigration officials were instructed to tell the islanders about the arrangements, but not the reasons. Some absconded but most, assuming that it was the 'king' or 'bishops' or some higher authority that had ordered their deportation, made their way to the embarkation ports without protest.

Seventy per cent of the Solomon Islanders were from Malaita and many had lived in Australia for years. They had put down roots, made relationships and regarded themselves as Australian. Some took to the bush and others simply refused to move. They were brought before magistrates, formally sentenced to deportation and taken in chains to the waiting boats. One young white

Australian witnessed the final scenes at the dockside:

> Two by two they came through a passage made in the crowd from a gateway in the fence to the foot of the gangplank, black shoulders topped by black curly-tufted hair, with bare chests and torn trousers. Their sweaty bodies gleamed in the thick yellow light and the iron shackles on their wrists and ankles clinked and clanked as they shuffled forward, breathing heavily and without a word. In the background the wails of their womenfolk persisted. The human stream pushed forward . . . up the gangplank they stumbled. 'Thank Christ that's over and that's the last of the black bastards,' I heard a man exclaim.

Dismissed with a curse, white Australia turned its back on the thousands who, for almost half a century, had manned the engine rooms that had created Queensland's wealth.

Woodford was aware of the dangers of returning the thousands of deportees directly to their native roots, so a depot was built near to the British administration's capital on the Floridas. Here the bemused, angry, or the simply fearful were given the chance to reflect and decide where they wished to take up the threads of their past lives. Many chose to join a community that would mirror in some way the world they had left behind and throughout the Solomons Christian enclaves sprang up, even on Malaita, the most pagan of the islands.

Nevertheless, despite Woodford's planning, the impact of this sudden importation of thousands of people was grievous. In *Barchester Towers*, Anthony Trollope wrote: 'The islanders who are brought from Queensland all return, and not a man of them returns without taking with him the lessons of civilization.' Unfortunately many who returned were time expired and had lived in Queensland for considerably longer than the initial three-year contract period and, whether Christian or pagan, the first experience of these repatriates was sickness. Too many had been away too long and had lost their capacity to fight malaria and intestinal infections. Those few Europeans who were honest enough to record morbidity and mortality rates paint a dispiriting picture. Almost none of the children who had been born in Queensland survived the first year. In an effort to rid themselves of the black man, and despite Woodford's strictures, medical screening in Queensland had been a charade and hundreds of adults returned with tuberculosis, influenza and other diseases. With only Geddie's records on Aneityum providing any empirical data, it is impossible to be precise about the effect the repatriation of these deportees had on the resident population.

A 1906 census in Queensland estimated that of the remaining 4,800 Solomon Islanders due for deportation about 2,500 were Malaitans. Although valued as the workhorses of the cane fields, they had the reputation of being the most volatile, arrogant and fractious of the Pacific Islanders and their home was viewed as one of wildest places in the British Empire. The Protectorate was only a few years old and was entirely dependent on 'big men' like Kwaisulia to provide the veneer of order. When asked, they would do the Administration's bidding but for the rest of the time *kustom* life continued as usual. The island that was about to feel the full impact of repatriation was the place least prepared to absorb it.

Doorey and Renton were the only white people who had ever

been permitted to survive on the island. Ever mindful of the lessons of history, both had had to endure a period of quarantine. When the recruiters arrived, all negotiations were carried out on board ship and none of the ship's company, with the exception of the recruiter, was permitted to disembark. This cordon sanitaire was applied by the two other passage masters on the island, Foulanger in the south and Mahoalla on the west coast and, as all returnees would be inspected prior to disembarkation, Malaita had remained disease-free – until the mass repatriation.

Walter Ivens worked as a missionary during this period in the Sa'a mission enclave on Foulanger's territory. Twenty years later he returned to write a book on the area. His is the only empirical evidence that exists of the depopulation of the island. During the creation of the Protectorate in the 1890s, the British estimated Malaita's population to be 150,000. When Ivens returned in 1924 it had fallen to 65,000. He concedes that: 'The white man must be held responsible for the considerable diminution in the number of the people. Mala [sic] was a great recruiting ground for the vessels of the Labour Trade and since the cessation of the Trade, dysentery and influenza spread from visiting ships have caused considerable mortality on Mala.' In Sa'a, where he had lived at the turn of the century, he had estimated the village's population to be 250. When he returned it had shrunk to less than a hundred 'owing to various epidemics'.

Increasingly, Kwaisulia found himself having to do Woodford's bidding, not out of conviction, but in a desperate attempt to preserve his pagan stronghold. In 1899 he was given a graphic demonstration of the benefits of his collaboration. As Woodford's tough Irish deputy Mahaffy toured through the

Solomons in a gunboat, he systematically broke up every war canoe he could find, yet he pointedly bypassed the Lau Lagoon. Eighteen months later he deputed Kaiviti, one of Kwaisulia's sons, to arrest two murderers who had taken refuge in the Ataa Lagoon, fifteen miles south of Ada Gege. Kaiviti duly obliged and Mahaffy reported to Woodford: 'It is quite plain that Quaisulia [sic] is able to keep order in this district and I impressed upon him that he would in future be held responsible for the peace in this part of Mala.'

Kwaisulia's attempts to delude himself into thinking that he was running a parallel administration finally evaporated when he was sent an instruction to arrest a group of Lau people on the island of Funafae. He played for time and Woodford, eventually tiring of his excuses, sent a gunboat to shell the island, causing considerable loss of life. Not only was he unable to protect his people from the wrath of the British but he also discovered later the same year that he was impotent in the face of their ambitions for their religion.

On the mainland at Fou'ia, directly opposite Ada Gege, a Mission station was established with the Administration's blessing. His sense of outrage was compounded when he discovered that the Mission's pastor was a man from Ada Gege who had acquired the virus of Christianity after he had offered his services to Kwaisulia's recruiting business six years earlier. Faced with this affront, yet fearing Woodford's explosive displeasure, Kwaisulia refused to sanction the sale of any land and subjected the man to constant harassment – everything, short of killing him. With his relationship with the British clearly in danger of further undermining his prestige, he now deputed his son Kaiviti and his nephew Kaa to deal with them and turned his attention to shoring up his authority in the one arena in which he excelled – supply and demand.

Since the 1880s the soap manufacturers, Lever Brothers, had been actively purchasing copra from plantations in the New Hebrides, which was now jointly administered by the French and the English. Amongst the traders, this new Condominium had soon earned the sobriquet of 'the Pandemonium Government' and Levers, deciding that it was time to control the means of production, turned to Woodford. Anxious to demonstrate to his masters in Whitehall that the Solomon Islands had the potential to pay for themselves, he offered Levers a 999-year lease on a group of islands to the north of Isabel. The Russell Islands cover an area of two hundred square kilometres and are virtually flat – perfect plantation terrain.

For the task of clearing and planting, Levers turned to the most reliable source of labour in the Solomons. Kwaisulia duly obliged and when the palms had matured, a steady stream of recruits took ship from the Urassi Passage. Contracts were for two years and for a fifty-hour week they were paid £8 per annum, slightly more than the old Queensland rates. For Kwaisulia the success of that arrangement was an augury that clearly demonstrated ancestral favour. Fired by auspiciousness, he sent a party of warriors to Fou'ia who duly gathered up all the Mission's clothing, tools, prayer books and bibles and threw them into the lagoon. It was a premature celebration. Within a year, the arrangement with Levers began to unravel. Although Kwaisulia understood European greed, he was far too respectful of their abilities to make provision for a weakness common to all races – stupidity.

Attracting overseers to work in one of the wildest corners of the British Empire proved an impossibility and Levers had to accept almost anyone who applied. The inevitable result was that they ended up employing the dregs of white Australia; bitter failures conditioned by the racist rhetoric of the Labour Party and prone to take out their loneliness and frustration on their charges. One newcomer recorded the advice of an old hand: 'treat them as muck. Remember that a white man's the only human being here and that there isn't any other kind.'

Woodford's ever vigilant deputy Mahaffy warned in 1908 that most of the Australian managers employed by Levers were '. . . for the most part unable to deal with native labour, and it is not surprising when it is remembered that they have every opportunity to manifest their dislike of 'niggers' upon some of the most isolated plantations of the firm, desertions are not infrequent . . . and it is not denied that floggings take place upon the estates, and to put such power into the hands of ignorant and prejudiced persons constitutes a real danger.'

Reports reached Kwaisulia, not of the behaviour of the whites, which, since Queensland, had been accepted as an occupational hazard, but of the conditions. They were housed in airless huts built of corrugated iron, their beds flat pieces of wood. The work was dull and repetitive and the bulk of what they earned was retained by Levers and only handed over at the end of the contract when deductions had been made. Nothing could be purchased except from the company store which charged exorbitant prices – or 'native prices' as Levers euphemistically put it. There was no social life as there were no other islanders, male or (more importantly) female. The place was a wasteland and when they had completed their two years in the fractious, bored, single-sex community they discovered that there were no

275

firearms that they could purchase with their hard earned cash, only tinned meat, cheap watches, mirrors, razors and the inevitable beads. Above all there was no kudos. They had not been to the white man's world and they had no stories to tell except of an island prison less than one hundred miles away.

Nonetheless Kwaisulia remained an optimist. He knew Woodford had to make the Solomons pay for itself and, as he would constantly point out to Kaiviti and Kaa, Levers needed to make a profit and, as it was clear that no other island in the Solomons had a reputation that could match the Malaitans when it came to plantation work, they had the monopoly of the labour market.

He was old now and he knew that it was not the problems of the labour market that posed the greatest threat to his people. Somehow the Missions had come up with a religion that celebrated individuality, yet at the same time promised eternal life to its adherents. It profoundly insulted his sense of order and the central tenet of the sanctity of communality. Nothing happened in the lagoon that was individually ordained. Knowledge and power were indivisible and only acquired through the sanction of ancestral favour. No one struck out on their own, except a big man.

It was perhaps too much to have expected them to tell him to his own face but he should have guessed. On numerous occasions both Kaiviti and Kaa had made it clear to him that their efforts to shield the lagoon from the new order were becoming increasingly difficult. Although they would carry out Woodford's bidding when asked, they discovered that they were often bypassed by an administration intent on seeking assistance from the Missions. They had both explained to Kwaisulia that these people were effectively sponsored by the British who were doing everything in their power, short of confrontation with Kwaisulia, to foster an alternative nucleus of authority and influence in the lagoon. If Sulufou and Ada Gege were to retain control of the economic activity there would have to be some rapprochement with the Christians. Each time the subject had been brought up Kwaisulia made it clear that it was not a move he was prepared to sanction. But as the months went by he became aware that the two young men were establishing contact with the missions, yet he said nothing. As he waited for the inevitable, all three of them knew that he had no alternative strategy and, in 1909, both Kaiviti and Kaa converted to Christianity.

In the evenings, as Kwaisulia sat on the quayside in Ada Gege, he could hear the hymns from the Mission house at Fou'ia wafting across the lagoon – a nightly reproach to his leadership. He had husbanded his flock through the turmoil of the last thirty years and many had grown wealthy through his efforts. Now they stood, row upon row of them, singing their dreary songs and none of them, as he knew very well, were attending out of religious conviction but from some vague notion that this new belief would make them richer. This was the god of all things white who, courtesy of his book, would open the way to stone houses, effortless travel, food from tins, books, writing, money and advancement; above all, he would make them like the white man. And now his own family had succumbed. One evening, in late summer 1909, he left Ada Gege with a party of fishermen bound for Basakana Island in one of Lever's early gifts, a twenty-foot whaleboat.

The channel between the island and the mainland is less than half a mile wide. The sheltered waters teem with fish, many of them from the open sea. Tiger sharks, barracuda, bonito and dorado make their way through a deep-water channel on the island's western approach. By contrast, the eastern end of the channel is a continuation of the adjacent lagoon. They arrived just after dawn, moored off a small beach, carried their nets through the shallows and laid them out on the sand. Some of the fishermen wandered off along the shoreline in search of slabs of rock coral to weight their nets. Kwaisulia sat alone in the whaler as it drifted in the gentle offshore swell. He took up two oars and, seating himself on the centre thwart, manoeuvred the boat into the channel. It sat low in the water and was difficult for one man to handle despite the fact that it carried nothing except their net of last resort, a box of dynamite. He had ordered it twenty years earlier for a purpose entirely unrelated to its present role. An old recruiting friend, Jock Cromer, had taken him out to demonstrate its effectiveness on tuna. Gazing at the two hundred fish that lay stunned on the surface, he had been impressed by the demonstration and not least by the fact that the substance worked in water. Cromer's demonstration in the lagoon was even more spectacular. Not only did the shock waves travel horizontally, but vertically as they bounced back off the seabed.

The box had become a talisman, a symbol of his own ambivalence. As it had been moved from boat to boat over the last twenty years, it had remained unopened. Sulufou and Ada Gege would continue to fish in the sea as saltwater people had for centuries. Iron tools might change their relationship with the land but the sea was sacred. Without the butterfly nets shaped like the Southern Cross, the porpoise hunts, the great rituals at low and high tide, the priestly sanctions for the great group endeavours, their world would fall apart. And so, over the decades, the box had mutated into a symbol, not of the white world, but of their own – there was to be no 'last resort'.

Yet over the last two years the box had lost its power. The priests had neither sanctified it nor, like their own totems, did it possess the force of ancestral *mana*. It was simply a utilitarian object from a world that was about to overwhelm them. The flood of repatriates, the proliferation of Missions, reports from the interior of death and dying, Levers' betrayals and Woodford's contempt – all had leeched away at his certainties. He, Kwaisulia, the most acculturated, had kept his faith yet the two young men to whom he had entrusted the future of his people had secretly bowed to the new dispensation. He knew now that the only way back for him would require an act of apostasy. He reached into his ornate shell belt, extracted his tobacco pouch and matches and knelt down beside the last resort. Leaning forward he struck a match on the box's metal clasp.

On the beach, the fishermen had completed their preparations. The huge net lay on the sand secured at each end by the Southern Cross braces, each to be manned by a Watcher of the Cross. Now they waited for their chief to return and take up the right-hand station.

He was standing now, in the middle of the boat, facing away from them. His grey head was very still and he appeared to be looking intently at some object far away on the towering coastline of the island. The fishermen noticed a thin wisp of smoke curling over the right shoulder of the statuesque figure. He appeared to be holding some object in his right hand but as he lifted it to his face it exploded. The fishermen followed the trajectory of his head as it skimmed across the lagoon and disappeared amongst a startled shoal of kakarai. A moment of complete silence followed and then the booming echo of the explosion reverberated through the mountains of the island of Malaita.

Endnotes

Chapter Three – Landfall

1. This wishful thinking was not uncommon. In 1524 Verrazzano returned from America with gold which, on closer examination, turned out to be iron pyrites. Paris in 1542 saw the staging of an exhibition of Cartier's finds from his exploration off the coast of Canada. The centrepiece was a display of diamonds which later turned out to be simple quartz crystals – making the phrase 'un diamont du Canada' forever synonymous with worthlessness.

   In 1577 Martin Frobisher had found gold-bearing rocks on the south coast of Baffin Island. Bringing two hundred tons of it back to London, the load was assayed at £25 a ton. (Given that the average annual income of a labourer was £5 per annum, this was a sensational discovery.) Not surprisingly investors rushed forward to fund a mining expedition to England's new-found Mexico and a year later Frobisher returned with a fleet of fourteen ships. He spent a month mining a heavy black rock from seven locations, including one so rich in the rock 'that it might reasonably suffise all the golde gluttons of the worlde'. In early September, having extracted 1,350 tons, he made a dash for home, hoping to avoid the winter storms. His fleet was decimated and, one month later, just two ships limped into Harwich harbour. The cargoes were offloaded and shipped to London and Bristol. The rock was assayed, then crushed and smelted and re-examined. From these black lumps, as a contemporary historian recorded, 'neither gold, silver, nor any other metal could be drawn and they were thrown away to repair the high-way'.

2. Once a victim had contracted the 'disease of the heart' there appeared to be no cure and the twenty-five-year-old Mendana was no exception. His symptoms were further aggravated when Phillip II made him a marquis five years after he returned from the Solomons granting him absolute gover-norship of the islands, as well as all mineral rights. He followed this up with a decree authorizing Mendana to return to his discovery with five hundred men (fifty of whom should be married with families), together with cattle, horses, pigs and sheep 'and there to found three cities'. Politics inter-vened – his uncle was no longer governor and Spain was becoming disenchanted with the expense of colonial expan-sion and exploration.

For years Mendana planned, petitioned and pleaded with the persistence of one truly afflicted. In 1595, twenty years after he had returned, he set sail for the Solomons with four ships and three hundred men, women and children, including his own wife and her three brothers. Now, in place of soldiers and sailors used to the hardships and discipline of shipboard life, his expedition comprised a ragbag of the vulnerable and the desperate.

En route to their destination they landed on a number of islands including the Marquesas, which they named. But with inadequate supplies on board ship and stoked by sixteenth-century contempt for all races other than their own, they left a trail of theft, destruction and cruelty.

Mendana was horrified by the needless slaughter but, dominated by his wife and her relatives, his authority was gradually leaching away.

Exhausted by the bickering and ill-discipline, he landed at a group of islands five hundred miles short of his intended destination. Here, in the Santa Cruz group, he decided to make the best of a bad job and establish a colony. Ever the diplomat, he reached an agreement with the local chief, Malope, and the settlers began to build a camp in an inlet which they named Graciosa Bay.

Within a fortnight, despite being liberally supplied with food by Malope, the settlers began to steal. Mendana's entreaties could do nothing to mitigate the contempt that his companions, and particularly his wife, felt for their naked hosts. Within a few days a number of the settlers mutinied and killed Malope.

Although the natives had few answers to European firearms, nature was about to intervene. The settlement had been built near a swamp and soon disease overwhelmed the little community. Mendana himself was one of the first to die and, after eight weeks, the settlers voted to abandon their ill-fated colony.

Passing among the sick, and mindful of their behaviour, the expedition's priest commented: 'the natives will triumph over us and remain, enjoying our cloths and arms and all we possess in this place, where God holds us prisoners, to chastise us according to our desserts.'

One incident perhaps exemplifies the sickness at the heart of this expedition. As the survivors struggled westward towards the Philippines, Mendana's widow kept her prize pigs well fed whilst the crew and passengers starved.

Chapter Four – Savage Civilization

1. Magical death has attracted a considerable amount of comment, most of it anecdotal, however in Melanesia one physician did keep clinical records of a victim hospitalized in a military clinic in Papua New Guinea.

When the patient was admitted to hospital, he explained that he was the victim of magic because he had broken a taboo. He had been treated as if excommunicated by the tribe, and his relatives totally avoided and neglected him. Upon admission, he did not appear severely ill, but was clearly depressed and apathetic. He refused to eat and would drink no fluids, remaining inert on his bed. His pulse rate was sixty-five, and his blood pressure only slightly elevated. The doctors were able to get a potion from the tribe, which they assured would bring back his health. He tried some mixture but rejected it.

Over a few days he became increasingly apathetic and seemed detached, barely moving. His skin and mouth were dry, his urine had a high specific gravity, and he stopped defecating altogether. He received penicillin, arsenicals and digitalis. No one came to see him, and he showed no interest in the other patients. He was found dead on the ninth day after admission.

The autopsy showed cirrhosis of the liver, enlargement of the spleen, and widespread arteriosclerosis. The spleen, kidneys, pancreas, and liver showed damage, but no immediate cause of death was apparent. The doctors decided that his death was suicide through voluntary rejection of fluids. His tribe, however, believed he died because he had broken a taboo. (From *Medical Anthropology in Ecological Perspective* by Ann McElroy, Duxbury Press, Massachusetts, 1999)

Chapter Five – Headhunting

[1.] In western societies war trophies have by and large enjoyed a good press, being almost invariably associated with the walls of a fighter squadron's mess or the personal effects of a battlefield casualty. In a 1940 report to the *British Journal of Medical Psychology* a field study had observed that a combatant was 'as careful to collect souvenirs from his dead enemy as from the girl he left behind'. During the First World War, buttons, epaulettes, medals, helmets, photographs and personal effects were common trophies but from 1942 onwards the collecting of body parts became more common, particularly in the Pacific theatre of war. It appears that where 'Japs' or 'Gooks' were concerned it was open season, their being somehow less human than 'Huns' or 'Krauts'. In the Pacific islands and the Philippines the gold teeth of dead Japanese soldiers became the trophies of choice.

This tendency to collect human trophies escalated during the Korean and Vietnam wars. Most favoured were ears, teeth and fingers. However heads, penises, hands and toes were also reported. A Vietnam paratrooper who collected about fourteen ears and fingers which he strung round his neck found that once he returned to base camp he 'would get free drugs, free booze, free pussy because they wouldn't want to bother you 'cause this man's a killer. It symbolized that "I'm a killer." And it was, so to speak, a symbol of combat-type manhood.'

Another marine who wore a string of ears recalled: 'we used to cut their ears off. We had a trophy. If a guy would have a necklace of ears, he was a good killer, a good trooper. It was encouraged to cut ears off, to cut the nose off, to cut a guy's penis off. A female, you cut her breasts off. It was encouraged to do these things. The officers expected you to do it or something was wrong with you.' (From *An Intimate History of Killing* by Joanna Bourke, Granta Books, London, 1999.)

Chapter Seven – The Arms Race

1. Murray's partners, Armstrong and Dowden, were convicted on his evidence and sentenced to death. Five seamen were found guilty of assault on the high seas and sentenced to two years imprisonment. Then, after some months, Henry Mount and Arthur Morris, his two original partners, were arrested and charged with having committed wilful murder on the high seas.

   In the course of the trial the Chief Justice, Sir William Stawell, commented, referring to the scene when the wounded men were thrown overboard: 'I cannot understand how any man understanding the words used by Murray could stand by and do nothing. It won't do for a man to stand by and say he will wash his hands of the whole affair when he sees murder committed before his eyes.'

286

Mount and Morris were committed to fifteen years penal servitude. On appeal the sentence was quashed on the grounds that there was no such thing as penal servitude in the state of Victoria. Later the Privy Council decided that the sentence was correct by which time the two gentlemen had wisely left the state. At this point the legal arm of the state decided to remain foreshortened enough to allow the two men to live out their lives elsewhere, particularly as public opinion was crying out for the blood of the man who had turned Queen's Evidence.

It was left to Murray's father to sum up the character of his son in a widely published letter to the *Sydney Press*:

> As regards Dr Murray, the celebrated *Carl* man-catching approver whom I have for years cut off as a disgrace to creed, country and family – your condemnation of that cruel unhappy being I fully endorse and add, although opposed to capital punishment on principle, that if any of the *Carl* crew murderers ever ascend the gibbet for the seventy kidnapped and cruelly slaughtered poor Polynesians [sic], Dr Murray should be the first, as head.

Murray, by this time, was long gone. Abandoning his wife and children, he took ship for England where, full of contrition, insights and a wealth of experience in the 'sad' business of recruiting for a colony 'desperately in need of labour', he was invited to advise the Secretary of State for the Colonies, Lord Kimberley, upon a more effective method of suppressing the rampant practice of blackbirding that he claimed was the scourge of the Pacific. Later he had detailed discussions with an ecclesiastical lord who is said to have found the doctor a most charming person.

Chapter Eight – Between Two Worlds

1. Frank Wickham was born in Somerset. In 1878, the year Renton was rescued, he ran away to sea and was shipwrecked in the Western Solomons a year later. Alexander Ferguson, the first resident trader on the islands, rescued him. Ferguson set the young man up with a trading post in Roviana Lagoon. In exchange for turtleshell, he supplied the local chiefs with firearms, a symbiotic relationship that ensured his survival. Frank married a Solomon Islands woman, Ameriga, an arrangement that conferred additional protection. They produced a son, Alick. By the late 1890s Wickham's activities had become so profitable that he was able to send his teenage son to a Sydney boarding school to complete his education. In the evenings and weekends he swam in the sea baths on Bronte Beach using a stroke that was widespread in the Pacific.

   One day, the leading swimming coach, George Farmer, saw Wickham swimming and is reputed to have shouted out: 'Look at that kid crawling over the water'. Other swimmers quickly appropriated a stroke that Solomon Islanders knew as *taptapalla* and changed its name to the Australian Crawl. Alick Wickham went on to become Australia's first swimming champion and held a couple of world records before the First World War. He also introduced body surfing and skin diving to the colonials.

   After the war, in the tradition of Houdini and Blondin, he made a living undertaking stunts. One involved sitting at the bottom of a transparent water tank for seven minutes. In Melbourne he accepted the challenge of diving from a 100-foot tower into the Yarra River. When he arrived he discovered that the tower was at least 105 feet high. He made the dive and set a record that stood for forty years.

Wickham retired to Gizo, the British administrative capital of the Western Solomons and set up a barber's shop. Right up until the 1960s he was part of the furniture of the little community. Nobody passing the shop could miss him – his stooped gait, chin permanently thrust down on his left shoulder, sidling round his customers. Alick had broken his neck attempting to better his Yarra River dive.

2. From Professor David Whittaker's forensic examination, July 2002:

'The necklace consists of 59 human anterior teeth. Each tooth has been drilled through the root apex and threaded on a two strand laid cord, knotted by 'reef knots'. Separating each tooth are usually three shell beads mostly arranged black/white/black, but at one end pink/white/pink.

All the teeth are human permanent teeth, both upper and lowers. All except four are anterior teeth (i.e. canines, lateral and central incisors). The other four are premolars.

The degree of wear on the teeth biting edges is similar and probably relates to about three decades of life (this is a crude estimate because I have no information on diet). However, I believe the teeth are *not* individuals of great age, but of mature age. The wear (attrition) is just into dentine. There is virtually no evidence of decay (caries) in any teeth.

The teeth are identifiable with reasonable accuracy below:

Upper left central incisor 9	Lower right central incisor 1
Upper right central incisor 8	Lower left lateral incisor 5
Upper left lateral incisor 3	Lower right lateral incisor 4

Upper lateral incisor 3   Lower left canine 6

Upper right left canine 6   Lower right canine 4

Upper right canine 5   Lower left first premolar 2

Upper left second premolar 1   Lower right second premolar 1

Lower left central incisor 1

These are, therefore, teeth from a minimum of nine individuals'.

Examining the teeth seventy years ago, Dr Gunn observed that 'the business end is jet black, as if enamelled. This is due to the chewing of betel, which is universal in these islands and is said to preserve as well as decorate the teeth.' The teeth are stained, but not by betelnut, which leaves a pale pink residue.

Jock Cromer's memoirs of his life as a recruiter during the period of Kwaisulia's ascendancy describes a scene on entering a hut on Ada Gege:

> Two boys were lying in the house, spread out on mats, and at first sight I thought they were dead. They lay perfectly still, and their lips were propped back from their teeth by pieces of wood. They would be there for three or four days, I learned, while a paste that was applied to their teeth performed its work of turning them black.

The fashion survived the suppression of headhunting. Walter Ivens, writing about Malaita in the 1920s, commented: 'young men or girls, who wish to give themselves airs, blacken their teeth with a pigment from a river rock called *lawa* which is roasted and pounded.'

Chapter Ten – Sex and Death

1. What do we taste like?' It has, of course, been a source of endless fascination to white people and nineteenth- and early twentieth-century literature is full of highly dubious descriptions. The following description carries far more weight than many.

Malekula, in the New Hebrides, is the home of the Big Nambas, a well known tramping ground for three of the most respected British anthropologists of the 1920s and 30s, Leyard, Deacon and Harrisson. All three maintained that cannibalism was still rife on the island. MacClancey spent a number of years there in the 1970s and recorded this statement from the Big Nambas chief Anahapat in 1978.

When a man is cut, he is cut in a different way from bullock or sheep or pig or goat. Cut out the navel, then cut the fingers at all the joints, then the wrists, then the elbow, then the shoulder, then all toe and foot joints, then the knee, then pull out the stomach, then cut the neck, then cut out the legs. Then cut everything into pieces. Give the legs to the chief [it is up to him if he takes both or not]. The rest of the body is divided among the Naml [different lodges within the village].

When you cook a man, it is very yellow, very greasy, very sweet. It cannot be cooked like normal meat. It tastes better if hung for a couple of days. Put the meat in *a lap lap* [grated tuber pudding wrapped in banana leaves like a long flat packet and cooked in an earth oven].

You must be very careful when eating human flesh because when you eat man, if any bit sticks in the middle of your teeth, if you use a stick to remove the bits, someone from another village will shoot you [in other words, subsequent misfortune will be attributed to breaking this taboo]. You make a special drink from *nesu*, a special kind of sugar cane, and use it to clean your mouth if human flesh is stuck.

(From *Consuming Culture* by J. MacClancey, Chapmans, 1994).

Chapter Twelve – Kwaisulia of Ada Gege

1. Outside Kwaisulia's territory little changed, as Jack London discovered thirty years later during the cruise of the *Snark*. Forbidden by the British administration to sail his boat in Malaitan waters, he left her and her crew in southern Isabel whilst he and his wife joined Captain Jansen on the recruiting ship *Minota* bound for Malaita. There was a frisson of anticipation as the ship approached the village of Su'u on the western coast. It had been less than six months since a group of islanders had overrun the ship and chopped up the previous captain.

Captain Jansen did not like the anchorage. It was the first time he had been to Su'u and it had a bad reputation. He explained at length that no white man was sure of his Malaitan crew in a tight place; that the bushmen looked upon all wrecks as their personal property; that bushmen possessed plenty of Snider rifles; and that he had on board a dozen 'return' boys for Su'u who were certain to join in with their friends and relatives ashore when it came to looting the *Minota*.

In vain did the whaleboat ply about the shores of the bay in quest of recruits. The bush was full of armed natives, all willing enough to talk with the recruiter, but none would engage to sign on for three years plantation labour at six pounds per year. Yet they were anxious enough to get our people ashore. On the second day they raised a smoke on the beach at the head of the bay. This being the customary signal of men desiring to recruit, the boat was sent. But nothing resulted. No one recruited, nor any of our men lured ashore. A little later we caught glimpses of a number of armed natives moving about the beach. Outside these rare glimpses, there was no telling how many might be lurking in the bush. In the afternoon, Captain Jansen, Charmain and I went dynamiting fish.

We were close in to the shore and working in closer, stern-first, when a school of fish was sighted. The fuse was ignited and the stick of dynamite thrown. With the explosion the surface of the water was broken by the flash of leaping fish. At the same instant the woods broke into life. A score of naked savages, armed with bows and arrows, spears, and Sniders, burst upon the shore. At the same moment our boat's crew lifted their rifles. And thus the opposing parties faced each other, while our extra boys dived over after the stunned fish.

Three fruitless days were spent at Su'u. The *Minota* got no recruits from the bush, and the bushmen got no heads from the *Minota*.

Chapter Thirteen – The Last Resort

1. 'Their religion was viewed as a tool to be used to maintain their place in the cosmic order.' One of the characteristics of animist religions, where much of the material culture is suffused by profound spiritual belief, is its extraordinary delicacy. Remove one brick from the wall and the whole system collapses. In *Tristes Tropiques* Levi-Strauss describes the

original complex circular arrangement of a Bororo village, which mirrored their cosmology.

The Salesian missionaries in the Roi das Garcas region were quick to realize that the surest way to convert the Bororo was to make them abandon their village in favour of one with the houses set out in parallel rows. Once they had been deprived of their bearings and were without a plan which acted as a confirmation of the native lore, the Indians soon lost any feeling for tradition; it was as if their religious systems were too complex to exist without a pattern which was embodied in the plan of the village and of which their awareness was constantly being refreshed by their everyday activities.

Bibliography

────── ○ ──────

Allen, Colin, *Marching Rule: a Nativistic Cult of the British Solomon Islands*, vol. 3, Corona, 1951.

Amhurst, Lord and Basil Thompson, eds., *The Discovery of the Solomon Islands by Alvaro de Mendana in 1568*, 2 vols., Hakluyt Society, London, 1901.

Beaglehole, John, *The Exploration of the Pacific*, A&C Black, London, 1934.

Bennett, Judith, *Wealth of the Solomons*, University of Hawaii Press, Honolulu, 1987.

Bernatzik, Hugo, *Sudsee: Travels in the South Seas*, Constable, London, 1935.

Belshaw, Cyril, *Changing Melanesia: Social Economics of Culture Contact*, Oxford University Press, Melbourne, 1976.

Blackburn, Julia, *The White Man*, Orbis Publishing, London, 1979.

Boelaars, J. H. M., *Headhunters about Themselves*, Martinus Nijhoff, The Hague, 1981.

Bogesi, George, 'Santa Isabel, Solomon Islands', *Oceana* 18(3), 1948.

Bougainville, Louis de, *A Voyage Round the World*, Gregg Press, New Jersey, 1967 (reprint).

Bourke, Joanna, *An Intimate History of Killing*, Granta Books, London, 1999.

Brewster, A. B., *King of the Cannibal Islands*, Hale & Co., London, 1937.

Brown, George, *Melanesians and Polynesians*, Macmillan, London, 1910.

Burridge, Kenelm, *Mambu – A Melanesian Millennium*, Methuen & Co., London, 1960.

Callender, John, *Terra Australis Incognita*, Clark & Collins, Edinburgh, 1776.

Carter, Rita, *Mapping the Mind*, Weidenfeld & Nicolson, London, 1998.

Cattlin, E. *Journal of the John Bull*, Mitchell Library, Sydney, 1828.

Chase, Owen, *The Wreck of the Whaleship Essex*, Headline, London, 1999 (reprint).

Chewings, Hannah, *Among Tropical Islands: Notes and Observations during a visit of SS Moresby to New Guinea, New Britain and the Solomon Islands in 1899*, Bonython, London, 1900.

Clifford, James, *The Predicament of Culture*, Harvard University Press, Massachusetts, 1988.

Cochrane, Glynn, *Big Men and Cargo Cults*, Oxford University Press, Oxford, 1970.

Codrington, R. H. *The Melanesians: Studies in their Anthropology and Folk-Lore*, Clarendon Press, Oxford, 1891.

Connolly, B. & Anderson, R., *First Contact*, Penguin Books, London, 1987.

Conrad, Joseph, *Heart of Darkness*, with Introduction and Notes by Hampson, R., Penguin Books, London, 1995.

Collinson, Clifford, *Cannibals and Coconuts*, George Philip, London, 1929.

Coombe, Florence, *Islands of Enchantment*, Macmillan, London, 1911.

Corris, Peter, 'Kwaisulia of Ada Gege: A Strongman in the Solomon Islands', in *Pacific Island Portraits*, eds. Davidson, James and Scarr, Derek, Australian National University Press, Canberra, 1970.

—*Passage Port and Planatation: A History of Solomon Islands Labour Migration, 1870–1914*, Melbourne University Press, Melbourne, 1973.

Clune, Frank, *Captain Bully Hayes: Blackbirder and Bigamist*, Angus & Robertson, London, 1970.

Coote, Walter, *The Western Pacific*, Sampson Low, London, 1883.

Cromar, Jock, *Jock of the Islands*, Faber & Faber, London, 1935.

Davidson, James and Scarr, Derek, eds. *Pacific Island Portraits*, Australian National University Press, Canberra, 1970.

Deacon, Bernard, *Malekula*, George Routledge & Sons, London, 1934.

Derrick, R. A., 1952. *A History of Fiji*, Printing and Stationary Department, Suva, Fiji, 1952.

Dickinson, Joseph, *A Trader in the Savage Solomons*, Witherby, London, 1927.

Docker, Edward, *The Blackbirders: The Recruiting of South Seas Labour for Queensland*. Angus & Robertson, Sydney, 1970.

Dunbabin, Thomas, *Slavers of the South Seas*, Angus & Robertson, Sydney, 1935.

Durrad, W. J., 'The depopulation of Melanesia' in *Essays on the depopulation of Melanesia*, ed. W. H. R. Rivers, Cambridge University Press, 1922.

Eagen, Brian, *Clash of Cultures*, W. H. Freeman & Co., New York, 1984.

Edge-Partington. T. W., 'Ingava, Chief of Rubiana, Solomon Islands', *Man Magazine*, London, 1907.

Edridge, Sally, *Solomon Islands Bibliography to 1980*, University of the South Pacific, Suva, Fiji, 1985.

Evans, Julian, *Transit of Venus*, Secker & Warburg, London, 1992.

Festetics von Tolna, *Chez les Cannibales*, Plon-Nourrit, Paris, 1903.

Fieldhouse, David, *Unilever Overseas: The Anatomy of a Multinational, 1895–1965*, Croom Helm, London, 1979.

Fifi'i, Jonathan, 'World War II and the Origins of Maasina Rule', in *The Big Death*, Akin, D., ed., Institute of Pacific Studies, Suva, Fiji, 1982.

Firth, Raymond, *We the Tikopia*, Allen & Unwin, London, 1963.

Fox, Charles, *The Threshold of the Pacific*, Kegan Paul, London, 1924.

Gallego, Hernando, *A true and correct account of the voyage to the Western Isles of the Southern Ocean made by Hernando Gallego*, Hakluyt Society, London, 1901.

Gardiner, Margaret, *Footprints on Malekula*, Free Association Books, London, 1987.

Goodenough, V., ed., *Journal of Commodore Goodenough: 1873–1875*, Henry King, London, 1876.

Graves, Adrian, *Cane and Labour – The political economy of the Queensland sugar industry, 1862–1906*, Edinburgh University Press, 1993.

Guppy, Henry, *The Solomon Islands and their Natives*, Swan Sonnenschien, London, 1887.

Hardy, Norman, and Elkington. E. W., *The Savage South Seas*, A&C Black, London, 1907.

Harrisson, Thomas, *Savage Civilization*, Gollancz, London, 1937.

Herbert, Walter, *Marquesan Encounters*, Harvard University Press, Massachusetts, 1980.

Hickman, John, *The Enchanted Islands: The Galapagos Discovered*, Anthony Nelson, Shropshire, 1985.

Hocart, Arthur, 'The Cult of the Dead in Eddystone in the Solomons', *Proceedings of the Royal Anthropological Institute*, vol. 52, 1922.

Hogbin, Herbert, 'Culture Change in the Solomon Islands: Report of Field Work in Guadalcanal and Malaita', *Oceana 4* (3), 1934.

—*Experiments in Civilization*, Routledge & Kegan Paul, London, 1939.

Holthouse, Hector, *Cannibal Cargoes*, Angus & Robertson, Adelaide and London, 1969.

Hopkins, Arthur Innes, *In the Isles of King Solomon*, London, 1928.

Ivens, Walter, *Melanesians of the south-east Solomon Islands*, Kegan Paul, London, 1927.

—*The Island Builders of the Pacific*, London, 1930.

Jack-Hinton, Colin, *The Search for the Islands of Solomon, 1567–1838*, Clarendon Press, Oxford, 1969.

Jackson, K. B., 'Headhunting in the Christianization of Bogotu 1861–1900', *Journal of Pacific History*, 10 (1), 1975.

Johnson, Osa, *I Married Adventure*, Hutchinson, London, 1940.

—*Bride in the Solomons*, Harrap & Co, London, 1945.

Keesing, R. and Corris, P., *Lightning Meets the West Wind*, Oxford University Press, Oxford, 1980.

Kent, Janet, *The Solomon Islands*, Wren Publishing, Melbourne, 1996.

Knibbs, S., *The Savage Solomons*, London, 1929.

Kuipers, Joel, *Power in Performance*, University of Pennsylvania Press, Philadephia, 1990.

Laracy, Hugh, *The Maasina Rule Movement*, Institute of Pacific Studies, Suva, Fiji, 1983.

Lawrence, Peter, *Road Belong Cargo*, Manchester University Press, Manchester, 1964.

—*Gods, Ghosts and Men in Melanesia*, Oxford University Press, Melbourne, 1965.

Leslie, Edward, *Desperate Journeys, Abandoned Souls: True Stories of Castaways and Other Survivors*, Houghton Mifflin, Boston, 1988.

Levi-Strauss, Claude, *Tristes Tropiques*, Penguin Books, London, 1992.

Lindstrom, L. & White, G. eds., *Island Encounters*, Smithsonian Institution Press, Washington, 1990.

London, Jack, *The Cruise of the Snark*, Mills & Boon, London, 1913.

—*South Sea Tales*, Mills & Boon, London, 1912.

MacClancy, Jeremy, *Consuming Culture*, Chapmans, London, 1994.

Markham, Albert, *The Cruise of the Rosario*, Samson Low, London, 1873.

Martin, John (with William Mariner), *An Account of the Natives of Tonga Islands* (2 vols), John Constable, London, 1817.

Marwick, James, *The Adventures of John Renton*, Kirkwall Press, Orcadian Office, 1935.

Maude, H. E., *Of Islands and Men*, Oxford University Press, Melbourne, 1968.

Melville, Herman, *Omoo: A Narrative of Adventures in the South Seas*, Library Classics, New York, 1982 (reprint).

—*Typee: A Peep at Polynesian Life*, New American Library, New York, 1979 (reprint).

McArthur, Norma, *Island Populations of the Pacific*, Australian National University Press, Canberra, 1968.

—'New Hebrides Population 1840–1967: a Re-interpretation', *South Pacific Commission*, Occasional paper No. 18, Noumea, New Caledonia, 1981.

McElroy, Ann, *Medical Anthropology in Perspective*, Duxbury Press, Massachusetts, 1999.

McKinnon, John, 'Tomahawks, Turtles and Traders: A reconstruction in the circular causation of warfare in the New Georgia group', *Oceana* 45 (4), 1975.

Melanesian Mission, 'Journal of the Mission Voyage to the Melanesian Islands by the schooner *Southern Cross*, made in May–October 1866', Auckland, printed at the *Daily Southern Cross* office, 1866.

Miller, R. S., *Misi Gete, Pioneer Missionary to the New Hebrides*, The Presbyterian Church of Tasmania, Launceston, Tasmania, 1975.

Mitchell, Andrew, *A Fragile Paradise*, Fontana/Collins, London, 1989.

Moresby, John, *Discoveries & Surveys in New Guinea and the D'Entrecasteaux Islands*, John Murray, London, 1876.

Nicholls, F., 'Journal aboard *Dauntless*'. Government agent's

301

journal, No. 19, Fiji National Archives, Suva, 1880.

Palmer, George, *Kidnapping in the South Seas*, Dawsons, London, 1971.

Penny, Alfred, *Diaries*, Mitchell Library, Sydney, 1886.

Pitt-Rivers, Henry, *The Clash of Cultures and the Contact of Races*, George Routledge, London, 1927.

Raabe, H. E., *Cannibal Nights*, Geoffrey Bles, London, 1927.

Rannie, Douglas, *My Adventures among South Sea Cannibals*, London, 1912.

Renton, John, 'The Adventures of John Renton', *Australasian Supplement*, Sydney, 1875 (Oct.).

—'The Adventures of John Renton', *Australasian Supplement*, Sydney, 1876 (Jan.).

Rice, Edward, *John Frum He Come*, Doubleday & Co., New York, 1974.

Rivers, William, 'The Psychological Factor', in Rivers, W. H. (ed.) *Essays on the Depopulation of Melanesia*, Cambridge University Press, Cambridge, 1922.

Roberts, Stephen, *Population Problems of the Pacific*, George Routledge, London, 1927.

Rogers, Stanley, *Crusoes and Castaways*, George Harrap, London, 1932.

Romilly, Hugh, *The Western Pacific and New Guinea*, John Murray, London, 1886.

Sale, Kirkpatrick, *The Conquest of Paradise*, Hodder & Stoughton, London, 1991.

Sahlins, Marshall, *Islands of History*, University of Chicago Press, Chicago, 1985.

Salisbury, Edward, 'Napoleon of the Solomons', *Asia: Journal of the American Asiatic Association*, 22, 1922.

Sanday, Peggy, *Divine Hunger: Cannibalism as a cultural system*, Cambridge University Press, Cambridge, 1986.

Scherzer, Karl Ritter von, *Narrative of the Circumnavigation of the Globe by the Austrian Frigate Novara*, Saunders, Otley, London, 1861.

Searle, G. S., *Mount and Morris Exonerated – a narrative of the Brig Carl*, Evans Brothers, Melbourne, 1875.

Seton, K. W., 'Francis Drake of the Bourgainville Straits', *Pacific Islands Monthly*, 16 (1), 1945.

Shineberg, Dorothy, *They Came for Sandalwood*, Cambridge University Press, Cambridge, 1967.

Somerville, Boyle, *Will Mariner: A True Record of Adventure*, Faber & Faber, London, 1936.

Spriggs, Matthew, *The Island Melanesians*, Blackwell, Sydney, 1997.

Stannard, David, *Before the Horror*, Social Science Research Institute, University of Hawaii, 1989.

Suggs, Robert, *The Hidden Worlds of Polynesia*, Cresset Press, London, 1984.

Tippet, A. R., *Solomon Islands Christianity*, Lutterworth Press, London, 1967

Toohey, John, *Captain Bligh's Portable Nightmare*, Fourth Estate, London, 1999.

Trollope, Anthony, *In Australia and New Zealand*, London, 1873.

Wawn, William, *The South Sea Islanders and the Queensland Labour Trade*, Swann & Sonnenschien, London, 1893.

Wallis, Helen, ed., *Carteret's Voyage Round the World, 1766–1769*, Cambridge University Press for the Hakluyt Society, London, 1965.

Williamson, Robert, *The Ways of the South Sea Savage*, Lippincott, Philadelphia, 1914.

Wood, George, *The Discovery of Australia*, Macmillan, London, 1922.

Woodford, Charles, *A Naturalist among the Headhunters*, G. Philip, London, 1890.

Woodford, Charles, 'The Canoes of the British Solomon Islands', *Journal of the Royal Anthropological Institute*, Vol. 39, pages 506–16, 1909.

Worsley, Peter, *The Trumpet Shall Sound*, MacGibbon & Kee, London, 1957.

ORAL HISTORIES (Solomon Islands)
Malaita Island
(Sulufou)

Nelson Jack Boe	Jacob Selo
Henry Furage	Grace Sosoe
Thomas Gwageni	Malachi Tate
Patrick Inoke	Loinel Tole
Anthony Jack	George Wate
Leonard Mare	
Anathanasias Orudiana	

Malaita Island
(Ada Gege)

Stewart Diudi
Ashley Kakaluae
James Kakaluae

New Georgia and Vella Islands.

Robertson Batu
Nathan Kera
Falataou Levi
Charles Panakera
Kenneth Rongga

Vanuatu (formerly The New Hebrides)

Peter Afoa
Dick Kaitani
James Quiero
John Tamanta

Selected Sources

— o —

Introduction

D. F. Maude's *Of Islands and Men* contains, by his own admission, an incomplete list of 20 'beachcomber' books published between 1788 and 1850. Half of them were published in a 16-year period between 1831 and 1847. The 1847 publication is Herman Melville's *Typee*, the only one still in print.

During one of my visits to the archipelago of Vanuatu, (formerly the New Hebrides), researching Renton's subsequent career, I came across a number of oral histories relating to an unrecorded castaway. Pentecost lies in the middle of the archipelago. On the far north of the island, around the town of Laone, stories abound of 'Jimmy' – a teenage castaway. As this book is peppered with extracts from oral histories I have included a verbatim transcript of one of the Jimmy narratives as the appendix.

307

Chapter One 'The Island'

The John Bull. Smith's account was given added weight by papers that recently came into the possession of the Mitchell Library in Sydney. *Journal of a Voyage from Port Jackson to the Northward kept by Edward Cattlin – Mate*, supports Smith's account of the capture of three seamen from the *Alfred*.

Chapter Two 'Escape from the *Reynard*'

Marwick's researches. John Renton is still very much part of Stomness' history. Two guidebooks on the Highlands and Islands contain photographs of the family house. The Stromness Museum displays a number of artefacts that he brought back from the Solomons. Sadly, since Marwick's researches in the 1920s, all Renton's brothers and sisters either died without issue or left the little port.

Chapter Three 'Landfall'

Discovery. Mendana's discovery of the Solomon Islands is particularly well documented and one is left with the impression of all the major figures on the expedition busily at work every evening on their journals of self-justification. Published in 1901 by the Hakluyt Society, *The Discovery of the Solomon Islands* is a collection of these journals that, for the most part, conceal more than they reveal. The main contributors were the expedition's leader Alvero de Mendana, the Chief Pilot Hernando Gallego, his deputy and competitor Pedro Samiento and Gomez Catoira, the Chief Purser.

Colin Jack-Hinton's *The Search for the Solomon Islands* examines in detail the expedition's errors in longitudinal reckoning that effectively 'lost' the Solomon Islands for over 200 years.

The indigenous accounts of the expedition's arrival on Santa Isabel were collected by the anthropologist George Borgese in 1947 and were published in *Oceana*. At that time there were still a few inhabitants who claimed to be related to the original Ghene people. One of Borgese's informants maintained that he was a direct descendent of Belenbangara, Mendana's reluctant host.

The Generations. A large number of the 'Generations' of Malaita were transcribed after the Second World War during a period of anti-colonial unrest known as Maasina Rule. After the British fled the Solomon Islands in 1942, the Japanese decided that the island, having little strategic importance, could govern itself. Maasina Rule grew out of a refusal by the islanders to return to their status as colonial subjects following the cessation of hostilities. The bloodless and partially successful rebellion centred on the issue of land ownership and the 'Generations' were, in effect, a statement of the non-transferability of customary lands. Hugh Laracy's *The Maasina Rule Movement* contains the 30-page 'Generation' of the People of Oau.

Chapter Four 'Savage Civilization'
Sulufou. Much of the information not supplied by Renton can be found in Walter Ivens' *Island Builders of the Pacific*. Throughout 1927 this missionary-turned-anthropologist collected information in North Malaita, using Sulufou as his base. It had been barely twenty years since the coastal region had been pacified by the British and most of the information he obtained, relating to their social organization, religion and history came from men and women who had been alive during the later period covered by this book. Additional information, relating to

cosmologies and belief systems, can be found in Lawrence and Meggitt's *Gods, Ghosts and Men in Melanesia*.

Canoe building held a particular fascination for Charles Woodford. This naturalist turned administrator was appointed the first Resident Commissioner of the British Solomon Islands. His 1909 paper *The Canoes of the Solomon Islands* was published by the Royal Anthropological Institute.

Chapter Five 'Headhunting'

Headhunting. Surprisingly, given its title, Professor Tippet's *Solomon Islands Christianity* contains the most detailed and lucid review of the cultural and religious imperatives that drove men to decapitate each other. Unlike more politically correct commentators, he does not shy away from examining the central tenet of pre-Christian Solomon Islands culture – namely, in his words, *the slavery complex.*

The role of the *ramo*. Roger Keesing and Peter Corris' extraordinary *Lightning Meets the West Wind* charts the final confrontation between a Malaitan *ramo* and a representative of the British colonial government. In 1927, whilst Walter Ivens was living peacefully on Sulufou, inland, the District Administrator William Bell was attempting bring the bush people under British rule. From oral histories and their own researches amongst the Kwaio people, Keesing and Corris paint a vivid picture of Basiana, the last of the Malaitan *ramos*. In the face of a pervasive threat to their ancestral way of life, he and his followers resolved to challenge the power of the Empire and murder Bell.

Chapter Six 'Grief, Terror and Rage'

Blackbirding. Peter Corris' *Passage, Port and Plantation* is a scholarly analysis of what the labour trade was like for the islanders concerned and draws on the reminiscences if eighteen migrant workers. Thomas Dunbabin's *Slavers of the South Seas*, published in 1935, within a generation of the events described, is a powerful, if somewhat episodic account of the worst abuses. Docker's *The Blackbirders* and Holthouse's *Cannibal Cargoes*, published within a year of each other (1969-70), cover the same territory and are equally valuable in their analysis of the political and economic forces that fuelled and prolonged this enterprise.

James Murray. By far the best book about this strange and deeply disturbed man was published in Melbourne in 1875. *Mount and Morris Exonerated – A Narrative of the Voyage of the Brig Carl in 1871, with Comments upon the Trial* uncovered the seedy aftermath of this voyage. The author, G. S. Searl, was clearly incensed that, given the events aboard the *Carl*, the only people to stand trial were two of Murray's underlings, whilst the real villain had long since departed the continent [see Endnote].

Chapter Seven 'The Arms Race'

The voyage of the *Peri*. Published in 1937 under the misleading title of *King of the Cannibal Islands* A. B. Brewster's book is a series of sketches of colonial life in Fiji after the First World War. Ploughing through this obscure functionary's reminiscences of recalcitrant natives, hunting parties and portraits of obscure and long-forgotten colonial administrators, Chapter 26 produces a gem. 'When my friend Mr C. R. Swayne, CMG., died in 1920 many of his notes and papers were given to me by his widow.' Written in 1893, eighteen years after the events it describes, one

311

of the papers was a testimony transcribed by one of Swayne's Fijiian clerks. It was a deposition by Aliverete and recorded his ordeal on the *Carl* and the voyage of the *Peri*.

Captain Morseby's account is taken from the opening chapter of *Discoveries and Surveys in New Guinea and the D'Entrecasteaux Islands*. Over the next two years Moresby placed on the chart more then 100 islands, including the D'Entrecasteaux Group off the south-east coast of Papua New Guinea. Along its southern coast Moresby surveyed the last spaces on the chart, including a huge enclosed bay that now bears his name and it the capital of that country. Almost a century after Cook's death, Moresby's was the last great Pacific voyage of discovery.

Arboreal Villages. An excellent description of Santa Isabel's defences against headhunters can be found in a news-sheet published by the Melanesian Mission in 1866. It recounts the first visit to Santa Isabel by the mission ship *Southern Cross*. In general the usefulness of mission reports in the Pacific are somewhat blunted by the exigencies of their own agenda. It is only when describing natural phenomena or, in this case, people in whom they have no pastoral interest, that they are in any way helpful . . . or accurate.

Chapter Eight 'Between Two Worlds'

'The tricks of the trade'. In the heyday of labour recruiting the practice generated numerous articles and tracts from the opposition. The first book written by a participant appeared in 1893, by which time the whole operation was winding down. William Wawn's *The South Sea Islands* is an account of a business from which he had long since retired. Douglas Rannie's *My Adventures among South Sea Cannibals* is, like Wawn's book, an exercise in self-exculpation, pointing the finger at other ships' captains, long since dead.

John Cromer's *Jock of The Islands* published by Faber in 1935 is by far the best book on Blackbirding. Academic reaction to it at the time of publication was dismissive, however its wealth of ethnographic detail has, in the light of subsequent knowledge, proved to be faultless. Written forty years after the events described and from contemporaneous notes, it is book rich in incident and unfettered by the racism and a lack of candour that is a characteristic of books written earlier. Importantly, for this author, he knew Kwaisulia well.

On page 166 I have included a complete quote from Tom Harrisson's *Savage Civilization*. This piece of oral history encapsulates the whole drama of recruiting, particularly its fatal misunderstandings. Published by Gollancz in 1937 it remains the best book written about Melanesia. Sadly, given the above, my copy was acquired in a second-hand bookshop in Los Angeles – sold on by *The gifts and exchange division of Harvard University Library*.

Chapter Nine 'The Benighted People'

Geddie. When it come to the Missionary presence there are few better examples of their inability to face up to the lethal nature of that presence than *Misi Gete*. Published by the Presbyterian Church of Tasmania in 1975, Miller's book dutifully reproduces, without comment, Geddie's catalogue of epidemics that devastated the island of Aneityum. Clearly, even as late as the 1970s, some members of the missionary movement were still finding it impossible to face up to cause and effect.

Bernard Deacon. Posthumous author of *Malekula, A*

Vanishing People in the New Hebrides, Deacon lived there from January 1926 until his death from blackwater fever in March 1927. A Cambridge Double First, he was too young to sit the examination for the Consular Service and decided to read anthropology 'for amusement'. In 1925 he was awarded another First in the Anthropological Tripos and arrived in Malekula on his 23rd birthday. A gifted linguist he was soon fluent in the island's two main languages. Time and again he hints at a much darker world but in his 700-page book only three are devoted to the widespread practice of cannibalism. As his book was assembled by colleagues in Cambridge after his death it is a matter of speculation what weight Deacon would have ascribed to the practice. It would take the mercurial Harrisson, following in Deacon's footsteps ten years later, to confront the issue head-on.

Chapter Ten 'Sex and Death'

The death of Renton and cannibalism. Harrisson's *Savage Civilization* deals with both in some detail. As a recent Oxford graduate he joined a field trip to the New Hebrides in 1934 where he took an instant liking to the wife of the professor leading the expedition. Volunteering one day to stay behind to mind both the camp and spouse while the rest of the party set off into the bush, Harrisson and the lady settled down in her tent. What happened subsequently is a matter of some dispute but the livid professor departed with his wife and his undergraduates, abandoning Harrisson. 'I had no money. And I was fascinated by the islands. I hopped a lift to Omba, where I found the natives Europeanized but splendid people'. Here he unearthed the facts behind Renton's death. Then; 'All this time I was hearing about

314

the Big Nambas [Big Penis Wrappers] tribe of North Malekula. They were constantly fighting amongst themselves and eating each other. I went for looksee. It was, for once, true.' Unlike Deacon he then devotes thirty pages to the practice. 'In the year I was around, 30 men were killed in various wars that were going on'. Many have claimed to witness this ultimate expression of otherness (including the American film-maker Martin Johnson who spent six months in Malekula manoeuvring for the 'money shot') but only Harrisson witnessed the ceremony. His description bares a striking resemblance to the story of Renton's death I obtained from the nearby island of Aoba [Omba]. I have therefore conflated to two accounts – one European, the other, indigenous.

Chapter Twelve 'Kwaisulia of Ada Gege'

Kwaisulia. The ex-missionary Walter Ivens in *Island Builders of the Pacific* has nothing complimentary to say about Kwaisulia. Commenting on his 'overbearing style and hectoring ways' he paints a picture of a man who was a thorough menace. What Ivens does not say is that in his previous incarnation as a missionary, twenty-five years earlier, Kwaisulia was one of the major impediments in Ivens's attempts at evangelization.

For much of the information about Kwaisulia's rise to prominence I am indebted to Peter Corris's researches, in particular his chapter 'Kwaisulia of Ada Gege' that he contributed to *Pacific Island Portraits*. Further information was furnished by Kwaisulia's great-grandson and his great-nephew, Ashley Kakaluae and Stewart Diudi.

Chapter thirteen 'The Last Resort'

Soga of Isabel. K. B Jackson's 1975 paper 'Head-hunting and the Christianization of Bogotu 1861-1900' in the *Journal of Pacific History* explores Soga's apostasy in detail and provides a vivid commentary on the determined and remorseless infiltration of the missionary presence.

Aliferete's death. A. B. Brewster, clutching his, as yet, unpublished manuscript of *King of the Cannibal Islands* attended a lecture in Torquay given by Walter Ivens in 1932. 'I lent him the manuscript of the chapter "How We were Kidnapped" and learned from him that he knew some of the actors in that ghastly tragedy'. Having been a missionary at the time of Aliferete's death, Ivens provided the details of the fatal results of Aliferete's 'abstemious' sign.

The mystical power of education [p. 266]. Ian Hogbin was an Australian anthropologist working in the Pacific in the 1930s. The British mandarins in the Colonial Office, feeling slightly queasy about their unsuccessful attempts to 'Westernize' Malaita, asked Hogbin to examine the impact of colonial rule on the island. His 'Experiments in Civilization' was never officially released. Hogbin, however, had retained the copywrite on his researches and went ahead with publication. His conclusions were devastating and it was probably the last time the Colonial Office asked a neutral anthropologist to undertake such a survey.

Kwaisulia's death. Ivens in *Island Builders of the Pacific* and Hopkins in The *Isles of King Solomon* both refer to Kwaisulia's death. There were no other casualties. Hopkins points out that, in true Melanesian fashion, 'the search for the author of his death was being sought and that it was in vain to point out that Kwaisulia had killed himself.'

Appendix

———— o ————

THE following is an oral history from the island of Pentecost that has been passed down through (probably) five generations. Apart from providing a remarkable example of much of the material used in this book, this story tells of an escape from Fiji by a group of recruits and its aftermath.

Pentecost is a finger-shaped island in the middle of the New Hebridean archipelago, now the Republic of Vanuatu. As Renton is to Sulufou, so 'Jimmy' is to North Pentecost, a person who lived amongst them for many years and who is remembered with affection. However 'Jimmy' is an elusive quarry simply because there is no documentary evidence of his existence. When he took ship, he simply disappeared into history. I have reproduced this story verbatim to give a flavour of how many of the oral histories used in this book were recounted.

My name is John Tamanta. I am from the village of Ataleva on Pentecost. I am happy that you have asked me to tell this story. I learned it from my father Paul Ara fifteen years ago and I have held it in my head for all that time. My father hoped that one day people would be interested in this tale.

The story starts with a group of men from Pentecost who were blackbirded to work on the island of Fiji, hundreds of miles away. After a number of months they were desperate to return home and had escaped from the plantation where they had been indentured. They fled to the port of Suva and started hanging about the wharves.

One night they saw a sailing boat that looked unguarded. Their leader told them that they should all go and collect enough food for a week and then return and wait for nightfall. That night they rowed out to the boat, quietly cast off and raised the sails. As they left the harbour, the movement of the boat awoke the owners. From the cabin, two people came on deck – a man and his son. They were astonished to see men handling their boat and putting out to sea. The father's name is lost, but the boy's name was Jimmy.

They did not try to resist as there were too many men on the boat. They were forced by sheer numbers to agree to sail them to Pentecost. The journey took longer than expected, there was little wind and they ran out of food. The leader decided that they should kill Jimmy's father. They seized him and killed him – there was nothing Jimmy could do but he was determined that they would not cook his father so he went into the cabin found all the matches and threw them into the sea.

They ate Jimmy's father anyway. They cut him into small strips and ate him raw. They thought of killing Jimmy too but then they realized that he was the only one who knew how to navigate. The days wore on and soon they had finished Jimmy's father. Although they were all too weak to move, Jimmy steered them to Pentecost.

As the boat blew towards a reef they were too weak to handle the sails and they wanted to jump overboard. Jimmy told them not to as they would drown. So he steered the boat onto a reef where it stuck fast. Then he told them to jump. They took his advice and all were saved. It was at a reef by Lavousi.

They staggered onto the beach and lay there exhausted amongst the rocks. Jimmy found a long flat boulder the length of a man. He then found a piece of dried wood, placed it under his head and went to sleep.

The stone Jimmy had chosen to lie on was a *kustom* stone – it had a meaning. In those times there were many wars between people and this stone was a stone of peace. If anyone came to it, whether he was an enemy or not, he must not be killed.

The people of Lavousi had seen the ship crash onto the reef and Chief Viramata sent his people to find out what the ship was. When they arrived they saw men on the beach, some eating raw leaves, others sleeping. They were going to kill all the intruders but one man said: 'Look, the white man is sleeping on the stone of peace.' When the chief was told this he said: 'We must not kill them, we must look after them.'

Chief Viramata looked after them all for many months until their strength was restored and then they left for their different villages on Pentecost. But Jimmy stayed and was adopted by chief Viramata. He lived there for many years. Viramata took him to marriages, festivities and taught him the ways of Pentecost and soon he learned the language. Jimmy's clothes were soon rags so they gave him a *mal-mal* [Penis wrapper] to wear.

One day chief Viramata took him to a killing ceremony in the middle of the island. Jimmy saw the women with their painted faces and bodies who danced at the ceremony. He asked his hosts if they knew where the dyes came from, but none of them knew. Jimmy said they came from white man's countries and sang a song about them. This song, Jimmy's song, is still used at Pentecost dances today.

One evening he went to wash in the sea at a place called Awalayu. In our old stories there are devils. They saw this white man with his long straggly hair and were astonished. They made up a song, which they communicated to our priests. (I can't sing the song but my brother Robin knows it and more of Jimmy's.) It is said that the people of Pentecost were very kind to him and they gave him an island. Jimmy called it Oretape.

After many years a ship anchored at Laone. It was a ship that burns coal. Jimmy went on board the ship and told them his story. They were astonished, for he was dressed like a Pentecost man. They asked him if he wanted to go back to his own people. Jimmy said, 'Yes.' So they washed him and shaved him, cut his hair and dressed him like a white man and he went on shore to say goodbye. The people were afraid and ran away for they did not recognize him but he reassured them that he was the same Jimmy that they knew.

He came up to chief Viramata and they embraced and they cried. And when they had finished crying the chief took a pig and killed it and gave Jimmy the cut for food for his journey. Then they said goodbye but they did not shake hands as we do today. The chief only said, 'Now you are leaving' and Jimmy said, 'Yes, I am going', and the chief said, 'Yes, and I am staying here.'

This is the end of the story I know.

Index

'R' indicates Renton

321